Animal Natural History Series
Victor H. Hutchison, General Editor

NORTH AMERICAN
BOX TURTLES

Charlie, a Gulf Coast box turtle kept by the author, in autumn.
Illustration by Dale Johnson.

NORTH AMERICAN
BOX TURTLES

A Natural History

C. KENNETH DODD, JR.

UNIVERSITY OF OKLAHOMA PRESS

NORMAN

LIBRARY OF CONGRESS CATALOGING-IN-PUBLICATION DATA

Dodd, C. Kenneth.
    North American box turtles : a natural history / C. Kenneth Dodd, Jr.
        p. cm. — (Animal natural history series; v. 6)
    Includes bibliographical references (p. 203).
    ISBN 0-8061-3294-9 (cloth)
    ISBN 0-8061-3501-8 (paper)
        1. Terrapene. I. Title. II. Series.

QL666.C547 D63 2001
597.92'5—dc21   00-061596

DESIGNED BY ELLEN BEELER

North American Box Turtles: A Natural History is Volume 6 in the Animal Natural History Series.

The paper in this book meets the guidelines for permanence and durability of the Committee on Production Guidelines for Book Longevity of the Council on Library Resources, Inc. ∞

    2   3   4   5   6   7   8   9   10

Dedication

In order to appreciate the natural world, one must pay homage to those who have preceded us. Therefore, this book is dedicated first to the great naturalists Roger Barbour, Archie Carr, Roger Conant, Henry Fitch, Ernie Liner, and Hobart Smith, all of whom I have had the privilege to know. They have shown us that biology begins with a fascination with nature and continues throughout a lifetime of discovery.

Second, this book is dedicated to my late parents, Clifford and Mary Dodd, who tolerated the amphibians and reptiles that I brought home, including many poor box turtles, and who encouraged me to pursue an education so that I could have the opportunity to do what I wanted to do in life. Words cannot say enough.

Last but most important, I dedicate this book to my wife, Marian Griffey, who is my best friend, companion in the field, and love.

Contents

Color Plates

Unless otherwise noted, all photos are by the author.

Following page 110

Figures, Maps, and Tables

Figures

Maps

Tables

Preface

I grew up in the fields and woods of northern Virginia not far from Washington, D.C. At that time, the local area offered a great many places for nature exploration, and box turtles seemed rather common. I remember bringing home frogs and snakes, but most of all I remember the box turtles. They did not always fare well in my hands; I was far too ignorant of their needs. In many ways though, those box turtles, in habitats long asphalted and "developed," set me on a course to a life of study and observation of the herpetofauna of many parts of the world. Children growing up in concrete and brick jungles will never have the pleasure I had as a child in those almost forgotten woods and fields.

After moving to Florida, I fell in love with this naturalist's Eden, much as those before me have been captivated. Although my research initially focused mostly on amphibians, Dick Franz of the Florida Museum of Natural History invited me to join him in a brief survey of the reptiles and amphibians on Egmont Key, a national wildlife refuge leased to the Florida state park system. The survey revealed a large box turtle population, and so began our studies on the then little known Florida box turtles. Egmont's unique population reignited my curiosity about the biology of these friendly, plodding turtles and initiated a desire to fill in gaps in knowledge of their natural history. We began the study in January 1991, a study that continues today with more than fifteen hundred turtles marked. Much of the basis for this book rests on the shells of Egmont's box turtles. Thanks, Dick.

Throughout the book, I found myself switching between the pronouns *I* and *we*. Although I am the sole author, much of the data gathering on Egmont Key was a collaborative effort. The vertical pronoun seems inappropriate when so many others were involved, particularly Marian Griffey, Dick Franz, Lora Smith, Bob Baker and the park personnel on Egmont, and various friends and students at the University of Florida. I hope readers will keep this in mind.

A few more provisos are in order. Some readers may object that a favorite popular turtle book is not referenced in the literature cited. In every case, I have tried to cite the original source when referring to particular facts. All original citations have been read, checked, and verified. Unfortunately, some popular works that include information on box turtles do not cite the authority from which detail was obtained, and one gets the impression that the author is the original source, which is often not the case; I aim to avoid ambiguity about citations here. Further, this is not a book about the care of captive box turtles. People interested in this subject should consult de Vosjoli (1991), Patterson (1994), or Lowe (1996). Box turtles generally make poor pets, and the collection of specimens from wild populations is strongly discouraged.

Finally, it is sometimes difficult to address a professional and a nonscientific audience at the same time. To future authors, I offer the wisdom of Henry Pilsbry (1949:36) writing in the *Nautilus*: "If you want to learn how much you can overlook or forget, just write a book."

Acknowledgments

Writing a book is very much a collaborative effort. I thank the following individuals whose help and advice has been indispensable.

For providing illustrations and the beautiful frontispiece of this book: Dale Johnson.

For offering photographs: Kraig Adler, Noah Anderson, Matt Aresco, Richard Bartlett, Cathy B. Slack, Barbara Bell, Bruce Bury, James Buskirk, Sarah Converse, Russ Hall, Hannah Hamilton, James Harding, George Heinrich, Robert Hansen, Sandra Hildebrand, John Iverson, Dale Jackson, John Jensen, Julian Lee, John Legler, Ernie Liner, Peter May, Peter Mayne, Martha Messinger, Elizabeth Schwartz, Norm Scott, Jim Snyder, Ann Somers, Martin A. Tuegel, Jens Vindum, Robert Webb, Robert Zappalorti, George Zug.

For providing references and unpublished information: David Auth, Ellin Beltz, I. Lehr Brisbin, Jr., James Buskirk, Charles Carpenter, Robert Cook, Jon Costanzo, Brian Duracka, Wayne Frair, Michael Frick, J. Alan Holman, Martha Messinger, William Montgomery, Stephen J. Mullin, Max Nickerson, George Patton, John Sealy, William C. Sturtevant, Susan (Genie) White.

For providing postage stamps or classic color plates: Kraig Adler, Jacqueline Bonnemains, Elliott Jacobson, Don Riemer.

For the loan of specimens: David Auth and Russell McCarty (Florida Museum of Natural History), Steve Gotte and Roy McDiarmid (U.S. National Museum, Smithsonian Institution), Peter Pritchard (Chelonian Research Institute).

For reviewing sections of the manuscript: I. Lehr Brisbin, Jr., Terence Farrell, Russ Hall, Peter Pritchard, Craig Weatherby.

For her careful attention to editorial detail and readability: Sally E. Antrobus.

For advice and assistance in various other aspects of the project: J. Whitfield Gibbons, Robert Hansen, Vic Hutchison, Mark Jennings, Heather Kalb, Richard Seigel, George Zug.

For providing assistance in covering illustration expenses: Anders Rhodin and the Chelonian Research Foundation.

In addition, I thank my wife, Marian Griffey, for reading and editing the entire manuscript, organizing the photographs, sending out correspondence, preparing illustration 8-3, and offering advice and counsel. Her help has been invaluable.

NORTH AMERICAN
BOX TURTLES

1 A Most Amiable Reptile

An Introduction to Box Turtles

Everybody likes box turtles.
ARCHIE CARR, 1994

 In his famed book on his beloved Florida, naturalist and renowned turtle researcher Archie Carr penned the words that set the theme for this book. Archie called the box turtle "sticky heels," supposedly a name of Delaware Indian derivation that acknowledged the slow walking gait of the eastern box turtle (Carr, 1994). Carr noted that despite this animal's familiarity to both biologists and the lay public, there was surprisingly little written on the biology of the so-called common box turtle. Although the "Sticky Heels" essay was probably penned in the early 1940s, the situation had not changed much by the early 1990s when I began my studies of Florida box turtles on Egmont Key, a small island at the entrance to Tampa Bay (fig. 1-1). Indeed, what I could find in the literature on Florida's box turtles I often learned later was wrong, pirated from studies carried out hundreds or thousands of kilometers away.

Today there has been a reawakening of interest in the study of box turtles, and it is coming none too soon. Some of the interest is derived from the same sort of inquisitiveness that motivated naturalists in the past—that is, simply a keen curiosity about the inhabitants of the world around us. Another interest, more urgent, is motivated by a desire to conserve this most amiable reptile in the face of a tidal wave of humanity. With human populations expanding and a booming economy, it seems as though no habitat is truly protected. Although there are only four species of box turtles, their familiarity, their stoical, benign nature, and their vulnerability as they helplessly plod along make them symbols of the fragility of nature and the threat to biotic diversity in temperate and subtropical North America. Everybody likes box turtles.

This book has two purposes. The first is to introduce the amateur naturalist and other interested people to the biology and natural history of North American box turtles. The second is to summarize the scientific literature as much as possible in order for the work to serve as a reference for the professional biologist. Although these objectives are by no means mutually exclusive, difficulties may arise. In case technical terms are unfamiliar to some, a glossary is provided. Professionals may want to skip explanations of concepts already familiar. My larger overall purpose is to celebrate the natural history of box turtles, to make people aware of their biology, behavior, and requirements, and to cultivate an appreciation of them that will help conserve the animals and their habitats.

Figure. 1-1. Aerial photograph of Egmont Key, Hillsborough County, Florida, looking south. Mullet Key (Fort DeSoto State Park) is to the lower left, Passage Key is directly south of Egmont, and the mainland is to the upper center-left. Egmont Key is the home of large Florida box turtle and gopher tortoise populations. Research carried out since 1991 on Egmont's turtles forms the basis for much of the information in this book. This is a very special place, a crown jewel in the national wildlife refuge system.

To the amateur, I say learn about nature, but do it carefully and with commitment. There is nothing mysterious about science; and although many professionals forget it, the scientific method begins with careful observation and curiosity, not dry hypotheses. Amateur naturalists have much to offer the scientific community in understanding the ways of box turtles. Ultimately, it will be up to the public to forge the will to protect them. To the professional, I say get outdoors and observe nature. A bond with the animal under study is not inappropriate, and natural history has much to offer in terms of understanding the foundations of ecology and conservation. Although we tend to get wrapped up in test statistics—our means, medians, and normal distributions—an important part of ecology and evolution is the variation we see, and not necessarily the mean or average. Natural history should be celebrated. After all, we are dealing with life in all its complexity. A study of box turtles is the perfect place to begin.

What Is a Box Turtle?

NOMENCLATURE, SPECIES, AND SUBSPECIES

The name by which we call an animal should tell us something about the animal. The common name *box turtle* indicates what this animal generally resembles: it is a box with a head on a moderately long neck, four powerful legs with sharp claws, and a short little tail. Many turtles may be said to resemble a box, however, so scientists have devised a system whereby there can be no doubt about which animal is under discussion. Biologists use a two-word (binomial) nomenclature to designate the scientific name of a species. Scientific names contain both a generic (genus) name and a specific epithet. All North American box turtles are placed within the genus *Terrapene* (a name derived from an Algonkian Indian word for turtle). There are four recognized species: *T. carolina*, *T. ornata*, *T. nelsoni*, and *T. coahuila*. Placing the four within the same genus implies a shared evolutionary history. Table 1-1 gives their accepted common names.

Some researchers recognize phenotypic variation (differences in appearance) among regional populations of a species and give such populations a third name, the subspecies name. No subspecies are recognized for the Coahuilan box turtle, *T. coahuila*, but several

TABLE 1-1. Standard English common names for turtles of the genus *Terrapene*. Nomenclature follows Collins (1997). Common names in other languages are found in the Species Accounts.

Terrapene	Box turtle
T. carolina	Eastern box turtle
T. c. carolina	Eastern box turtle
T. c. bauri	Florida box turtle
T. c. major	Gulf Coast box turtle
T. c. mexicana	Mexican box turtle
T. c. putnami	Giant box turtle (fossil)
T. c. triunguis	Three-toed box turtle
T. c. yucatana	Yucatán box turtle
T. coahuila	Coahuilan box turtle
T. nelsoni	Spotted box turtle
T. n. nelsoni	Southern spotted box turtle
T. n. klauberi	Northern spotted box turtle
T. ornata	Ornate box turtle
T. o. ornata	Ornate box turtle
T. o. luteola	Desert box turtle

are recognized for the other species. The species *T. carolina*, the eastern box turtle, includes the subspecies *T. c. carolina*, *bauri*, *major*, *triunguis*, and *putnami* (fossil); *T. ornata*, the ornate box turtle, includes *T. o. ornata* and *luteola*; and *T. nelsoni*, the spotted box turtle, includes *T. n. nelsoni* and *klauberi*. Again, a shared evolutionary history, or lineage, is implied by grouping subspecies within a nominate species (see glossary).

In the past, other species and subspecies of recent and fossil *Terrapene* have been described. However, additional evidence has shown either that these taxa are not valid or that they are not sufficiently distinct to merit recognition. More information on invalid names is presented in chapter 2 and in the synonymies in the species accounts. As information in chapter 2 shows, our concepts of box turtle systematics, and therefore nomenclature, are far from settled. As recently as 1980, recommendations were made to elevate some subspecies, such as *bauri*, to full specific status (Ward, 1980). I have chosen not to follow this recommendation since the information supporting the change was not published in the peer-reviewed scientific literature and the suggestion has not been followed by chelonian systematists (*chelonian*, meaning turtle, is derived from the Greek name for the animals). Still, the question of how many species and subspecies of *Terrapene* should be recognized is by no means closed.

Indeed, the definitions of species and subspecies are open to much debate for all forms of life. In this book, I use an essentially biological species concept definition; that is, a species is a group of organisms that are capable of interbreeding, that produce fertile offspring in the wild, and that share a common evolutionary lineage. There are other species concepts, such as the evolutionary and phylogenetic concepts, which seek to recognize evolutionary lineages without necessarily invoking the criterion of reproductive compatibility. For box turtles, the determination of evolutionary lineages remains open to debate, and more data, especially molecular data, are required for a better understanding of relationships.

Likewise, I have chosen to recognize the subspecies of box turtles generally accepted by most chelonian researchers. The definition of a subspecies, or whether it is a taxon that should be recognized, is hotly debated (see Smith et al., 1997, for a review). In the present work, the concept of subspecies is used for a phenotypically distinct group of box turtles occupying a spatially defined region, but without reproductive isolation from other such groups of box turtles. There are many good arguments for not recognizing subspecies in biological nomenclature, but in this case I follow the advice of Smith and colleagues (1997:16) when they state that the use of a subspecies name is "a tool for conveying information about major patterns of variation within species, flagging opportunities for causal analyses. A subspecies name draws attention to a geographic segment of a species that is in some way recognizably different . . . and provides information about diversity to a variety of disciplines from genetics and ecology to conservation biology."

Certainly, the named subspecies of box turtles are recognizably very different across their range as regards a host of characters, such as shell shape, coloration, and cranial osteology. However, the named box turtle subspecies may also represent divergent evolutionary lineages (chapter 2), in contrast to classical notions of what constitutes a subspecies (Smith et al., 1997). There is considerable introgression (see glossary) in areas of subspecific contact that warrants detailed genetic, phenotypic, and ecological evaluation. In such areas, subspecific nomenclature becomes much more fluid and difficult to apply, and it may not be possible to attach a name to a particular specimen. In such areas of contact, where subspecific characters blend, those populations are referred to as intergrades. Turtles cannot be made to fit into type categories, no matter how hard we try; populations are dynamic and individuals are ever variable.

Until recently, biologists applied a rather Linnaean (after Carl Linnaeus, the originator of modern biological nomenclature) hierarchical system when discussing classification above the species level. Box turtles were classified as follows: Kingdom Animalia, Class Reptilia, Order Testudines, Suborder Cryptodira, Family Emydidae, Genus *Terrapene*. However, the Linnaean system itself has come under increasing criticism by some evolutionary biologists, who propose that its hierarchies be replaced by a lineage-based system employing clade and species (De Queiroz, 1995, 1997). It is not clear how phylogenetic nomenclature might replace the old Linnaean hierarchical system, but biologists agree that any system of nomenclature should reflect phylogenetic (evolutionary) lineages and historical relationships.

MORPHOLOGY

The most obvious morphological feature of box turtles is their bony, boxy shell, illustrated in figures 1-2 and 1-3. In times of danger, the turtle is able to withdraw its head, neck, tail, and limbs completely within the shell. It does this by expelling air in the lungs to allow room for the limbs and by twisting its neck into an S shape to bring the head into the enclosing shell. Box turtles are able to effect a tight seal by closing the plastron (bottom shell) upward to fit snugly against the carapace (top shell). A movable hinge between the pectoral and abdominal scutes (and between the hyoplastral and hypoplastral bones; see fig. 1-3b) assures closure of the front end of the plastron. Once inside its shell, a box turtle is virtually impossible to dislodge.

The shell of the turtle consists of scutes, composed of a keratinized substance covering the bony shell, and the bones of the shell. The scutes and bones are of different embryological origin and do not overlay exactly. Instead, they are offset to allow strong support. A turtle's shell coloration is due to pigment cells located within the epidermal scutes. Scutes are not shed as are the scales of many reptiles but grow concentrically outward from a central region, thus keeping pace with the growth of the underlying bony shell. This periodic growth gives the scutes of some species, including box turtles, a sculpted appearance. In old specimens the scutes may be worn smooth, but in younger specimens growth produces well-defined rings, which may or may not indicate seasonal or annular growth. The names of the bones and scutes are provided in figures 1-2 and 1-3.

Unlike in many turtles, the bones of box turtle shells fuse together, especially in older and larger specimens (see chapter 9). Thus, box turtle shells are found in natural settings long after the shells of other turtles would have disarticulated and scattered. As with all bony turtles, the ribs and vertebral column are fused with the bony shell. Otherwise, the skeletons of box turtles are similar to those of other turtles in the family Emydidae except for the skulls, which are diagnostic among the species and subspecies (fig. 1-4). These are

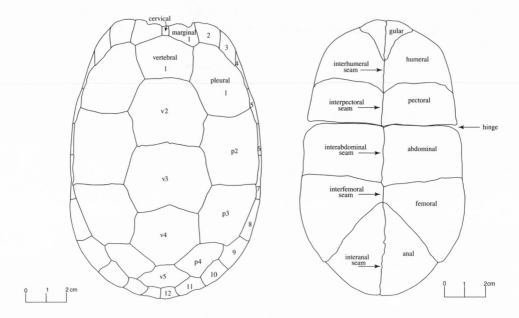

Figure 1-2a. Scutes of the carapace of a box turtle.

1-2b. Scutes of the plastron of a box turtle.

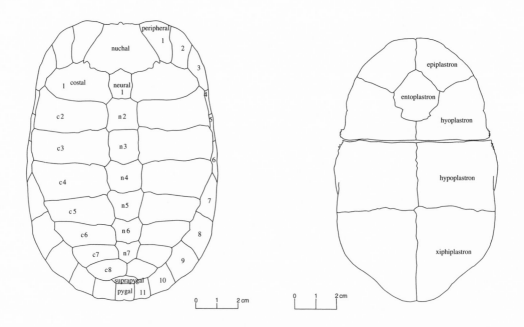

Figure. 1-3a. Bones of the carapace of a box turtle.

1-3b. Bones of the plastron of a box turtle.

illustrated in more detail in the species accounts at the end of the book. As with the skeleton, the internal anatomy of box turtles is similar to that of freshwater turtles, except that
box turtles either lack or have degenerative cloacal bursae, small pouch-like organs found
in other emydid turtles. This is not surprising since the cloacal bursae have a respiratory
function associated with hibernation in water (Smith and James, 1958). Inasmuch as
Terrapene pass the cold winter on land, the organ is unnecessary. Readers interested in
more detail on the internal anatomy of turtles should consult Noble and Noble (1940).

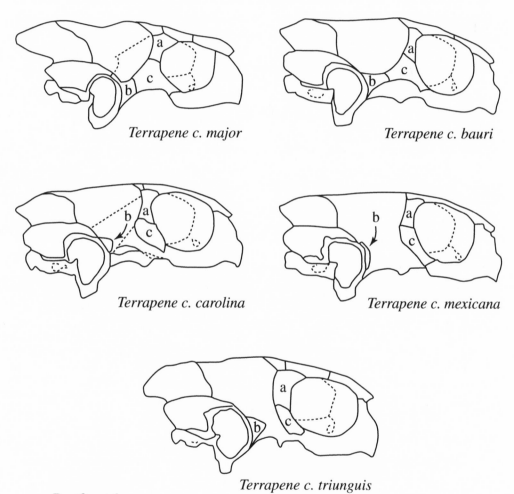

a. Postfrontal
b. Quadrato-jugal
c. Jugal

Figure. 1-4. Skull structure: variation in the three bones comprising the zygomatic arch among
subspecies of *Terrapene carolina*. After Taylor (1895).

HABITATS

Box turtles are generally terrestrial turtles, although they occasionally take to water and one species, *T. coahuila*, is highly aquatic. They eat a wide variety of foods, frequent many types of habitats, and are active as temperature and humidity permit. As such, nearly all box turtles are ecological generalists. The generalist approach to life has allowed them access to many areas of the Nearctic Region devoid of terrestrial turtles, and they seem adapted for a long and rather uneventful, quiet life. Box turtles are home-bodies living in a small, defined area and seem well aware of their surroundings and the locations of choice food, temporary shelter, and overwintering sites. These subjects are explored more fully in the chapters that follow.

NORTH AMERICAN VERSUS ASIAN BOX TURTLES

There are two groups of turtles commonly called box turtles in English, the North American *Terrapene* and the Asian turtles of the genus *Cuora*. Although a few other turtles have movable plastral hinges between the pectoral and abdominal scutes (*Emys* in Europe, *Emydoidea* in North America, and *Notochelys*, *Pyxidea*, and *Cyclemys* in Asia), only *Terrapene* and *Cuora* can completely close the shell into a tight box. Indeed, only some advanced *Cuora* (e.g., *amboinensis*, *flavomarginata*, and *galbinifrons*) can enclose the body as completely as can *Terrapene*, whereas the others attain only partial closure. Unlike in *Terrapene*, the shells of Asian box turtles usually have a median keel and two longitudinal keels as well as a smooth posterior rim of the carapace. In addition, the plastral scute ratios are different despite general impressions of close similarity in shape (Ernst et al., 1997). Some of the primitive *Cuora* are downright "unboxy" in appearance, with much more depressed and elongated carapaces than that of our familiar box turtle. In addition, the Asian box turtles are more aquatic than North American species, preferring marshes, ponds, and flooded fields. Thus, the development of the hinged plastron in these turtles represents a case of convergent evolution. The Asian and North American box turtles, although superficially similar, are not closely related.

Box Turtles through Human History

ARCHEOLOGY

Box turtle shell fragments are found abundantly throughout eastern North America associated with Native American trash middens (fig. 1-5). Nearly every site for which I have been able to examine archeological summaries of animal remains includes at least some box turtle bones (see also Adler, 1968). The charred nature of many of the early fragments suggests that the turtles were eaten rather than used solely for ceremonial purposes. In later cultures, such as those of the Middle and Late Woodland periods from 2000 to 400 years before the present (B.P.), use shifted primarily to ceremonial functions. In the Northeast, the oldest archeological record extends to about 5400 years B.P. (Adler, 1970).

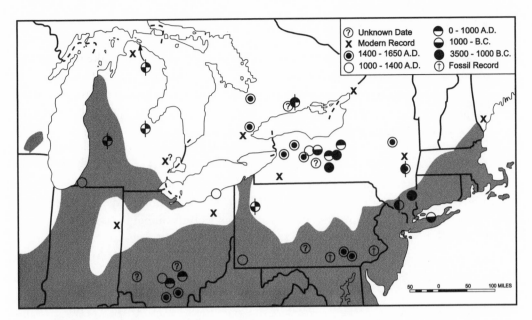

Figure. 1-5. Archeological sites in the upper Midwest and Northeast of North America containing remains of box turtles. The shading indicates the present range of Terrapene. Reprinted from Adler (1970).

The importance certain peoples attached to box turtles can be seen in the inclusion of box turtles in graves as burial items. In New York, box turtles were included with burials as late as the late 1600s, although the decreasing frequency with which they are seen in later sites suggests decreasing abundance. Burials sometimes contained dozens of individual turtles. Such box turtle shells likely were ceremonial in nature rather than indicative of a food preference.

It appears as though box turtles formed a minor part of the diet of certain Native American cultures, such as the Deptford of the Florida Gulf Coast (2300 years B.P.; Wing, 1968). Box turtles were probably gathered as they were encountered, perhaps by women and children tending gardens or during the course of land clearing for agriculture. In other cultures, such as those of New York state, adult and juvenile box turtles were harvested intensively (Adler, 1970). Some modern cultures avoid box turtles, such as the Hurons of the Great Lakes region, who associate them with bewitchment (Adler, 1970). Undoubtedly, there was a mosaic of beliefs associated with the turtles in pre-European times and far into the distant past, depending on period, region, local turtle abundance, and ancestral tradition. These beliefs would in turn affect whether and how box turtles were used as food.

Moving to their role as ceremonial objects, archeological evidence from the Mississippian period (ca. 1300–600 years B.P.) suggests that box turtle leg rattles were used at this early time. Box turtle shells also were used as hand rattles, with a shaft stuck into a hole drilled into the carapace. It seems likely that some southern turtle rattles were traded northward, since specimens found in Ontario and New York have holes in them where handles were attached (Bleakney, 1958). This is a common feature of the rattles of modern southern tribes, and shells have been found in archeological sites outside the known or presumed range of these species. Certainly their light weight and ease of transport made box turtle rattles amenable to trade among distant tribes. Box turtle bones with holes in them have been found as early as the Archaic (5800 years B.P.), suggesting that they were not associated with agricultural rituals when they first began to be used, as some authors have suggested (see Sturtevant, 1961).

In addition to serving as rattles, box turtle shells were shaped or fashioned into bowls and other forms of ornaments. By grinding down or removing the vertebral column and the heads of ribs, a smooth bowl or drinking ladle could be fashioned. Worked specimens likely were traded, so their presence in archeological deposits cannot be used to infer local turtle distribution (Adler, 1968). Still, archeological evidence suggests that box turtles were present in many areas outside their current range, especially in the Midwest and at their northern range limit in New York and perhaps even Canada. The range of ornate box turtles has receded due to the spatial reduction in prairie habitats (Adler, 1968), whereas the range of eastern box turtles likely has shifted southward as a result of overuse by indigenous peoples. In New York, for example, the decline in box turtles appears correlated with a large increase in Iroquoian populations at ca. 2700 to 2900 years B.P. (Adler, 1970). The use of box turtles largely ended by 350 years B.P. among northeastern Native Americans as box turtles became exceedingly scarce or disappeared altogether. In the Northeast, at least, the disappearance of box turtles does not appear correlated with climate changes. As in other regions around the world, use by indigenous peoples may have had profound effects on local chelonian distribution and survival.

In Mayan México, the Yucatán box turtle may have played an important role, at least judging from the number of stone carvings that seem to represent this species. In Uxmal, the Mayans built (ca. 1200 years B.P.) what is now called the House of Turtles. The upper cornice of the building contains a series of carved turtles closely resembling box turtles (fig. 1-6). Aside from the carved turtles, there is no elaborate decoration, and the building seems simple, yet elegant. Shells of Yucatán box turtles have been excavated from the Mayan city of Mayapan and closely resemble terra cotta figures found in the vicinity of the ruins. The Yucatán box turtle may have been used in rituals associated with the summer solstice and the beginning of the rainy season, and hence it may have been an important herald in Mayan society (Mills, 1970).

USE BY MODERN NATIVE AMERICANS

Box turtles were used in historic times and continue to be used by Native Americans. For example, the Sioux (Lakota) used them for food (Over, 1923) and the Kiowa Apache roasted them. The Kiowa also made amulets for young children by drying a hatchling or small box turtle, covering it with buckskin, and then beading the buckskin (Jordan, 1979a). The earliest mention that I can find in the North American literature perhaps referring to box turtles is the observation by Barton (1796) of Delaware Indians using turtle rattles in their dances. Although Barton does not explicitly name the turtle used, it

Figure 1-6. Carved stone box turtle from "House of the Turtles," Uxmal, Mexico. Photo by James Buskirk.

seems likely that box turtle shells were a readily available choice in the Middle Atlantic region.

Today, box turtle shells still are used in ceremonial function by Native Americans. Shells are painted with various designs, such as those of the Cherokee and Catawba. They also are used as rattles, although rattles made of tin cans and other containers are supplanting turtle shells to some extent. In the Northeast, the Seneca use the shell as a hand rattle (*ká?tya꞉skwa? kastáwĕ?shæ?*, box-turtle rattle); that is, without a handle. The shell is soaked and cleaned, internal body parts are removed, and small pebbles or shot are inserted to make the rattle sound. The hinge is then shut and dried forming the seal (Conklin and Sturtevant, 1953). Shells may be varnished. Box turtle rattles are owned only by women or the longhouse, although only men make them. Shells may be kept for generations. Box turtle shell rattles are used as part of the Women's Rite, which occurs during the Midwinter Festival. Detailed descriptions of the dance and songs associated with this rite are provided by Conklin and Sturtevant (1953). The Cherokee make similar handheld rattles, but they have handles (see photo in Leftwich, 1970). Modern seals and handle attachment are secured using aquarium sealer.

Many Native American tribes use turtle shell leg rattles during specific ceremonies. Women and girls wear elaborate shank or leg rattles containing from a few to five or more shells per leg (see, for example, the cover of the spring 1997 issue of *Native Peoples* magazine, featuring Wilma Mankiller, former principal chief of the Cherokee Nation of Oklahoma, wearing box turtle shell rattles). The rattles are worn during the rhythmic Stomp Dance, associated with the Busk or Green Corn ceremonies. Western tribes—

including the Cherokee, Creek, Seminole, Yuchi, Shawnee, Caddo, and Seneca-Cayuga, all of Oklahoma—use ornate and three-toed box turtles (see color plates), whereas eastern tribes such as the Cherokee of North Carolina use eastern box turtles. Even Plains tribes that had no historical equivalent of the Stomp Dance now have adopted it. Descriptions of the dance are provided by Jordan (1979b), and photographs of dancers and rattles are in Sturtevant (1954), Leftwich (1970), and Heth (1997) and on beautiful note cards available from the Museum of the Cherokee in Cherokee, North Carolina.

I can find only one major reference to box turtles in modern literature: John Steinbeck's elegant portrayal of a box turtle approaching and crossing a dusty Oklahoma road in *The Grapes of Wrath*. But there are many stories and myths featuring *Terrapene* within Native American traditions. The turtle in general, and among Algonkian tribes the box turtle in particular, was said to be the earth-bearer, the animal responsible for holding up the earth. Another mythic perspective views the turtle as a reminder to not judge by outward appearances: it may look like an animal of no great distinction, but the box turtle can smell and see reasonably well. Among the Cherokee, the "land tortoise" (*tûksĭ'*) was reputed to have been a great warrior, and ball players would rub their limbs with the turtle prior to entering the ball court (Mooney, 1900). There is also a well-known Cherokee story about how a lowly box turtle outwits a speedy and overconfident rabbit in a race over four mountain ridges; it seems the turtle used his friends, which of course resembled him, to appear to stay ahead of the rabbit and, in the end, to win the race. Mooney (1900) provides the complete text.

ART AND ILLUSTRATION

Today, representations of box turtles are commonly seen in every variety, from cheap plastic turtles with dancing heads to works of fine art. They are incorporated into sculptural stonework, cast as bronze figures, and carved from every wood imaginable. Some artists, such as in Tom McFarland's painting of emerging hatchlings (see color plates), closely convey the physical attitude and behavior of the turtle—faithful renderings are often attempted but rarely achieved. Other artists freely interpret the shape of the shell, the form and arrangement of carapace sutures, the coloration, and the demeanor into a free-form expression far removed from the turtle in the woods. Even with such extremes of artistic license, they still remind us of a box turtle. Perhaps this is not surprising, since so many people have at least a passing recognition of the appearance of a box turtle. Artists may be inspired by the stoical look of a contemplative turtle; indeed, capturing the exact facial features and demeanor of a turtle can be a much more daunting task than it initially appears. Perhaps this is the artistic challenge.

In many indigenous cultures, and even in Europeanized North America, turtles are perceived as totems or representations of longevity and fecundity. Not surprisingly, some of the finest artwork I have seen featuring box turtles is being produced by Native American artists in stone, wood, and pottery. In our personal collection, my wife and I have a stylized wood carving in buckeye by Cherokee artist Ernest Lambert, box turtle pottery by Catawba master potter Sara Ayers (Catawba Cultural Preservation Project, 1995), and a beautiful soapstone carved *Terrapene* by the Canadian Inik artist Augiak

Novalinga. These artists blend the realistic with the spiritual to produce a representation of the box turtle as both being and spirit being.

Turtles also are widely used as the subject of jewelry, perhaps subliminally in connection with their perceived powers of life. Turtle pins and earrings are common in galleries and at art shows, and undoubtedly box turtles often have inspired their creators in both form and appearance. Fine examples of contemporary jewelry featuring box turtles are the earrings and necklaces created by Barbara Bell of Philadelphia, Pennsylvania, from polymer clay (see plates).

One cannot leave the subject of box turtles in art without mentioning the often exquisite illustrations produced in connection with early explorations, publications, and contemporary meetings. For example, the color illustrations of Schoepff (1792–1801), Charles-Alexandre Lesueur in the early 1800s (Bonnemains and Bour, 1996), Georges Cuvier (in Duvernoy, 1836), John Holbrook (1842), Karl Bodmer in Wied-Neuwied (1865), Sowerby and Lear (1872), and J. Henry Blake in Babcock (1919) are certainly among the most beautiful of all wildlife illustrations as well as being scientifically accurate. Black and white illustrations of high quality can be found in early natural histories, such as DeKay's *Zoology of New York* (DeKay, 1842) and Agassiz's (1857) hatchlings in his *Contributions to the Natural History of the United States of America*.

The high esteem and recognition with which box turtles are associated within the scientific discipline of herpetology culminated in their selection as subject for the poster of the First World Congress of Herpetology, held in Canterbury, England, in 1989. David Dennis's portrait of an eastern box turtle looking upward at ripe blueberries is a classic in a long tradition of fine art as scientific illustration, a tradition that somewhat lamentably has given way to line drawings and photographs. Yet some contemporary postcards and journal covers featuring box turtles (e.g., *Herpetological Review* volume 26, number 3) approach the quality of photographic art. Box turtles have appeared on postage stamps in the United States, Cambodia, Scotland, and even Dagestan, a republic within Russia. They even have a beer named in their honor—Box Turtle Beer by Old North State Brewing Company of Youngsville, North Carolina. A most amiable reptile, indeed!

Important Contributors to Box Turtle Research

PALEOHISTORY

The most important contributors to knowledge of the paleohistory of box turtles have been Oliver Perry Hay, Walter Auffenberg, Wilbur Milstead, and J. Alan Holman. Hay (1846–1930), an associate of the Carnegie Institution of Washington, wrote voluminously on the Pleistocene vertebrates of North America. Although he published on all taxa, one of his best known works is his *Fossil Turtles of North America*, published in 1908. With regard to *Terrapene*, he published a number of papers from 1906 to 1924 describing new species (see chapter 2) and summarizing local faunas. Unfortunately, many of his descriptions were based on fragmentary pieces of shell or on a small number of individuals, and more recent systematists have suggested that the variation noted by Hay was not sufficient to warrant recognition of so many species.

Walter Auffenberg, emeritus curator of the Florida Museum of Natural History (FLMNH), studied all aspects of the herpetofauna of Florida but is perhaps better known for his studies of tortoises and of the giant monitor lizards (*Varanus*) of south and southeast Asia. Although his doctoral dissertation focused on Florida's fossil snakes, he published a series of papers beginning in 1957 on the rich fossil turtle fauna of Florida, including three papers dealing specifically with *Terrapene*. Auffenberg reviewed the myriad box turtle fossils in the FLMNH collection and clarified the systematics of the many fossil Florida box turtles described by Hay.

Wilbur W. Milstead (1928–74; fig. 1-7) was a colleague and friend of Auffenberg's and with him coauthored a summary of the Quaternary reptile fauna of North America. Milstead is well known for his studies on lizard ecology, but he also had an interest in the evolution of both modern and fossil *Terrapene*, culminating in his 1969 "Studies on the Evolution of Box Turtles (Genus *Terrapene*)." Milstead's research on fossil *Terrapene* focused on the central and south-central portions of North America. Like Auffenberg, Milstead helped clarify the systematics of some of the fossils originally described by Hay.

More recently J. Alan Holman of Michigan State University Museum has become the dean of the study of Pleistocene reptiles and amphibians. He has published books summarizing the Pleistocene herpetofauna of North America and Europe (e.g., Holman, 1995) as well as numerous papers describing fossil faunas from sites all over both continents. Although retired, he is studying fossil *Terrapene* from Nebraska, including perhaps the oldest known fossil that can be assigned to the genus.

LIFE HISTORY

The most important life history studies not connected with long-term studies are those of William Brown, recently retired from Skidmore College, on *T. coahuila*, and of John Legler (fig. 1-8) of the University of Utah, who studied ornate box turtles. Brown (1974) conducted his work in the late 1960s for his master's degree, extensively examining the life history of the then little known Coahuilan box turtle. His research followed much the same outline as Legler's Ph.D. work on the Kansas prairie in the late 1950s (Legler, 1960). Both studies examined nearly every aspect of the ecology of their respective species of box turtles, including food, reproduction, habitat use, movement, predation, social interactions, and activity patterns. These studies still form the basis for what we know about both species, and the results of these studies are referred to again and again in the chapters that follow.

Other significant natural history contributions were made by Artie and Edna Metcalf (in southeastern Kansas) and Angela Doroff and Lloyd Keith (in Wisconsin), both on *T. ornata*; by Douglas Reagan, who worked on *T. carolina* habitat use in Arkansas; and by H. A. Allard, who reported on the natural history of his captive herd of box turtles in the Washington, D.C., area in the 1930s and 1940s. Movement patterns have been studied using radio telemetry in several of the species, but these studies still are mostly unpublished. The most comprehensive, perhaps, are those of Robert Madden and Robert Cook, both of whom conducted box turtle telemetry research on Long Island as part of their Ph.D. program at City University of New York.

Figure 1-7. Wilbur W. Milstead. Photograph courtesy of Kraig Adler.

Figure 1-8. John Legler. Photograph courtesy of George Zug.

Long-term Studies

The first long-term study on the life history of box turtles began around 1911 when John Treadwell Nichols (1883–1958; fig. 1-9) of the American Museum of Natural History began inscribing box turtles on his estate on Long Island, New York (now called the Floyd Estate). He published some of his results in 1939 (Nichols, 1939a, 1939b), and they formed the earliest reliable information on growth, movements, and activity. Nichols continued to mark turtles until his death. In 1989, National Park Service biologist Richard Stavdal was continuing Nichols's study and had marked an additional four hundred eastern box turtles (Lipske, 1989). Although information has been collected on the Floyd Estate since 1915, little of it has been published.

In 1944, Lucille Stickel (fig. 1-10), who would become director of the Patuxent Wildlife Research Center of the U.S. Fish and Wildlife Service, began a study of the box turtles of the center's lands near Laurel, Maryland. Stickel continued the study until her retirement. Her major contribution to our knowledge of *Terrapene* is a monographic study published in 1950, which forms the basis of what is known about *T. carolina* ecology in eastern deciduous woodlands (Stickel, 1950). This paper remains an excellent source of basic natural history. Among other things, Stickel introduced the term *form* for the indentation that a box turtle makes in the leaf litter and ground cover while it is resting (chapter 3). Later she published papers on morphology, growth, home range, and population trends after thirty years of data collection. Stickel's population has been resurveyed

Figure 1-9. John Treadwell Nichols. Photograph courtesy of the G. S. Myers/A. Leviton portrait file, California Academy of Sciences.

Figure 1-10. Lucille Stickel. Photograph courtesy of Patuxent Wildlife Research Center, U.S. Geological Survey.

by Russell Hall of the U.S. Geological Survey, who recently reported on fifty-year population trends (Hall et al., 1999). Stickel's data are being computerized for future access (R. Hall, pers. comm.).

From 1958 to 1983, Eliot C. Williams of Wabash College studied the three-toed box turtles of Allee Memorial Woods in Indiana. Preliminary results were published in 1961 (Williams, 1961), but the bulk of the information on the natural history of this population was published in 1987 in collaboration with William S. Parker (Williams and Parker, 1987). During this time, six hundred turtles were marked, and 1,915 recaptures were recorded. Long-term trends showed a box turtle population decline and helped direct attention to the impacts on resident fauna of adverse land use adjacent to protected areas.

Finally, this brief account of the history of research on box turtles cannot end without mention of the work of Charles and Elizabeth Schwartz of the Missouri Department of Conservation (figs. 1-11, 1-12). The Schwartzes conducted research on the habitat use, home range, and population characteristics of the three-toed box turtles inhabiting their land near Jefferson City, Missouri, from 1965 to 1983 (Vance, 1985). Results of their work appeared in a series of publications by the Missouri Department of Conservation (Schwartz and Schwartz, 1974; Schwartz et al., 1984) and are presented throughout this book. To see the realm of colorful variation in *T. c. triunguis*, Schwartz et al. (1984) is a "must" for its impressive selection of color photographs. The Schwartzes also perfected the use of dogs—black Labradors—to find turtles. This box turtle population has recently been reexamined by Julie Miller of the University of Idaho to determine its status.

Figure 1-11. Charles W. Schwartz. Photograph courtesy of Elizabeth Schwartz.

Figure 1-12. Elizabeth R. Schwartz and turtle-hunting field crew. Photograph courtesy of Elizabeth Schwartz.

Research Techniques

Although it is impossible to describe in detail all the research techniques used to study box turtles, a brief introduction seems appropriate.

IDENTIFICATION

Perhaps the most important information a researcher needs when studying the natural history of a population of animals is "who am I looking at?" Repeated observations of individuals through time allows biologists to gather data on individual traits (e.g., how individuals change physically through time; growth; how many eggs a particular female lays in a particular year); ecological changes (e.g., do turtles change their habitat and activity patterns as they grow?); and population characteristics (e.g., survival rates, population sizes, trends in populations). Individuals must be identified accurately, identification must be possible through time and through a range of body sizes, and the marking technique should not influence the animal's activity or harm it.

Currently, there are three main ways of identifying box turtles in field studies. One is purely visual: the varied color and unique marking patterns of a box turtle's shell allow individual identification; no two patterns are alike in certain subspecies, such as the Florida box turtle (*T. c. bauri*). Strictly visual identification techniques work well in small populations, although as numbers increase it becomes difficult to keep track of individual variation. To avoid making errors, field biologists either sketch the pattern, which is time-consuming, or photograph the carapace and plastron of each specimen. Researchers even report success in identifying individuals by using a copying machine to obtain black and white images; color copies are expensive, and it is hard to get a box turtle to sit still for a good color image.

Early researchers, such as J. T. Nichols, initially marked box turtle shells by carving the date, identification number, and collector's initials directly into the turtle's shell (Lipske, 1989). Undoubtedly, this time-consuming process was traumatic for the turtle. Today, the most commonly used identification method is to notch or drill holes in the marginal scutes (Cagle, 1939), a process that can be completed in a few seconds and is permanent. Note in figure 1-2a that the marginal scutes are distributed in bilateral symmetry around the margin of the carapace. By counting around the circumference from the cervical scute either left or right, numbers can be assigned. For example, going left, the first marginal is assigned 1,000, the second 2,000, the third 4,000, and the fourth 7,000; one can notch two scutes to get to the number 9,000 (notching scutes 1 and 2 would yield an identification number of 3,000, which is why scute 3 is assigned 4,000; notching scutes 1 and 3 would give 5,000; and so on). Going right, the same 1-2-4-7 combination is used to indicate 100s. In the rear of the carapace, the dividing line is the junction of the number 12 marginals (see fig 1-2a). Going left, the number scheme is assigned to 10s, whereas going right yields unit values. Thus, 9,999 turtles can be marked in a population using this scheme. Notches are made with a file (to produce a V) a hacksaw blade (to produce a slit) or a drill bit (to produce a hole); they last throughout the turtle's life and have no long-term effects. On our Egmont Key study site, where we have marked more than sixteen hundred animals, we have never observed a box turtle with any problems associated with making the notches, but I suggest that instruments should be cleaned in alcohol between markings. In conjunction with the notching sequence, unusual patterns, scars, or injuries are noted directly on field data sheets.

Finally, passive integrative transponder (PIT) tags offer promise of long-term marking in turtle populations. PIT tags are magnetically encoded tags that provide a readout when activated by a handheld reader. Each tag has a unique identification number. Using a syringe, tags are inserted in box turtles under the skin of the lower abdomen just in front of the rear leg. The technique is invasive and certainly causes the turtle discomfort, but it is probably no worse than shell notching. Tags are long lasting and small enough to be inserted in small turtles, and the magnetic readout assures that the number can be read unambiguously. However, the glass capsules enclosing the tags sometimes break after insertion, occasionally a tag may be shed, and PIT tags cost about four to six dollars apiece, depending on the number ordered.

IN THE ENVIRONMENT

Finding box turtles when you want to study them can be difficult. One can search for them while walking transects or riding roads through habitats where they are suspected to occur, but their propensity for burrowing under surface debris makes finding them haphazard. Some researchers have employed turtle-sniffing dogs to search out hidden turtles, and as already noted, Labrador retrievers in particular have proven quite effective (Schwartz and Schwartz, 1974; Schwartz et al., 1984). In their publications, Elizabeth and Charles Schwartz have some wonderful photographs of their canine survey crew in action.

Once turtles are found, biologists may take a great many measurements related to the physical characters of both the turtle and its habitat. Our data sheets include diagrams on which we mark unusual color patterns, scars, injuries, and shell anomalies. We take straight-line measurements of carapace length (CL), plastron length (PL), shell depth, the number of toes on the rear feet, and body mass. Other researchers have recorded the lengths and widths of various scutes, tail length, eye color, and a variety of other meristic characters. We note what the turtle was doing, the time of day, and whether the head was in or out. For habitat variables, we measure the temperature of the air, substrate, and water (when appropriate), and we record relative humidity, weather conditions, and the nature of cover, habitat type, and substrate. Recently, we installed long-term data loggers to measure air temperature and relative humidity at fifteen-minute intervals for seven months. Data loggers can also be used to monitor nest temperatures and environmental variables associated with overwintering sites. Again, other researchers have employed different measurements, depending on the questions asked and the funds available. Naturalists should always put their observations into the context of the environmental conditions when the observations were made.

Once turtles are found and data recorded, it is useful to be able to find those individuals again. The best way to do that is to attach a transmitter on the back or side of the turtle's shell and to follow the animal's movements with a telemetry receiver. Transmitters have become smaller, less intrusive, longer lasting, and cheaper through the years, a trend one hopes will continue. The main drawbacks to using transmitters are that they fail on occasion, they are expensive if many turtles are to be followed, they have to be replaced periodically, and battery life may be relatively short (months rather than years). Battery size limits the size of turtles to which a transmitter can be attached. Small turtles normally cannot be tracked using radio telemetry; instead, some form of thread-trailing device or the use of a metal detector (chapter 4) may be possible.

POPULATIONS

In the past, the only way to tell much about certain aspects of the life history of box turtles, such as their diet, reproductive characteristics, or the presence of toxic compounds, was to examine dead specimens. These techniques are destructive and provide only a snapshot of what the turtle was doing or of its body condition at a point in time. Fortunately, there are new techniques available to examine turtles harmlessly and allow them to return to wild populations. For example, diets can be examined by using stomach flushing, feces examination, and sophisticated biochemical nutritional analyses to see what turtles eat. The reproductive system can be inspected using radiographs, ultrasound, laparoscopy, or even hormone levels in the blood. Biopsies allow toxicologists to extract tissues harmlessly and with a minimum of discomfort or pain. New techniques in field and laboratory biology are being developed all the time, especially borrowing from the medical sciences. Not only are they accurate, but such tools also allow characterization of life history variables through time (seasonally, annually) for single individuals. Modern researchers recognize that the destruction of large numbers of turtles cannot be justified on the basis of scientific inquiry.

The ability to derive a great deal of information about the history of a species from the tissues of organisms, even of a single individual, is a relatively recent phenomenon. By looking at the structure of how individual genes are put together (the nucleotide base sequences) and comparing them, levels of relatedness can be examined at multiple scales. Molecular biologists use a suite of highly complex biochemical procedures, including gene sequencing and mitochondrial DNA analysis, to determine the evolutionary history, approximate time of clade (lineage) divergence, population origin, and levels of genetic variability on a local or regional scale. Although molecular techniques have not been used extensively to examine *Terrapene*, they hold great promise.

To obtain proteins, molecular biologists use tissues from a variety of sources, including muscle, organs (especially the liver), and blood. New biopsy or extraction techniques and sample handling procedures that may not even require refrigeration allow field samples to be taken with a minimum of handling time; animals can be returned immediately to the environment. In addition, other information can be gathered using tissue samples—for example, the sex of juvenile turtles can otherwise be impossible to determine; secondary sexual characters do not develop until the turtle reaches maturity, only after many years. However, endocrinologists are able to use the ratios of various hormone titres to determine sex, even in small animals. Knowledge of juvenile sex ratios could become important in the development of conservation programs.

Finally, the advent of microcomputers and the development of statistical programs capable of analyzing large amounts of data have revolutionized the way field biologists study natural history. Data have always been easy to gather, but analyzing large amounts of information was difficult because of the sheer volume and complexity of statistical calculations. Now, with fast coprocessors and sophisticated mathematical programs, biologists have new tools to examine demographic parameters, such as survivorship and abundance. In addition, biologists are better able to examine the assumptions underlying different statistical models and to determine which model best fits the data gathered. It is possible to identify capture biases (sex, habitat, season) to see whether some animals are capture prone or shy and even to determine subtle changes in a population resulting from transients or environmental perturbation. Mathematical models allow herpetologists to monitor trends in turtle populations and to determine the precision of their results. Such tools give researchers greater confidence in estimates of abundance, survivorship, biomass, sex ratios, and a host of other parameters. With such an arsenal available, the study of the natural history of box turtles has opened up exciting, challenging, and thought-provoking areas of research.

Future Directions

Each of the chapters that follow includes a section titled Future Directions to point out unresolved questions regarding the natural history of box turtles. Of course, there may be a great many additional aspects of the biology of *Terrapene* awaiting discovery. Some questions require the use of sophisticated equipment or an advanced knowledge of statistics. Others need only a keen sense of observation, a notebook, and an inquiring mind. I hope this material will help stimulate both research on and appreciation of box turtles as dynamic members of their environment. In this regard, we might keep in mind the contributions of those naturalists who preceded us, no matter how simplistic their observations may appear today. As Isaac Newton (in Turnbull et al., 1959:416) said in correspondence to Robert Hooke on February 5, 1676: "If I have seen further it is by standing on ye shoulders of giants."

2 | # The Evolution of Box Turtles

> As *T. major* demonstrates so clearly, the carapace of a box turtle is an exceedingly variable thing, and the many changes of shape and proportion which it may assume cannot be regarded as of specific value.
>
> THOMAS BARBOUR AND H. C. STETSON, 1931

 In one of my early vertebrate zoology courses at the University of Kentucky, I remember Roger Barbour, my professor, telling the class that turtles were a remarkable group of animals because they accomplished a feat matched by no other vertebrate: moving the shoulder girdle and neck inside the rib cage. This allowed the development of the shell, a formidable protective device for a small animal. He further stated that turtles must have been very smug with their accomplishment; since the basic framework was set forth, turtles have used the same body plan ever since. Still, it must have been a successful strategy as turtles have persisted throughout an extremely long evolutionary history. One can always identify a turtle, whether it be one of the earliest kinds, *Proganochelys, Palaeochersis,* and *Proterochersis* of the Late Triassic (210 million years ago) or our present 260 or so extant species.

So it is with box turtles. Of our four living species, all are readily recognized as box turtles, and the earliest Miocene box turtle fossils are easily seen to be *Terrapene*. The link between its emydid, presumably aquatic ancestors and *Terrapene* is not at all clear and is subject to ongoing evaluation. Indeed, the relationship between the only recognized fossil taxon, *T. carolina putnami*, and the modern taxa is unclear. In evolutionary terms, box turtles seem to be a rather conservative group of turtles. Their morphological conservatism, however, suggests a generalist approach to life; perhaps that is their key to survival.

In this chapter, I outline the fossil history of the genus and current ideas of phylogenetic relationships. I then relate this information to biogeography and show how the present distribution mirrors phylogenetic history. Finally, I suggest numerous questions that remain to be answered concerning box turtle evolution and relationships. There have been a number of estimates presented in the literature concerning the dates of boundaries and the duration of the various Tertiary geologic epochs. In this discussion I follow Holman's (1995) time sequence. The acronym *m.y. B.P.* means million years before present.

Fossil Record

Fossil box turtles have been found from eastern Pennsylvania to southeastern Arizona and from Florida through western Nebraska. The locations of major fossil deposits containing remains of *Terrapene* are shown in fig. 2-1. Although *Terrapene* fossils have been found as isolated fragments on the surface, most good remains have been found in caves or fissures. Several important fossil sites even suggest that box turtles hibernated communally underground (Milstead, 1956; Auffenberg, 1959).

The distinctive shell of North American box turtles makes identification to generic level quite easy; fossil box turtles look like modern box turtles. Unfortunately, carapace and plastron fragments are most often found and, while recognizable, such fragments often do not lend themselves to specific or even unqualified generic identification. Shell fragments from the only other "boxy" North American hinged-plastron turtle, *Emydoidea blandingi*, have at times been confused with *Terrapene* and vice versa (Moodie and Van Devender, 1977).

The science of paleoherpetology has progressed much since its early days. Prior to the mid-twentieth century, paleontologists working with box turtle fossils were hampered by several factors that inhibited them from interpreting the fragments in hand accurately. For one, only a few researchers had access to only a few fragments. These researchers often worked in geographic isolation and some did not have the means to travel widely and view comparative material. Thus, very similar specimens from widely separated areas were sometimes described as different species. Second, fossils from a series of individuals generally were not available, and key diagnostic material, such as the skull,

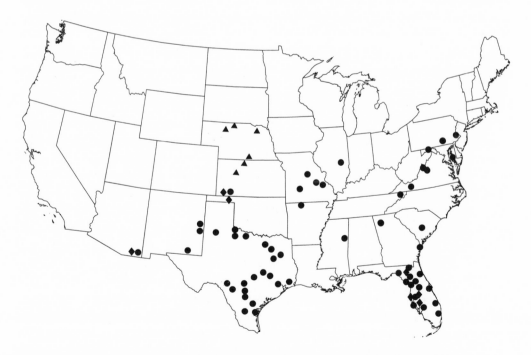

Figure 2-1. The locations of major fossil sites in North America containing bones of *Terrapene*. Triangles represent Miocene locations; diamonds represent Pliocene locations; and circles represent Pleistocene locations. Sources: In addition to text citations, see Jackson and Kaye (1974) and Preston (1979).

usually was not present. This meant that aberrant specimens or those distorted through time via geologic processes could be mistaken for different species. Third, researchers did not have a good grasp of the range of variation inherent within a taxon, even within modern species. Thus minor differences were mistakenly considered important, sometimes among specimens found in close spacial and/or temporal proximity. These three factors led to a proliferation of species descriptions based on minute differences in shell shape or size. We now know that modern box turtle species show a wide range of character variation, even within a single population. It is likely that fossil *Terrapene* did likewise.

Interpreting the biogeographic and evolutionary significance of fossils also was difficult for early researchers. Ideas concerning the age of the boundaries between geologic epochs have changed as more information has come to light. Also, paleontologists describing box turtle fossils did not have access to recent sophisticated methods for dating the age of deposits. Hence some early estimates of the age of fossil material were in error, and evolutionary events now must be reanalyzed in terms of revised age estimates. Likewise, a great deal of comparative information is now available on the paleoecology of entire communities and geographic regions. This allows modern researchers greater confidence in interpreting the timing of speciation events and in speculating upon the climatic mechanisms associated with those events.

MIOCENE (25–5 M.Y. B.P.)

The earliest fossil box turtles known are from mid-Miocene (Barstovian) deposits in Webster and Keya Paha counties, Nebraska, dating from around 15 m.y. B.P. (Holman and Corner, 1985; Holman, 1987). The Webster County fossils superficially resemble *T. coahuila* and perhaps substantiate a rather early date for the divergence of this isolated Mexican species from a proto-*Terrapene* ancestor (Auffenberg, 1958; Legler, 1960; Minx, 1996). J. A. Holman (Michigan State Univ., pers. comm.) thinks that it represents a distinct ancestral species and he is presently studying additional material from Nebraska.

Other fossils of *Terrapene* are known from the Late Miocene of Kansas and Nebraska (5 m.y. B.P.; Parmley, 1992). These fossils have been allocated to *T. carolina* (Holman, 1975) and *T. ornata* (Holman and Corner, 1985). As such, the two major evolutionary lineages of *Terrapene* (Carolina and Ornata) were present in modern form at least by the late Miocene.

Terrapene ornata longinsulae was described from Late Miocene deposits in Phillips County, Kansas (fig. 2-2; see Hay, 1908a). Unlike most fossil finds of box turtles, however, the Phillips County material included a skull. Hay (1908a) noted similarities among the skulls of *carolina*, *ornata*, and the new taxon but readily distinguished its greater affinities with *ornata*. Thus he described *longinsulae* as a subspecies of *ornata* but stated that it differed from *T. o. ornata* in having a narrow rather than wide carapace near the transverse hinge line at the eighth peripherals; not having a ridge line on the carapace; having parallel rather than converging rami of the lower jaw; and not having a median carina. These characters are quite variable in modern *ornata*, however, and the variation is such as to negate their diagnostic usefulness in identifying *longinsulae*. Accordingly, this subspecies is not currently recognized (J. A. Holman, pers. comm.), and no other fossil *Terrapene* of the Ornata group has been formally named and recognized.

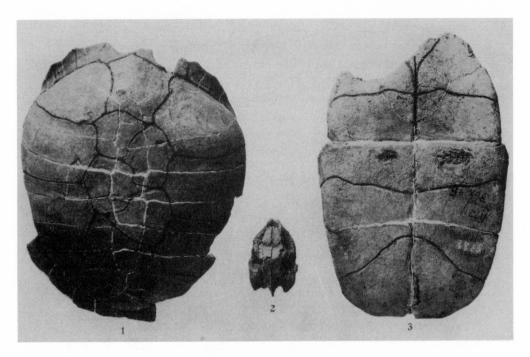

Figure 2-2. Terrapene ornata longinsulae. From Hay (1908a).

PLIOCENE (5–1.9 M.Y. B.P.)

Fossil *Terrapene carolina* are known from Columbia, Pinellas, Polk, and Hardee counties in Florida (all are in the Vertebrate Paleontology Collection, Florida Museum of Natural History, Gainesville). One new species of box turtle, *T. antipex*, was described from a partial plastron and associated fragments found in what were thought to be Pleistocene deposits in Indian River County, Florida (Hay, 1916a). A partial plastron and fragments found in questionably Middle Pliocene deposits in St. Johns County, Florida, later were referred to this species (Hay, 1923). However, *T. antipex* is now considered conspecific with *T. carolina putnami* (see Gilmore, 1927) and the age initially assigned to the fossils is in error. Fossil *T. carolina* previously reported from the Wakeeney Local Fauna in Trego County, Kansas, as Early Pliocene (Holman, 1975) are now known to be of Miocene age (J. A. Holman, pers. comm.). Pliocene fossil *Terrapene ornata* are known from Oklahoma and Kansas (Milstead, 1967) and Arizona (Moodie and Van Devender, 1978).

PLEISTOCENE (1.9 MILLION TO 10,000 YEARS B.P.)

Most named fossil box turtles have been described from Pleistocene deposits. These, listed chronologically, include:

> *Cistudo* (= *Terrapene*) *eurypygia*. Cope, 1869. A *T. c. carolina* from Talbot Co., Maryland. See Milstead (1965). Hay (1908b) previously placed the fossil turtle *Toxaspis anguillulatus* (Cope) from Pennsylvania in synonymy with *T. eurypygia*.

Cistudo (= *Terrapene*) *marnochi*. Cope, 1878. An intermediate between *T. c. put-nami* and *T. c. triunguis* from Atascosa County, Texas. See Milstead (1965).

Terrapene carolina putnami. Hay, 1906 (often incorrectly cited as 1908). The only currently recognized fossil taxon in the genus *Terrapene* (but see later discussion). *Terrapene carolina putnami* was a giant box turtle reaching more than 300 mm in carapace length and was found from Florida through Missouri, Kansas, and Texas to as far west as New Mexico (see fig. 2-3).

T. canaliculata. Hay, 1907. Originally described from Skidaway (spelled Skedaway in some literature) Island, Georgia. Now considered *T. c. putnami*. See Auffenberg (1958).

T. antipex. Hay, 1916a. A *T. c. putnami* from Indian River County, Florida See Auffenberg (1958).

T. formosa. Hay, 1916a. A *T. carolina* from Marion County, Florida. Barbour and Stetson (1931) considered this form a young *T. c. putnami* (under the name *T. canaliculata*). Placed in *T. c. carolina* or *bauri* by Auffenberg (1958).

T. innoxia. Hay, 1916a. A *T. carolina* from Indian River County, Florida. Barbour and Stetson (1931) considered this form a young *T. c. putnami* (under the name *T. canaliculata*). Placed in *T. c. carolina* or *bauri* by Auffenberg (1958). The carapace shape suggests that this fossil can be allocated to the modern *T. c. bauri*, but its flattened dome indicates that further work is necessary to evaluate taxonomic distinctiveness (Ernst et al., 1998a).

T. whitneyi. Hay, 1916b. A *T. c. triunguis* from Travis County, Texas. See Milstead (1965).

T. bulverda. Hay, 1920. A *T. c. triunguis* × *putnami* from Bexar County, Texas. See Oelrich (1953) and Milstead (1956).

T. impressa. Hay, 1924. A *T. c. putnami* from Brazos County, Texas. See Oelrich (1953; incorrectly spelled *impensa*) and Milstead (1956).

T. singletoni. Gilmore, 1927. A *T. carolina* from Brevard County, Florida. See Barbour and Stetson (1931).

T. llanensis. Oelrich, 1953. A *T. carolina* from Meade County, Kansas.

T. culturalia. Yeh, 1961. This subfossil box turtle was described from China. Milstead (1965) noted that it did not possess characters of *Terrapene*. McCoy and Richmond (1966) place it in the Asian genus *Cuora*, specifically *Cuora flavomarginata*.

As is evident, most named taxa refer to specimens now considered either fossils of the giant box turtle *T. c. putnami* or to one of the subspecies currently recognized as *T. carolina*. Often the fossil material is indistinguishable from the modern species and, as others have pointed out, it is easy to form linkages between small and large fossil forms. The fossil material appears to give credence to the phylogenetic species concept, whereby fossil taxa form lineages through time (vertical species). Unfortunately, this sameness among fossil material has led to a great deal of speculation as to how species and subspecies are related (see Phylogeny later in this chapter).

Fossil *T. carolina* have been found in abundance in Florida and Texas, and isolated

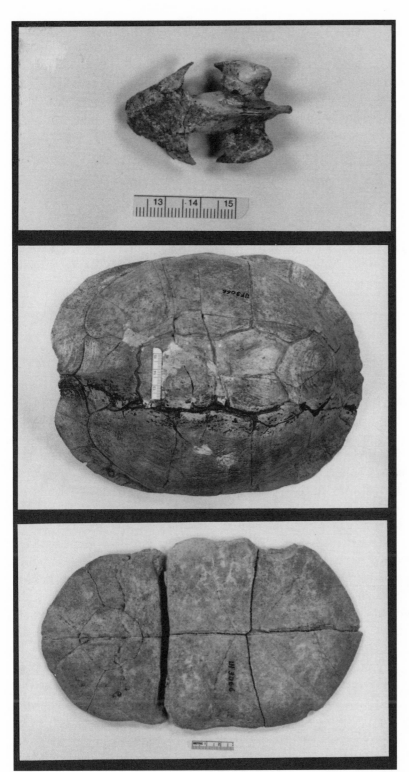

Figure 2-3. Fossil *Terrapene carolina putnami* of Late Pleistocene age. Florida Museum of Natural History, UF/FLMNH 3066 (carapace and plastron) and UF/FLMNH 47462 (skull), Haile VIII A, Alachua County, Florida.

finds extend the range in the Pleistocene from Maryland through Kansas and Missouri to southeastern New Mexico. Fossils west of the Appalachians have sometimes been referred to the modern subspecies *T. c. triunguis* (e.g., Milstead, 1969; Gillette, 1974), whereas southeastern specimens have been referred to *T. c. carolina*, *T. c. bauri*, or *T. c. major* (e.g., Auffenberg, 1958; Bentley and Knight, 1998). Pleistocene *T. ornata* are known from southeastern Arizona to Texas and eastern Missouri. Specimens from the southwest part of this range are sometimes referred to *T. o. luteola* (e.g., Moodie and Van Devender, 1978). Whether it is valid to refer fossils millions of years old to modern subspecies is questionable.

HOLOCENE (RECENT)

In addition to fossil material, box turtles have been found frequently in Recent deposits, both naturally and in an archeological context (chapter 1). Examples of Recent material reported in the literature include finds of *Terrapene* in Florida sinkholes (Hirschfeld, 1968).

Phylogeny

RELATIONSHIPS WITH OTHER TURTLES

The phylogenetic relationship of North American box turtles to other modern turtle genera is unclear. Although it is generally accepted that the four genera considered in the following discussion are closely related, it is by no means clear which is the likeliest direct ancestor to *Terrapene* or exactly when the clades (lineages) separated. Box turtles, after all, appear rather abruptly in the fossil record essentially in modern form.

Based on a variety of morphological characters, turtles of the genera *Emydoidea* (Blanding's turtle of North America), *Emys* (a mostly European and western Asian genus of pond turtles), and *Clemmys* (a group of semiaquatic North American turtles) have all been suggested as sister taxa of *Terrapene*. However, morphological similarities may by due to convergence rather than phylogeny, or perhaps certain morphological "similarities" are simply by-products of small sample size. For example, McDowell (1964) proposed that *Terrapene* and *Clemmys* were most closely related among modern genera since both have a large foramen caroticopharyngeale (an opening in the skull that allows the passage of a pharyngeal branch of the carotid artery). However, Milstead (1969) pointed out that there is much variation in the size of this opening in all four genera.

Instead, Milstead (1969) argued for a connection with *Emys* since it shares with *Terrapene* similarities of major skeletal characteristics—for example, in possessing a plastral hinge, in adsorption of plastral buttresses, and in having similarly shaped posterior plastral lobes and plastral scutes. However, other researchers have presented convincing evidence that *Emydoidea* is the most closely related modern genus (Bramble, 1974; Seidel and Adkins, 1989). Based on an exhaustive analysis of the mechanisms of shell closure, Bramble (1974) demonstrated that the turtles *Clemmys*, *Emys*, *Emydoidea*, and *Terrapene* formed a sequence of complexity in the morphology of shell kinesis. The similarity in the ways that these turtles close their shells, in conjunction with their morphology, was such as to cast evolutionary convergence into question as an explanation for the similarities. As such, these genera must be closely related. Seidel and Adkins (1989) also used an analysis of turtle myoglobins to detect similarities between these genera. These studies support the creation of a separate subfamily for them, the Emydinae, as originally proposed by Gaffney and Meylan (1988).

RELATIONSHIPS WITHIN *TERRAPENE*

The proto-*Terrapene* ancestor of modern box turtles evolved well before the mid-Miocene, since box turtles of this age are clearly recognized as *Terrapene*. As already noted, the identity of the ancestral box turtles is unknown. Paleoherpetologists have assumed that the ancestor was aquatic and that the complete shell closure of box turtles evolved in response to increasing terrestriality. Complete shell closure seems ideally suited to a turtle venturing onto land. However, Bramble (1974) has pointed out that Asian box turtles (*Cuora* and allies) and other emydids (e.g., *Emys*) are fully or partially aquatic and have full or partial shell closure thanks to a hinged plastron. This suggests that complete closure evolved prior to the time when box turtles left the water for a terrestrial existence. As such, the earliest box turtle may have looked like and lived a life similar to that of *T. coahuila* of Mexico, the only fully aquatic extant species. Morphological similarities between the earliest known *Terrapene* fossils and this species may not be coincidental.

There are two major lineages of extant box turtles. The Carolina group is composed of *T. carolina* and all its subspecies and *T. coahuila*, whereas the Ornata group is composed of *T. ornata* and *T. nelsoni* and their respective subspecies. These groups are separated from each other by a series of well-defined characters (table 2-1; Milstead and Tinkle, 1967; see also fig. 2-4). As noted, both lineages were present in the Late Miocene. The relationships among turtles in the Carolina group have always proven difficult to interpret, and there are nearly as many phylogenetic scenarios as there are published papers. The distribution of fossil locations suggests that the Carolina group evolved in southeastern North America in deciduous woodland or marshy habitats, perhaps in the northern Gulf Coast region inhabited by *T. c. major* today. The Ornata group is a grassland-adapted assemblage of turtles that evolved in Miocene-Pliocene grasslands either in the Great Plains or in the area of the old Rocky Mountain corridor where *T. o. luteola* lives today.

The close relationship between *T. ornata* and *T. nelsoni* seems never to have been seriously doubted, although the specific status of *T. nelsoni* has occasionally been questioned (Müller, 1936; McDowell, 1964). For example, Müller (1936) synonymized *nelsoni* with *T. mexicana* (now *T. c. mexicana*), but he used limited characters without considering geographic variation (Smith and Smith, 1979). Both *ornata* and *nelsoni* share a variety of morphological characteristics, including a 2-2-2-2-2 forefoot phalangeal formula (Minx, 1992, 1996). It is likely that *T. nelsoni* evolved from an *ornata*-like ancestor as a result of isolation due to climate changes during the Pleistocene (see later discussion; Milstead and Tinkle, 1967).

Box turtles resembling *T. coahuila* appear earliest in the fossil record, and modern

TABLE 2-1. Morphological characters distinguishing the Ornata and Carolina groups in the genus *Terrapene*. Data from Milstead and Tinkle (1967).

Ornata group	Carolina group
Postorbital bar absent; posterior border of orbit smooth	Postorbital bar usually present although the central portion (squamosal) may be cartilaginous; when postorbital bar is absent, the postorbital bone has a posteriorly directed process
Interfemoral suture long	Interfemoral suture short
First central scute concave or straight along midline	First central scute convex along midline
Highest vaulting of carapace anterior to bridge; carapace flat in both sagittal and cross section	Highest vaulting of carapace posterior to bridge; carapace rather high in both sagittal and cross section
First marginal scute irregularly oval or triangular in shape	First marginal scute usually rectangular in shape
Dorsal keel usually absent, but a weak keel may be present on the fourth central scute	Dorsal keel usually present and prominent; rarely absent
Inner toe of male capable of being turned inward at sharp angle to foot to serve as clasper (fig. 2-4)	Inner toe of male similar to other toes
Posterior lobe of plastron not or only shallowly concave (bowed dorsally) in males	Posterior lobe of plastron deeply concave (bowed dorsally) in males
Posterior margin of plastron usually straight	Posterior margin of plastron rounded
Bridge opposite the contact between the 5th and 6th marginals or opposite the 6th marginal when viewed laterally; infrequently opposite the 5th marginal	Bridge opposite the 5th marginal or, infrequently, opposite the contact between the 5th and 6th marginals when viewed laterally
Margin of plastron entire	Margin of plastron frequently indented at the pelvic-anal seam
Carapace generally round in overall appearance, except in *T. nelsoni nelsoni*	Carapace elongate except in some *T. carolina carolina*

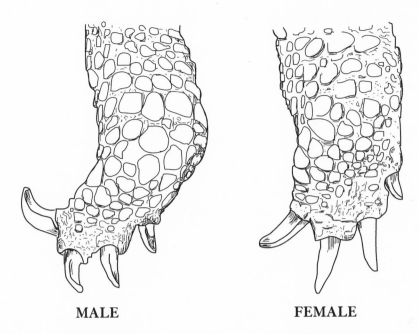

MALE   **FEMALE**

Figure 2-4. Contrasting position of the inner toes of male and female *T. ornata*. The male's inner toe (left) can be turned inward to serve as a clasper during mating. Figure shows a right hind foot of each sex. After Legler (1960).

T. coahuila have the most ancestral morphological characters. Today there is agreement that the aquatic box turtle is the most generalized of the box turtles and probably the closest to the ancestral clade within the genus *Terrapene* (Auffenberg, 1958; Legler, 1960; Minx, 1996). Brown's (1974) hypothesis that *T. coahuila* is actually the most derived of the box turtles because it adapted to a wetlands ecosystem as habitats became more arid in the Pleistocene seems untenable. It is more parsimonious to suggest that *T. coahuila* is a Pleistocene relict, as proposed earlier (Milstead, 1960; Auffenberg and Milstead, 1965; Milstead, 1965).

The earliest box turtles in the Carolina group were similar in size to the modern species. However, as mentioned, a giant box turtle found in Pliocene-Pleistocene deposits from Florida through Texas and Missouri reached carapace lengths of more than 300 mm (e.g., Holman, 1965). Hay (1906) described it as *T. c. putnami*. Although its main systematic character has been its great size, it was said to differ from *T. c. carolina* by the presence of an axillary scute, an urn-shaped first vertebral, and greatly flared peripherals (Moodie and Van Devender, 1977). However, these characters are known to be present in other members of the Carolina group, particularly in modern *T. c. major*. Indeed, other than size and perhaps shell thickness (some of the shells I have examined in the Florida Museum of Natural History are truly thick and massive in comparison to modern *Terrapene*), there appears to be no conclusive character that separates *putnami* from *major*, and both are thought to have inhabited similar environments—that is, marshes, swales, and extensive wet lowlands. If indeed *major* is the direct descendent of *putnami* as some have suggested (Barbour and Stetson, 1931; Moodie and Van Devender, 1977), there may be no taxonomic basis for recognizing *putnami* (see Bentley and Knight, 1998), although it is difficult to imagine a subspecies persisting for millions of years virtually unchanged.

The most plausible hypothesis for the evolution of modern Carolina group *Terrapene* was put forth by Milstead (1969), although minor modifications have since been made to correct certain age estimates (e.g., Gillette, 1974). In this scenario, *T. c. putnami* (or *major*, following Bentley and Knight, 1998) was present in the upper Gulf Coast region by mid-Pliocene to Pleistocene times. To the west, it seems clear that *putnami* gave rise to *T. c. triunguis* during the mid-Pleistocene since there is a clinal variation in morphological characters from *putnami* through *triunguis* in the fossils of the Midwest (Milstead, 1967). Morphological change occurred in concert with a reduction in shell size, so that *triunguis* was essentially modern by late Wisconsinan to Recent times (40,000–10,000 years B.P.).

To the east, the situation becomes less clear. Milstead (1969) suggested that *putnami* intergraded with *T. c. carolina* to produce *T. c. bauri* in the Florida Peninsula. However, Auffenberg (1958) had pointed out previously that there appeared to be two sympatric Florida *Terrapene* in the Pleistocene: a small form, which he allocated to either *T. c. carolina* or *T. c. bauri*, and a large form, which he allocated to *T. c. putnami*. On the basis of a skull, in part, Auffenberg speculated that there had been intergradation between these two, such as seems to be the case involving the species *T. singletoni*, which he suggested was *T. c. carolina* × *T. c. putnami* (Auffenberg, 1958, 1959). However, Auffenberg went further and proposed that *major* was also an intergrade between *T. c. carolina* and *T. c. putnami*. Biologists have had a hard time reconciling the large size of *putnami* with the lack of distinctive characters separating it from *major*. It is intriguing that there has been a corresponding size reduction from *putnami* to *major* and from *putnami* to *triunguis* during the Pleistocene.

Interpretations of the relationship between the northern *carolina* turtles (*bauri*, *carolina*, *major*, *triunguis*) and the Mexican Gulf subspecies (*mexicana*, *yucatana*) also have been muddled. Milstead (1969) proposed that a *putnami* × *triunguis* intergrade gave rise to *yucatana*, noting its affinities with *major* × *bauri* intergrades and with *putnami* itself. Although he once also considered *mexicana* to have arisen through intergradation between *putnami* and *triunguis* (Milstead, 1967), he later proposed that it originated from a *triunguis* × *yucatana* intergrade (Milstead, 1969). Indeed, there are some morphological characters, such as the phalangeal formula of the forefeet, that support a *major-bauri-yucatana* and a *triunguis-mexicana* relationship (Minx, 1992).

There has been only one recent study assessing a variety of morphological traits in an attempt to elucidate relationships among modern *Terrapene*. Minx (1996) used thirty-two characters, including postorbital bone, zygomatic arch, phalangeal formula, and characters of the plastron and carapace, to determine the most parsimonious relationships. As a result, the basic differences between the Ornata and Carolina clades were confirmed, a close relationship between *T. carolina* and *T. coahuila* was postulated, and two separate clades within the Carolina group were identified. One of these includes *triunguis-mexicana-yucatana*, whereas the other includes *carolina* and *bauri*. Thus, unlike in Milstead's (1969) hypothesis, these latter species are considered sister taxa rather than *bauri* being envisioned as a by-product of intergradation. Figure 2-5 is a cladogram showing the phylogenetic relationships between modern taxa.

In Minx's (1996) phylogeny, both of the most aquatic extant species are considered basal, one to the genus as a whole (*T. coahuila*) and the other to the Carolina group (*T. c. major*). Unfortunately, the exact relationship of *major* to other members of the Carolina group remains enigmatic. For example, Minx (1996) noted that *major* seems to have three regional phenotypes, which show signs of intergradation with adjacent subspecies of *T. carolina* (*bauri*, *carolina*, *triunguis*; see individual subspecies accounts). A possible conspecific relationship between *T. c. major* and *T. c. putnami* also was mentioned. Thus, the phylogeny of *Terrapene* remains unresolved to a certain extent, although it is clearer now than in the past. Minx's (1996) phylogeny coincides well with fossil, morphological, and biogeographic data.

Climate, Biogeography, and Evolution

During the Miocene, many regions of the earth that had previously been forested became more open as grasslands, deserts, and parklands expanded. Temperate ecosystems in general were diverse. Beginning in the mid-Miocene, climates became warmer, followed

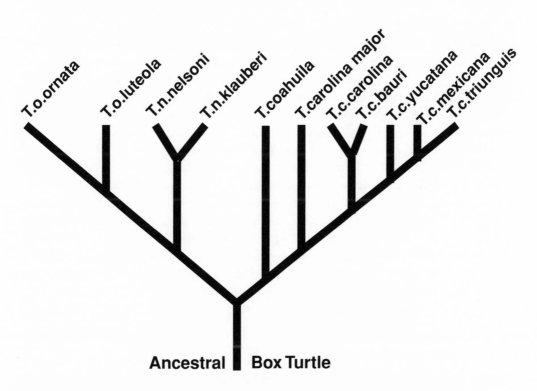

Figure 2-5. Cladogram showing phylogenetic relationships within modern *Terrapene*. Data from Minx (1996).

later by cooler periods, and seasonality became more prominent. Some paleoclimatologists consider Miocene climates most like our present climate. The herpetofauna was essentially modern, and included most families and many modern genera of reptiles (Holman, 1995). It was in such a climate that *Terrapene* first appeared and evolved into separate species groups.

The Pliocene was a rather short geologic period covering only a few million years. The epoch seems to have experienced a transition between the relatively warmer climates of the past and the cooler climates of the Pleistocene. Still, there were fluctuations, such as a mid-Pliocene warming followed by a late Pliocene cooling. Physiographically, the earth appeared essentially as it does today. According to Holman (1995), many of the modern herpetofaunal assemblages were present, at least at the generic level, although fossil amphibians and reptiles were poorly represented. Box turtles, already in essentially modern form, plodded along without obvious innovation.

The Pleistocene, although short in comparison with other Tertiary geologic epochs, was a time of substantial climate change. Extensive periods of glaciation were interspersed with much shorter periods of warming. Although it was once thought that there were four periods of major glaciation in North America (Nebraskan, Kansan, Illinoian, Wisconsinan), it is now recognized that there were glacial advances and retreats throughout the Pleistocene, even during the three recognized interglacial periods (Aftonian, Yarmouthian, Sangamonian). The advance and retreat of great ice sheets had profound effects on box turtle distribution and, in turn, speciation. In the following discussion I rely substantially on the reviews by Auffenberg and Milstead (1965) and Holman (1995).

During the glacial periods when vast sheets of ice covered much of North America, sea levels fell, allowing wide east-west corridors to form around the Gulf of Mexico and increasing Florida's land mass considerably. Much of the fauna and flora of present-day Florida was derived from western forms moving east; east to west dispersal also occurred. At the same time, grasslands spread across the Rocky Mountains in southern Arizona and New Mexico, forming a second important east-west corridor. A third corridor, the Prairie Peninsula, allowed western xeric-adapted species to move east. Eastern species moved west as climates became cooler but wetter. As climates changed during the interglacials, eastern and western forms were isolated, leading to the evolution of separate species and subspecies. At the same time, northern forms moved south in advance of glaciers, resulting in a mix of northern and southern faunas in areas such as northern Florida. When glaciers retreated, these species moved back north, as did some southern species. Thus, while communities changed, they did not change in unison. Whole faunas did not move; species did (Graham and Lundelius, 1984).

Although glacial ice spread south, eliminating much current habitat, southern climates were more equable and did not experience radical temperature fluctuations. Summers were cooler, but winters were warmer. Precipitation patterns likewise changed, with western regions receiving higher levels than they do at present. Grasslands spread west, reaching even the Sierra Madre of western Mexico. A more equable climate allowed subtropical conditions to persist in Florida, where giant tortoises roamed, while at the same time allowing the westward dispersal of mesic-adapted reptiles, such as box turtles, across what today is inhospitable desert and scrub.

It was during the series of Pleistocene glacials and interglacials that box turtles reached their present distribution. One of the species in the Carolina group, *T. coahuila*, is a Pleistocene relict, morphologically and ecologically similar to ancestral *Terrapene*. In the Carolina group, east-west corridors allowed *putnami*-like turtles to spread westward following the forests and marshes until they approached the Great Plains. The midwestern *T. c. triunguis* is the modern descendent of this range expansion. It is likely that a *triunguis*-like (or a *putnami*-like) box turtle moved south around the Mexican Gulf Coast when sea levels were much lower than today. As climates changed, isolated populations, which we now know as *T. c. mexicana*, and *T. c. yucatana*, evolved as phenotypically and ecologically distinct tropical descendants of this temperate turtle genus.

Eastward, the giant box turtles colonized much of the Florida Peninsula and up through the Atlantic coastal plain, at least to Georgia and the low country of coastal South Carolina. Their legacy here is *T. c. carolina* and *T. c. bauri*, although the phyletic relationship between *bauri* and *carolina* is unclear. If Auffenberg (1958) is correct in his hypothesis concerning the sympatric presence of both a large and a small species of box turtle in Pleistocene Florida, then it is unlikely that *putnami* is directly ancestral to *bauri* and/or *carolina*, depending on which was present in Florida at that time. As glaciers retreated, *T. c. carolina* moved north to its present distribution.

Also during the Pleistocene, grassland-adapted *T. ornata* moved eastward via the Prairie Peninsula through the Midwest and westward, along the Rocky Mountain corridor, to the Sierra Madre of western Mexico (Auffenberg and Milstead, 1965). It is thought that the subspecies *T. o. luteola* is phenotypically most like the ancestral ornate box turtle. If this is the case, then its present distribution is indeed relictual, representing remnant populations that had moved west along the Rocky Mountain corridor to colonize expanding mixed grassland-woodlands during Pleistocene glacial periods. Previous suggestions that *T. nelsoni* evolved from a *T. o. luteola*-like ancestor (Auffenberg and Milstead, 1965) seem doubtful if Minx's (1996) proposed phylogeny is correct, since *nelsoni* appears phyletically closer to the proto-*Terrapene* ancestor than to *ornata*. This relationship remains to be resolved.

Future Directions

In a time of high technology, it seems strange to call for field-level paleontological research of Tertiary deposits. This type of research is certainly arduous and not glamorous (even for paleontologists), but it is necessary if we are to understand the historical biogeography of present-day turtles. The upper Midwest has yielded valuable Miocene fossils; in this context, Early Miocene deposits should be carefully combed for remains of *Terrapene* or its possible ancestor. Likewise, Pliocene *Terrapene* fossils are not well described, and a careful examination of such remains should be undertaken.

It is clear, however, that simply finding more fossils probably will not help much to resolve the intrageneric relationships among extant *Terrapene*. Perhaps the best approach to understanding the phylogeny of box turtles is to commence a detailed molecular analysis. Mitochondrial DNA (mtDNA), in particular, has been used to examine the relationships of turtles both within and across genera. As Avise (1986) has pointed out, mtDNA is particularly useful in studying historical zoogeography, lineage phylogeny, reproductive isolation, and introgression and hybridization. Since intergradation has been invoked time and again to explain the relationships within *Terrapene*, an mtDNA study of the genus would appear to hold considerable promise. In the Ornata group, some of the topics that could be addressed are: (1) What is the relationship between the subspecies of *T. nelsoni* and between *T. nelsoni* and *T. o. luteola*; that is, who is correct—Auffenberg and Milstead (1965) or Minx (1996)? (2) Is *T. o. luteola* ancestral to *T. o. ornata*? (3) Is the actual introgression between subspecies of *T. ornata* as broad as is sometimes indicated on distribution maps?

In the Carolina group, the questions are: (1) What is the relationship between *T. c. major* and the three subspecies of *T. carolina* with which it interacts? (2) Is *T. coahuila* really ancestral to the genus *Terrapene*? (3) What is the relationship between *T. c. carolina* and *T. c. bauri*? (4) Is *T. c. triunguis* derived from *T. c. major*? (5) What is the relationship between the Gulf of Mexico subspecies and between them and the northern subspecies? Answers to these questions will certainly clarify the phylogeny of box turtles and help point the way toward interesting ecological studies in areas of critical contact and apparent introgression.

Finally, a careful examination of mtDNA in living *Terrapene*, in the Emydinae in general, and in those genera thought sister to the Emydinae (*Graptemys, Trachemys*) might lend a better understanding of the timing of speciation events. Although molecular clocks must be used cautiously in interpreting possible dates of lineage divergence (turtles, after all, seem to have "unusually low genetic variability and divergence among mtDNA lineages"; Avise et al., 1992:458), a molecular approach offers the best hope of understanding when important speciation events occurred in this morphologically conservative group of turtles.

3 | Habitats and Habitat Requirements

The similarity in temperature and humidity levels with those taken in form locations indicated that turtles exist within a relatively limited microclimatic range at all times during seasons of activity.

DOUGLAS REAGAN, 1974

Because they are close to the ground, box turtles maintain an intimate association with a relatively small part of the biosphere. Their vertical range extends from the subsurface soil layers where they escape cold, heat, and drought to a few centimeters above the carapace—that is, the extent of the reach of their long necks. As such, they are particularly sensitive to environmental variables that affect the litter and subsurface soils. In many species of animals, habitat structure, more than the actual composition of vegetation communities or soil types, plays a crucial role in how they use their environment. In others, variables such as pH, soil chemistry, or thermal requirements override or complement the importance of habitat structure. In this chapter, the types of macro- and microhabitats used by box turtles, both daily and seasonally, are discussed; information on habitat use in a regional landscape is presented in chapter 4. I also draw attention to how box turtles respond to adverse conditions, briefly touching on their physiological adaptations. Thus this chapter sets the stage for further detail in the life history of box turtles.

It is easy to fall into the trap of saying that "box turtles inhabit this or that type of habitat." However, habitats are not uniform in nature, either within a localized area or through time, and turtle populations are not distributed evenly throughout a regional landscape. Changes occur continuously, and what we see in a landscape may not be what is important to a box turtle. Some early reports on habitats of this species, such as Holbrook's (1842:34) statement that "in the southern states it is always found in dry places, and is very numerous in the immense pine forests of that country, and is hence frequently called pine-barren terrapin" clearly are in error.

Box turtles may use different habitats at different times of the year, particularly in eastern North America. During the spring and early summer, ornate and three-toed box turtles use open grasslands and pastures to forage and deposit eggs, generally avoiding agricultural croplands. As the summer's heat intensifies, they move toward adjacent mesic forest and bottomlands, where temperatures are more moderate and humidity is higher (Reagan, 1974; Doroff and Keith, 1990). Likewise, box turtles on Egmont Key,

Florida, use different habitats in the course of the year in response to changing thermal regimes and food availability (Dodd et al., 1994). Although the sabal palm (*Sabal palmetto*)–Brazilian pepper (*Schinus terebinthifolius*) forest is inhabited most often, the turtles readily use the open lawn and sea oats meadows during the winter and spring.

In another example of how habitat use changes with season, box turtles may use different habitats at they prepare to overwinter. As winter approaches, they move away from grasslands and forest-field ecotones and deeper into the forest, where protected sites are readily available (Reagan, 1974; Madden, 1975). Box turtle density also increases as succession takes place from more open to structurally diverse habitats—as when an old field reverts to forest. As these examples illustrate, box turtles prefer regions with more than one habitat type or with different types in fairly close proximity, and they particularly favor ecotones between habitats (Madden, 1975).

The habitats in which box turtles are found can change even with daily activity. On Egmont Key, the grassy lawn is favored in the morning at a time of cool temperatures and high humidity, whereas it is avoided during the heat of the day (fig. 3-1). In late afternoon, turtles are again encountered on grass or in the sea oats meadows as temperatures fall. They congregate in the morning to feed on sea grapes, but the location of the most prolific sea grape trees on Egmont—that is, in the direct afternoon sun—precludes much evening activity in this habitat. During most of the day, box turtles retreat to the cooler and more humid interior forest. In summer, Arkansas three-toed box turtles make similar movements from grasslands to more humid forests depending on time of day (Reagan, 1974). Changes in vegetation structure, temperature, plant composition, and topography likely have major influences on the habitat in which box turtles are found.

There also appears to be some differential use of habitats by box turtles at different stages of their lives: adults, subadults, and juveniles use habitats differently. Adults tend to roam over a greater variety of habitats, whereas juveniles prefer areas affording cover and concealment. For example, on Egmont Key juveniles were found most often in the thickly canopied Brazilian pepper–sabal palm forest through the year, whereas adults were found throughout the island (Dodd et al., 1994; Hamilton, 2000). In Wisconsin, subadult *T. ornata* used woodlands extensively, but juveniles did not (Doroff and Keith, 1990). In both cases, males and females generally used habitats similarly, although gravid females tended to inhabit more open areas, when available, for nesting. In contrast, Madden (1975) found no appreciable differences in habitat preferences between juvenile and adult *T. c. carolina* in New York.

Macrohabitats

Mesic Woodlands

Throughout much of eastern North America, the box turtle is an inhabitant of mesic (moist) woodlands. This type of biome includes hardwood (oak-hickory) forests, mixed hardwood-pine forests, maritime forests, pine flatwoods, and hardwood swamps. Common hardwood trees include birches (*Betula*, *Carpinus*), beech (*Fagus*), oaks (*Quercus*), elm (*Ulmus*), poplar (*Liriodendron*), sweetgum (*Liquidambar*), maples (*Acer*),

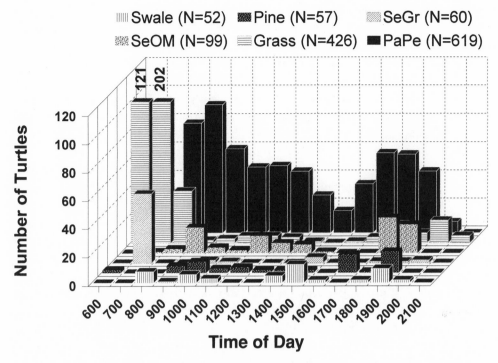

Figure 3-1. Temporal variation in habitat use by box turtles on Egmont Key. PaPe = Cabbage palm–Brazilian pepper forest. Pine = Australian pine groves. Swale = grassy swale on south of island. SeOM = sea oats meadow. SeGr = immediate vicinity of sea grape bushes. Grass = lawn at the Tampa Bay Pilots Association compound. Data from figure 8 in Dodd et al. (1994).

hickory (*Carya*), dogwood (*Cornus*), sassafras (*Sassafras*), and ash (*Fraxinus*). Understories include a mixture of shrubs and vines (*Lindera, Toxicodendron, Viburnum, Rosa, Rubus, Smilax, Vaccinium*); forbs (e.g., *Claytonia, Viola, Galium, Ranunculus, Laportea, Circaea, Aster, Geranium*); grasses (*Poa, Aristida, Festuca, Panicum*); and sedges (*Andropogon*), depending on location. Excellent descriptions of representative box turtle habitat in mesic forest are in Stickel (1950), Schwartz and Schwartz (1974), Reagan (1974), Madden (1975), and Doroff and Keith (1990).

Mesic forests usually have a relatively closed canopy that allows patchy sunlight to reach the surface, a well-defined leaf litter, moisture-retaining soils of varying depths, a sparse to moderate herbaceous understory, and plenty of cover (e.g., logs, woody debris, stumps, branches). Areas where sunlight reaches the ground are used as basking sites (Hallgren-Scaffidi, 1986) and possibly nesting sites (chapter 6). The closed-canopy forest may be interspersed with fields and other open areas forming a mosaic of habitat types across a landscape.

The thick canopy and intricate habitat structure of eastern broad-leaved forests undoubtedly facilitate thermoregulation by providing cool areas in summer and favorable habitats in which to overwinter; forests also maintain higher humidity than surrounding open zones (Reagan, 1974). Such forests are favored by *T. c. carolina*, *T. c. triunguis*, and

T. c. major. The Florida box turtle, *T. c. bauri*, likewise inhabits mesic woodlands (termed *hammocks* in much of its range; see Pilgrim et al., 1997), but it is also found in savanna-like grasslands, rimrock habitats, exotic forests of Brazilian pepper and Australian pine (*Casuarina*), and even out in salt marshes, such as at Merritt Island.

Box turtles occur from sea level (e.g., the surf line on Egmont Key) through the high ridges of the Appalachian Mountains. In regions with low hills, box turtles have been reported to be evenly distributed from "lowlands" through "uplands" (to 271 m in Strang, 1983), although it is not clear what "evenly distributed" means (see later discussion). However, they tend to become more and more infrequent as elevations increase. Box turtles are absent from several very high cold areas, such as Canaan Valley, West Virginia. The highest altitudinal record is given by Palmer and Braswell (1995) for North Carolina, and is from 2,007 m at the Mount Mitchell parking area. Palmer and Braswell (1995) suggested that this record might be suspect, but they provided additional high elevation records (1,387 m at Craggy Gardens and 1,341 m in Watauga County) that may represent the extreme in altitudinal distribution.

Within habitats of rolling or hilly terrain, most authors report that box turtles are *not* found distributed uniformly throughout the landscape. Turtles generally avoid ridges where moisture conditions are unfavorable, and they seem to prefer not to travel down steep embankments or hillsides, although they will do so if necessary. For example, Stickel (1950) found that eastern box turtles were present throughout the upland habitats she studied on the Maryland Piedmont but that they tended to congregate in the bottomlands and floodplain. Indiana *T. carolina* generally avoided power lines, a rocky gorge, and upland oak habitats but favored woodlands dominated by maples (Williams and Parker, 1987). It is likely that seasonal shifts and temperature influence the spread of turtles across the land.

Grasslands and Semiarid Desert

The ornate box turtle, T. *ornata*, comes closer to being a grassland species than the other species and subspecies of *Terrapene*, although *T. o. ornata* readily enters mesic forest and woodlands and *T. o. luteola* lives in desert or semidesert habitats in much of its range. Desert box turtles even have been found in pinyon-juniper-ponderosa woodlands at 2,200–2,300 m (Degenhardt et al., 1996). Ornate box turtles in Kansas and Oklahoma reach their greatest abundance in the western short-grass prairies, although they also are found in tallgrass prairies, pastures, open brushy woodlots, cedar glades, and open fields throughout the plains states (Webb, 1970; Johnson, 1987; Collins, 1993; Trail, 1995). In Nebraska, they are common in the sandhill prairies in the central and western part of the state (Hudson, 1942). Prairie grasslands are characterized by a wide diversity of grasses, such as *Andropogon, Agropyron, Bouteloua, Bromus, Panicum, Sorghastrum*, and *Buchloë*; species composition varies depending on rainfall. Reichman (1987) and Trail (1995) provide comprehensive descriptions of Kansas and Nebraska prairies, respectively, inhabited by *T. o. ornata*.

In New Mexico, *T. c. luteola* inhabits grasslands on the northern margin of the Chihuahuan Desert. Primary vegetation includes grasses (*Bouteloua, Sporobolous*,

Erioneuron, Muhlenbergia, Aristida), yucca (*Yucca*), cacti (*Opuntia*, *Echinocereus*), and various shrubs and bushes (notably *Gutierrezia*). In the range of the desert box turtle, the climate is characterized by summer rainfall and wide temperature fluctuations. *Terrapene c. luteola* are found both in the semidesert lowlands and on gravelly foothill slopes leading to surrounding mountains. Common plants within this habitat include creosote bush (*Larrea*), yucca (*Yucca*), mesquite *(Prosopis)*, juniper *(Juniperus)*, tarbush (*Flourensia*), and various grasses. Desert box turtles are found on a wide variety of soil types, including sand, red clay, silt, and gravels (Norris and Zweifel, 1950). During midday heat, turtles rest in the shade of bushes.

CUATRO CIÉNEGAS

The aquatic Coahuilan box turtle (*T. coahuila*) is known only from Cuatro Ciénegas in central Coahuila, Mexico. Cuatro Ciénegas is located in a broad basin of the Chihuahuan Desert dominated by mesquite, creosote bush, and many kinds of cacti on an arid plain. Permanent water is present in streams, ponds, and marshes, and aquatic box turtles are found in each habitat. Most Coahuilan box turtles, however, are found in the marshes, habitats of shallow water (less than 60 cm) overgrown with thick stands of cattails (*Typha*), herbs, grasses (*Cladium*, *Spartina*), and sedges (*Eleocharis, Fimbristylis, Scirpus*). Other plants include seep-willow (*Baccharis glutinosa*) and the halophyte grass *Distichlis stricta*. The substrates are typically composed of soft muds, marls, and decaying organic matter. Detailed descriptions of each habitat and the physical setting of this interesting biotic region are in Webb et al. (1963), Minckley (1969), and Brown (1974).

Aquatic box turtles usually are found in the water, although they occasionally make excursions in adjacent terrestrial habitats (chapter 4). Turtles are found buried in soft muds at various depths but at least to about 15 cm (Webb et al., 1963). From their hiding positions, they extend their necks so that they can peer about in the water. The dark color of their shells and the surrounding mud make these turtles difficult to spot.

TROPICAL MEXICO

Little information is available on the habitats of the two Mexican subspecies of the eastern box turtle, *T. c. yucatana* and *T. c. mexicana*, or those of the spotted box turtle, *T. nelsoni*. Yucatán box turtles inhabit open and forested environments but prefer the more open situations. They have been observed in marshes, pastures, thorn forest, and tropical evergreen forest (Lee, 1996). The area is generally a low, semiarid deciduous scrub forest interspersed by scattered grasslands (Smith and Smith, 1979). These turtles occasionally enter shallow water (Lee, 1996). *T. c. mexicana* lives in a mixed pine-deciduous forest tropical habitat.

Terrapene n. nelsoni is restricted to oak-savanna habitat at elevations below 1,220 m from central Sonora south to Nayarit. Myers (1945:172) records a specimen of *T. n. klauberi* in Sonora from "the western slope, among rolling granitic hills, with volcanic intrusions, covered with desert scrub." Burrows found on the southeastern slope of a 600 m hill in Sinaloa, Mexico, were attributed to this species (Hardy and McDiarmid, 1969).

Microhabitats

THE FORM

Most box turtles for which we have information spend the night and escape unfavorable climatic conditions in what Stickel (1950) termed a "form." The form is created by the turtle's shell and is simply a shallow depression in soil or leaf litter in which the turtle conceals itself. The turtle approaches a likely location and scrapes a shallow depression either vertically or horizontally, depending on conditions, with its front legs. It then slowly wedges itself into the substrate. By using a series of back and forth movements, the turtle creates a hollow into which its shell fits. The form may conceal only a small part, half, or all of the carapace. Forms may be dug into shallow soils of the forest floor, into the sides of depressions, under grasses or other vegetation, adjacent to logs, or under brush or leaf litter.

As the turtle enters the form, the rear of the carapace may be somewhat exposed, or it may be completely covered. On Egmont Key, I often have found box turtles by stepping on them as they rested within forms under Australian pine needles or beneath grass tussocks. Some turtles rest or sleep with their head and front legs extended into the depths of the form, whereas others may face outward. Turtles in forms are not necessarily asleep, however, except at night. During the day, they are invariably alert unless buried deeply. Sometimes, the turtle even extends its head up through the top of the form, which enables it to look around its environment without being conspicuous. A head appearing out of an otherwise uniform substrate can be difficult to see. At other times, the turtle may rotate its position sideways within the form and peer out from the litter. Turtles usually exit forms head first, either continuing in their original direction by pushing aside litter or rotating their shells and leaving the way they entered.

Box turtles may use several forms within the same day, awakening in one and moving to another after their morning's activity. They also may return to the same form repeatedly. In some instances, several turtles may use the same form from time to time; that is, one form may house different turtles on sequential days. On other occasions, turtles use the same form for days or even weeks at a time. There is no territorial defense of forms.

The method by which a turtle chooses a form is not clear. Certainly, the form must possess sufficient cover for concealment; if it is to be dug, soils must be friable; and it must contain favorable microhabitat conditions. Several studies have examined the microhabitat associated with forms, and it appears that the most important variable is moisture. Substrate temperatures are important to a lesser degree, since the turtles do not favor high temperatures. However, box turtles will not construct forms in locations with favorable temperatures if conditions are dry. With regard to moisture, the turtle selects habitats with a minimum of favorable conditions, even though more favorable moisture conditions may be found elsewhere in its nearby habitat (Reagan, 1974).

In addition to the form, box turtles in mesic substrates often make trails. The trails are exactly the width of the turtle's carapace and look as if they have been made by miniature bulldozers plowing through the leaf litter–soil interface. Box turtles on Egmont Key commonly are found by following the trails in the humid soils beneath non-indigenous Brazilian pepper. The trails are made as the turtles push through the litter, rather than over it. The purposes of the trails are not clear, but they could provide favorable temperatures (through conduction via the plastron), humidity, cover, and hunting ground (we have found box turtles in trails munching on freshly caught cockroaches). At the end of a day's bulldozing, Egmont Key box turtles simply push into the soil so that the carapace is covered, then resume their bulldozing the next day.

Substrate Use

Box turtles are found on a wide variety of substrates, usually leaf litter or the soil of the habitats in which they commonly are found. In deserts, the substrate may be quite rocky, offering few sites in which to burrow; desert box turtles do not appear to have specific substrate preferences (Norris and Zweifel, 1950). Indeed, it is not very easy to determine if any box turtles actually prefer different substrates or whether they are selecting preferred thermal and moisture regimes, sitting opportunistically while taking advantage of a favored food source, traveling over a substrate because it affords fewer obstacles, or occupying a convenient basking site (chapter 4).

In one area at least, box turtles are not found randomly distributed in terms of substrate availability. Florida box turtles on Egmont Key are found on a variety of substrates, including sand, organic soil, leaf litter, palm fronds, and grass. Each of these substrates has its own thermal properties, which probably influence turtle positioning. The type of substrate on which Egmont Key box turtles are encountered changes seasonally. In spring, adults are found most commonly on leaf litter and grass, whereas in autumn the most common substrates are soil and grass (fig. 3-2). In summer, adult males and females are most commonly found on grass and leaf litter, whereas juveniles avoid grass and live in contact with the moist, cool soil (fig. 3-3).

Overwintering Sites

Box turtles usually choose overwintering sites within their home ranges. Indeed, the same sites may be used both for overwintering and for escape from unfavorable environmental conditions during the summer. However, some turtles are known to move to a favorable site outside the home range (Stickel, 1989; see also chapter 4 of the present work). Often, the chosen site is very close to sites previously used (termed site fidelity), and this seems quite logical. If a turtle successfully overwintered at a site in the past, the site's favorable characteristics likely will allow the animal to survive future winters. In one example, eight of fourteen Wisconsin *T. ornata* overwintered within 1 m of previously used sites (Doroff and Keith, 1990). In some cases, turtles wintering regularly within a restricted area have been known to winter at a distant location (up to 0.5 km away) for a year, only to return to the original site during subsequent winters (I. L. Brisbin, pers. comm.).

The substrate of the overwintering site must allow the turtle to dig progressively into the ground; that is, the turtle gradually descends into the soil as the winter progresses (Legler, 1960). As such, the depth of the chamber varies from turtle to turtle within a

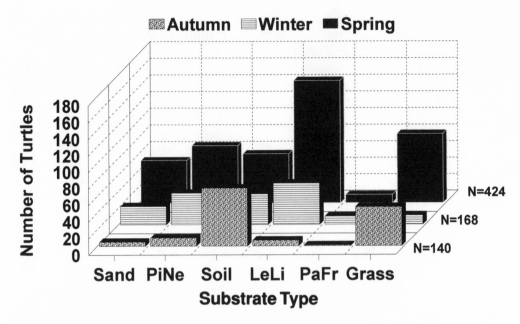

Figure 3-2. Substrate use by box turtles on Egmont Key during the winter, spring and autumn. No differences exist between the sexes or between adults and juveniles. Sand = shell sand. PiNe = Australian pine needles. Soil = organic soil. LeLi = leaf litter. PaFr = whole or nearly entire palm fronds. Grass = lawn grass. Data from figure 9 in Dodd et al. (1994).

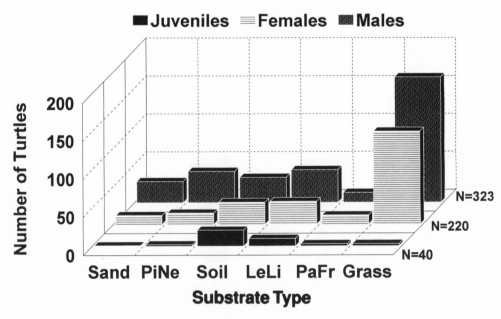

Figure 3-3. Variation in substrate use by box turtles on Egmont Key during the summer. Sand = shell sand. PiNe = Australian pine needles. Soil = organic soil. LeLi = leaf litter. PaFr = whole or nearly entire palm fronds. Grass = lawn grass. Data from figure 10 in Dodd et al. (1994).

locality. Even in northern climates experiencing cold and snow, the highest portion of the carapace is sometimes visible. Eastern box turtles dig shallow depressions, from barely concealing their carapace to about 10 cm below ground (Dolbeer, 1969, 1971; Madden, 1975; Gatten, 1987; Congdon et al., 1989); a recently hatched baby survived the winter by digging to a depth of 12 cm (Madden, 1975). Claussen et al. (1991) recorded a maximum depth of 14 cm (average 4–5 cm) for overwintering *T. c. carolina* in Ohio. In Oklahoma, *T. c. triunguis* burrow to a mean depth of 0.11 m with a maximum depth of 0.46 m (Carpenter, 1957). Even these shallow depths are effective at providing thermal insulation. In Tennessee one winter, the substrate temperature near box turtles buried in 10 cm of ground cover was 1.1°C, whereas the air temperature was −11°C (Dolbeer, 1969). The depth record for an overwintering eastern box turtle is 48 cm in Illinois (Cahn, 1937).

The ornate box turtle digs much deeper than its eastern counterpart. Depths recorded include a range of 0.05–0.56 m for Kansas *T. ornata* (Legler, 1960) and a mean of 0.7 m for male *T. ornata* and 1.1 m for females in Wisconsin, for a total range 0.5–1.8 m (Doroff and Keith, 1990). Even hatchling ornate box turtles do not remain in the nest (where temperatures reach −8°C) to overwinter, but burrow well below the nest cavity, to 68 cm below ground (Costanzo et al., 1995). Presumably, turtles at the more northerly extent of their ranges dig deeper into the substrate than do southern turtles, at least in the Midwest. However, there is significant variation even within a locality, and the depths descended are likely a function of the severity of the winter.

The exact features that a turtle uses to decide where an overwintering site should be located vary considerably from turtle to turtle. Leaf litter appears to be an important criterion, with depths averaging to about 10 cm (Carpenter, 1957; Dolbeer, 1971; Claussen et al., 1991). Some turtles choose sites on slopes, some in flat terrain, whereas others overwinter in water. Overwintering sites for Oklahoma *T. c. triunguis* were adjacent to some type of cover (rocks, shrubs, brush piles, logs, etc.), associated with depressions, and in soft soil conditions (table 3-1). *Terrapene c. carolina* and *T. c. triunguis* commonly use old stump holes, which fill with litter and surface debris; such depressions in Maryland were 15–40 cm deep (Stickel, 1989). On Egmont Key, I often have observed Florida box turtles dug down into depressions left by old palm stumps, so much so that my search image now is directed toward shallow depressions where turtles may be buried. Favored overwintering sites also are located in the litter that accumulates at the base of briar and blackberry thickets (Carpenter, 1957; Metcalf and Metcalf, 1970, 1979) and in old root tunnels (J. Sealy, pers. comm.).

The type of overwintering substrate, coupled with freeze tolerance (addressed later), is critical to the ability of some ornate box turtles to extend their ranges to the north, especially since turtles may spend as long as 140–160 days beneath the surface (Carpenter, 1957; Doroff and Keith, 1990; Claussen et al., 1991). At the northern extent of the range of *T. ornata*, Wisconsin ornate box turtles are found only in very sandy habitats where the turtles are able to dig deep below the frost line. Sandy areas within forest, and especially in native remnant prairies, are critical to their survival (Doroff and Keith, 1990). Turtles would not survive the winters if only shallower soils were available, despite the presence of favorable foraging habitat in summer. Even toward the south in Oklahoma, turtles favor sandy habitats in which to spend the winter.

TABLE 3.1. The relative importance of environmental features in dormancy site selection of *Terrapene carolina triunguis*. From Carpenter (1957).

Type of environmental feature	Number of individuals*	Percent in association
Cavity (stump hole, hollow, etc.)	179	39
Bushes and thick vegetation	153	33
Hillside	104	22
Gully bottom	60	13
Piles of brush and debris	50	11
Log	40	9
Base of hill	21	5
Sandy soil	23	5
Other	13	3

*The total number of indiviuals was 460, but this column totals much more because individuals' sites may have exhibited two or more recorded environmental factors. Thus the percentages do not total 100 but are greater for the same reason.

The box turtle digs its overwintering chamber much the same way as it creates a form, front end first. The front legs dig, and the rear legs push the dirt out behind the turtle. If the overwintering site is on a slope or under brush or tree roots, the turtle moves horizontally into the substrate. Progressive digging produces a tunnel, which may collapse or remain open throughout the winter. Burrow openings provide evidence of turtle occupation (e.g., Hardy and McDiarmid, 1969; Metcalf and Metcalf, 1970). In open locations, the turtle digs vertically until either the shell is covered or just a small portion of the carapace is visible. In Kansas, *T. ornata* dig at an angle of 30–40 degrees into the substrate and are able to conceal themselves in an hour or less.

Within their chambers, turtles may face in or out, or at an angle in relation to the opening, or may be in almost any position imaginable (Carpenter, 1957; Congdon et al., 1989; Claussen et al., 1991). Turtles may even be vertical, usually with the head up. During overwintering, shells are closed or very nearly so. In dry soils, a chamber forms around the turtle, but in wet conditions, the substrate packs close to the animal's shell. If a turtle is in close proximity to others, it may or may not be touching them; it may even be on top of or underneath other turtles! Carpenter (1957) records a number of vertebrates (turtles, lizards, salamanders) and invertebrates (beetles, earthworms, snails, sow bugs) in close association with overwintering *T. c. triunguis*.

Usually, there is only one box turtle in an overwintering chamber. However, there are cases of multiple turtles overwintering within the same chamber. Such chambers have been called "hibernacula," although the turtles do not hibernate in a mammalian sense. Instead, they undergo a period of dormancy more accurately termed torpor. At least one communal den has been reported for *T. ornata* in Kansas (Legler, 1960), and a fossil site in Florida suggested the use of communal dens by the extinct *T. c. putnami* (Auffenberg, 1959). At the Kansas site, seven turtles were found in a den at the end of a tunnel 76 m long; the opening to the den measured 30 × 23 cm. It seems likely that this was a mammal den taken over by the opportunistic reptiles.

Turtles often are found overwintering close to one another, even if not within the same chamber; Carpenter (1957) found up to six three-toed box turtles in a single stump hole measuring 0.61 m in diameter. Indeed, 53 percent of the turtles that he found overwintering were within 0.3 to 0.6 m of one another. In other examples, Doroff and Keith (1990) found five ornate box turtles in Wisconsin within 0.5 m of one another; in Kansas, Metcalf and Metcalf (1970, 1979) found three areas of concentration of overwintering *T. ornata*. Thus, some local areas may be particularly favorable, and box turtles use them accordingly. Even some chambers may be favored; Carpenter (1957) noted that certain overwintering sites were occupied by ten different individuals over the course of his three-year study. Still, the physical attractiveness of burrows can change over time due to erosion.

Overwintering chambers often are dug on south- or west-facing slopes where winter temperatures presumably are warmer than in other locations. In northern habitats, all overwintering chambers may be located facing south or west; in other areas, chambers are found facing in various directions in order to take advantage of local topography and microenvironmental conditions. Box turtles have also been observed to overwinter in wet bottomlands and, as noted, even in water.

The cues box turtles in natural populations use to emerge from their overwintering chambers are unknown but are likely related to soil temperature and perhaps moisture. Most turtles are near the substrate surface by the time spring arrives. Captive *T. c. triunguis* and *T. o. ornata* in an outdoor setting in Missouri emerged when the subsurface temperature remained at 7°C for at least five days. If the temperature dropped below 7°C just as the turtle was ready to emerge, it delayed its exit several days until conditions warmed. Occasional individuals emerged prematurely and died as a result of cold. After the first warm spring rains, the turtles left the vicinity of their chambers (Grobman, 1990). Presumably turtles overwintering in water also wait until water temperatures rise to a certain level over a period of days.

The preceding discussion applies generally to box turtles inhabiting mesic or prairie sites, where it is possible to dig overwintering burrows or depressions. In the dry Chihuahuan desert, however, digging may not be possible because of the soil's compaction. Desert box turtles (*T. o. luteola*) occupy and enlarge rodent burrows, such as those of the kangaroo rat *Dipodomys*, during unfavorable environmental conditions. Such burrows are positioned under bushes, particularly creosote bushes, which provide favorable digging conditions and shelter (in Norris and Zweifel, 1950; Degenhardt et al., 1996). Mammal burrows are also used by ornate box turtles in Nebraska prairies (Trail, 1995).

WINTER KILL

Box turtles generally overwinter safely, but they can be killed during severe winters. Harsh winter conditions may be ameliorated by snow cover; that is, the snow provides insulation against the cold. Turtles could be especially vulnerable during long periods of frigid temperatures without an overlying snow pack. There are reports of mass winter die-offs in Kansas *T. ornata*, and the most likely cause is freezing temperatures overtaking subterranean turtles before they could dig deeper to safety (Metcalf and Metcalf, 1979). Overwintering turtles also could be vulnerable to predators within their overwintering chambers. If a predator discovered how to find dormant turtles, it could have easy pickings at a time of potential food scarcity. Predators could scavenge turtles killed by cold temperatures. Thus, determining the cause of mass winter mortality may not be a simple matter.

Box turtles are also killed by sudden freezes, especially in the late winter and early spring (e.g., Allard, 1948). Turtles frequently change their overwintering position during winter warm spells, and they can be caught exposed by rapid cold fronts. Susceptibility to sudden freezing undoubtedly is more severe in the South, where turtles dig shallow overwintering chambers and frequently move during mild temperatures. Neill (1948a:114) states that in the early spring after sudden cold spells in Georgia, "vast numbers of the reptiles freeze to death at this time, and the woods are littered with their shells. I believe that more box turtles are killed by cold than by all other factors together." However, winter kill has never been observed across the Savannah River in South Carolina near where Neill made his observations (I. L. Brisbin, pers. comm.). Winter kill is thought to have detrimental effects on other turtle species as well (e.g., Christiansen and Bickham, 1989).

Box Turtles and Water

At one time, it appears that there was debate among naturalists as to whether eastern box turtles used water much (DeKay, 1842; Holbrook, 1842). Even experienced naturalists have stated that ornate box turtles are reluctant to enter water despite overwhelming evidence to the contrary. It seems well established at present, however, that all box turtles love a good soak and might be said to be fond of water (e.g., Allard, 1948). They are capable of swimming both at the surface and underwater (Overton, 1916; Norris and Zweifel, 1950; Brown, 1974). Indeed, true estivation—passing the hot or dry season in a state of torpor—has been attributed to turtles found buried 15–25 cm deep in underwater mud (Engelhardt, 1916; Brimley, 1943; Wood and Goodwin, 1954). Box turtles have even been found with algae (*Dermatophyton radians* and *Rhizoclonium hookeri*) on the carapace, indicating an extended stay in wet situations (Belusz and Reed, 1969).

In fact, box turtles like a variety of different wet habitats. In the heat of the summer, they congregate along the shallow edges of ponds, streams, and other wetlands (Overton, 1916; W. R. Potts, in Ditmars, 1934; McCauley, 1945; Wood and Goodwin, 1954; Blair, 1976)—sometimes in large numbers, making them vulnerable to predation (chapter 9). In West Virginia large numbers of eastern box turtles have been observed sitting in mountain streams at lower elevations (E. Knizley, pers. comm.). On dry Egmont Key, Florida box turtles move to water-filled ditches and swales after heavy rains and spend from hours to days in or near the water. *Terrapene ornata* have also been seen partially buried in muddy or sandy river banks along the North Canadian and Red rivers in

Oklahoma, near foraging grounds among nearby sedges (Ortenburger and Freeman, 1930; Webb, 1970). In Colorado, ornate box turtles inhabit the banks of the Cimarron River and freely enter the water to drink (Rodeck, 1949). John Sealy, a graduate student at Appalachian State University, even told me about a box turtle he found floating on a log 2.7 m from shore in Hanging Rock Lake, North Carolina. Presumably, water offers comfort, relief from high temperatures, concealment, and escape from biting flies and mosquitoes. It also offers a chance to replenish depleted water supplies, especially in arid lands.

Pet store box turtles are often dehydrated and lethargic. When offered the chance, they may sit alertly for hours in fresh water, drinking copiously, when they previously ignored water in a shallow dish. The low humidity at which captives are often kept makes them susceptible to dehydration from the dry heat of central heating; captives should always be given the opportunity for a full body soak.

Coping with the Environment

HEAT

In general, box turtles are not physiologically capable of sustaining extremely high body temperatures. The principal means by which a box turtle manages its heat load is to maintain a rather narrowly defined preferred body temperature. This temperature varies among species, but the narrowness of its range suggests that it results from an active response of the turtle rather than through a passive response to ambient temperature. Even so, the body temperatures of field-monitored *T. carolina* in Ohio closely tracked ambient temperatures and rarely exceeded 32°C (Adams et al., 1989). In Arkansas, the mean body temperature of active *T. c. triunguis* was 25.9°C (SD = 3.67; Reagan, 1974), whereas the mean summer body temperature of New Jersey *T. c. carolina* was 26–28°C (Russo, 1972).

Ornate box turtles are known to vary their temperature preference depending on their level of satiation. Well-fed box turtles chose preferred temperatures of 29.8°C, 1.5°C higher than box turtles that had fasted for seven to fourteen days prior to testing. Although their maximum temperature preference was similar to that of fed aquatic slider turtles (*Trachemys scripta*), the magnitude of the difference was far less (Gatten, 1974). However, a word of caution is in order, since the geographic origin of the specimens can influence thermal preferences. Wisconsin *T. ornata* have significantly lower preferred ambient temperatures (23.5 ±> 1.3°C) than Kansas *T. ornata* to the south (29.8°C) (Ellner and Karasov, 1993). Apparently, a lower preferred temperature allows the northern turtles a longer activity period at the cooler temperatures normally experienced in Wisconsin. Similar variation might be expected among individuals of the same species inhabiting different latitudes and, possibly, elevations.

Box turtles control their body temperature behaviorally by basking in the morning or on cool days to raise temperature and by becoming dormant or seeking cooler microclimates at higher temperatures. As such, the need to regulate body temperature probably accounts for shifts in seasonal habitat use, rather than these being a response to changes in habitat structure. For example, our Florida box turtles on Egmont Key were commonly found in the savannas of the island all day in winter during mild temperatures, but they retreated to the closed-canopy forest during summer's heat. In the late summer evenings, however, occasional turtles enter the savanna as the sun drops below the tree line and temperatures fall.

As long as box turtles have suitable microclimates into which to retreat, they likely never experience lethal ambient temperatures. Indeed, box turtles are creatures of moderate temperatures, their thermoregulation under active control via melatonin secreted by the pineal gland (Erskine and Hutchison, 1981). Although I have seen box turtles on Egmont Key moving rapidly across hot substrates (45°C and hotter), they do not linger in the late afternoon tropical sun. Their preferred body temperature seems to be about 28–30°C, at least under controlled conditions. Under stress, however, they have a few physiological mechanisms available to reduce internal heat loads.

Heat is stored in the body as temperatures increase. If the turtle is successful in finding a place to cool off, body temperatures fall as stored heat is dissipated via evaporation through the respiratory lining and oral cavity. In contrast to aquatic turtles, box turtles are able to dissipate heat more rapidly than they store it (Bethea, 1972; Spray and May, 1972). Until about 38–41°C, most box turtles do not exhibit outward signs of heat stress and remain fairly calm. At temperatures higher than 41°C, however, turtles pant (some begin the response sooner), which allows for cooling via evaporation along the respiratory and buccopharyngeal tracts. Box turtles urinate on their back legs and inguinal region, which also allows for cooling via evaporation on the exposed skin. At temperatures above 41°C, turtles start to foam at the mouth (termed frothing), which is the main source of cooling. They actively spread the froth around the head and front limbs, again to facilitate evaporative cooling (Riedesel et al., 1971; Sturbaum and Riedesel, 1977). As temperatures increase, turtles also become more agitated in their attempts to escape the high temperatures.

Evaporative cooling is effective at preventing core body temperatures from reaching lethal limits, at least for a period of a few hours. At an external temperature of 48°C, turtles maintained an 8.5°C temperature differential from core body temperature for three hours; at 51°C, they maintained a 10.5°C differential for an hour and a half (Sturbaum and Riedesel, 1974). Presumably, box turtles in most natural circumstances would have ample time to find refuge from such potentially lethal temperatures.

If a turtle is dehydrated, or if it uses up its body water reserves, it no longer is able to lower core body temperature and will succumb. Even at 38°C, a box turtle can lose 17 percent of its body weight through moisture loss (over a forty-five-hour period) without showing signs of heat stress (Bogert and Cowles, 1947). When core body temperatures reach about 42–43°C in ornate and eastern box turtles, death results (Hutchison et al., 1966; Sturbaum, 1981). A weight decrease due to water loss (as high as 5.6 percent of body weight per hour) is a much better sign of thermal stress than are physiological measures such as changes in heart rate (Sturbaum, 1972; Sturbaum and Riedesel, 1974). It has been suggested that the large bladder in box turtles allows water retention for heat stress thermoregulation (Riedesel et al., 1971), although most box turtles avoid excessive heat loads through behavioral thermoregulation. Heat-related mortality can occur if turtles fall into ditches (Wood and Goodwin, 1954) or become trapped between railroad ties. In addition, turtles that lose their scutes to fire or other factors are at a particular disadvantage since the scutes function, in part, to retain body water; turtles without scutes also lose heat faster on cool days than do turtles with scutes (Rose, 1969).

COLD

As with heat, the primary response to adverse cold conditions is to try to avoid them. Of course in cooler climates this is impossible, and box turtles have evolved measures to survive the frigid winters of the north. The first thing they do is to position overwintering chambers in favorable locations and to dig deep below the frost line. For Wisconsin *T. ornata*, overwintering chamber temperatures decline from about 5°C to 1.2°C from November through February, but lowest temperatures can reach to −3°C (Doroff and Keith, 1990). From late February to April, the mean overwintering chamber temperature rises to 2.9°C. Overwintering *T. carolina* and *T. ornata* experience similar minimum temperatures, that is, from −2.5 to −3°C (Russo, 1972; Claussen et al., 1991; Costanzo et al., 1995).

Box turtles in cold climates are routinely subject to temperatures below freezing for extended periods. For example, frost penetrates 60–70 cm below ground in Wisconsin. In laboratory experiments, Ohio *T. carolina* survived −2°C for forty-four hours without any obvious problems. Recovery occurs slowly for a frozen turtle. When an animal was returned to a 25°C room temperature, voluntary locomotion occurred in about 2.7 hours (Storey et al., 1993). When temperatures drop to freezing, the box turtle is able to shut down bodily functions. As the turtle cools from the outside in, blood is shunted toward the central core of the body. It mobilizes glucose produced in the liver and concentrates it in vital organs, such as the heart, eye, and brain, during the freezing process (Costanzo et al., 1993; Storey et al., 1993). The high glucose content in vital organs makes these organs the last to freeze and, in essence, vital organs are freeze-dried to protect their cellular structure. Under extreme cold, even the heart can cease to beat. To all intents and purposes the turtle appears dead.

The ability to sustain large amounts of ice within the body cavity is termed freeze tolerance, and box turtles are the largest animals so adapted. Freezing commences at about −8°C (Costanzo and Claussen, 1990). Cellular water is shunted into the body cavity, where it freezes. Ice also may surround the brain and skeletal muscles in limbs. Even the lungs can be a mass of icy tissue (Storey et al., 1993). A box turtle can have between 33 and 58 percent of its body water freeze for 18–50 hours and yet recover (Costanzo and Claussen, 1990). Box turtles do not mobilize or manufacture typical biological cryoprotectants, such as glycerol, sorbitol, and free amino acids, found in both vertebrates (e.g., wood frogs) and invertebrates. Indeed, no turtles are known to produce these cryoprotectants. Apparently, the fluid volume within a box turtle would require too much cryoprotectant to make supercooling effective.

DROUGHT

During prolonged periods of drought, box turtles retreat to protected environments, much the way they do in winter. They also may congregate in pools of water or even in running streams, as already noted. Some authors have stated that eastern box turtles undergo a terrestrial midsummer estivation to avoid heat and drought, but this does not seem to be the case, although individuals sometimes remain quiescent (dormant) for a long period. Areas that appear devoid of turtles during drought actually may have large populations once moisture returns. As with heat stress, turtles without scutes, perhaps because of fire or trauma, are particularly at risk during droughts because of the increased tendency to lose body water through the shell.

Future Directions

OTHER HABITATS, GRASSLANDS, AND MEXICO. Most of the research on habitat use by box turtles has been conducted in eastern North America in moist deciduous forests. Yet populations of box turtles inhabit different habitats in the east, such as southern Florida rocklands, barrier islands, and even suburban and other human-altered environments, such as greenways. Reports of box turtles foraging in salt marshes far from the nearest hammocks are intriguing. Do box turtles do different things in these habitats? Are they permanent residents or just passing through? In the Midwest and West, much more information is needed on grassland-inhabiting *T. ornata*; to date, there have been only a few good studies on this species in the vast prairie region, most notably in Kansas. To repeat a recurring theme, virtually nothing is known for any of the Mexican species, except for *T. coahuila*. Even obtaining good physical descriptions of their habitats would be a positive step in understanding how their spatial use of the environment compares and contrasts with that of their northern counterparts.

HABITAT PARTITIONING. There are many areas where phenotypically distinct species and subspecies come into local contact with one another. For example, *T. c. triunguis* and *T. ornata* often are found in close geographic proximity and even syntopically. Do they partition their habitats, and if so, what is the mechanism of such partitioning? In the Florida Panhandle, four subspecies of *T. carolina* come into contact: *bauri*, *carolina*, *major*, and *triunguis*. Based on my rather casual observations, it appears as if perfectly good *T. c. major* inhabit ridge tops, whereas phenotypic *T. c. carolina* are found in the deep ravines along the Apalachicola River. But is this a valid observation? If it is, then habitat partitioning, in addition to geographic barriers, helps keep these subspecies separate and makes them act like species. A great deal of introgression appears to take place in certain areas; how do the offspring partition habitats? Geographic partitioning based on habitat selection could be an important mechanism explaining some of the confusing distribution and phenotypic patterns observed

SUBSTRATE SELECTION. Does pH play any role in the microdistribution of box turtles and their selection of places to rest and retreat, as it does with terrestrial salamanders and other animals? In this line of thought, do box turtles actually "select" substrates at all, or do they respond solely to moisture and temperature conditions? It appears that ornate box turtles can extend their ranges northward if appropriate sandy soils are present in which they can dig to escape cold winters. Is the lack of sandy or otherwise friable substrates the reason eastern box turtles do not range as far north, as opposed to any innate genetic or physiological reason?

OVERWINTERING AND COLD. Over and over, I found reports that eastern box turtles do not dig deep into the substrate, even in rather cold climates. Yet there are other reports that turtles dig deeper in response to cold and that they change location during the winter. Given the thermal constraints on activity in winter, how do they do this? Are not shallow, cold turtles particularly susceptible to predation, as they certainly must be if they change locations at much less than optimum temperatures? There is only one report to suggest that this might occur (Metcalf and Metcalf, 1979), although other possible causes could not be discounted. How does a turtle know when to dig deeper because of oncoming cold? It would seem too late to respond to sudden cold once temperatures started to drop, especially if the turtle were already semitorpid or completely dormant. Do hatchlings respond like adults (that is, by digging deeper), or do they opt for special overwintering sites, such as tree root canals, mammal dens, or even in water or marshy areas? What are the effects of mass winter mortality on population structure? And finally, what causes a completely frozen box turtle to regain its spark of life? How a turtle comes back to life after being frozen—why it is alive and not a warm corpse—is one of the most fundamental questions a biologist or turtle watcher can contemplate.

4 | Activity, Movement, and Orientation

Movement in box turtles living in the desert is closely linked to the environment. However, there are still other factors…that are difficult to quantify, and a model that would predict when and where turtles move is far from being worked out. Obviously many factors are in operation, and no simple series of variables will explain fully the movements of turtles.

PIMMY NIEUWOLT, 1996

 Superficially, box turtles do not seem to do much. After nine years of studying them on Egmont Key, my foremost image is of a box turtle at rest, limbs tucked in, head out watching the world, plastron planted firmly on the substrate. Yet they eat, grow, find mates, and explore their world, just as we do. They deposit eggs, dig forms, and fend off heat and cold as necessary. Perhaps they seem so sedentary because in all my encounters with them, the box turtle concerned was already well aware of my presence, stopped what it was doing, and watched me approach from afar. Still, it is hard to shake the impression that box turtles are somehow much better than we are at economy of activity, leaving ample time for contemplation.

In this chapter, I describe the daily and seasonal activity of box turtles and review the related topics of home range, movement, homing, and orientation. Unfortunately, general overviews seem inadequate to characterize the variety of activities and movements made by individual box turtles (just as a general overview of human activity might fail to describe one's own daily round). More detailed descriptions of the activities of individual turtles are found in the work of Stickel (1950), Metcalf and Metcalf (1970), Schwartz and Schwartz (1974), and Schwartz et al. (1984).

Activity

DIURNAL ACTIVITY

Daily activity begins at various hours depending on weather conditions, latitude, and season. Box turtles in Florida become active at the slightest hint of daybreak, but Missouri *T. c. triunguis* do not leave their evening resting places until warmed by the sun (Schwartz and Schwartz, 1974). It may take a box turtle from forty-five to fifty minutes to warm from 18°C in a burrow to 24°C, the mean temperature of free-living box turtles in

Wisconsin (Ellner and Karasov, 1993). The earliest that I have seen box turtles active on Egmont Key is 6:30 A.M. in summer and 8:00 A.M. in winter, whereas others have seen box turtles active as early as 6:00 A.M. (e.g., Brown, 1974, for *T. coahuila*; Rose et al., 1988, for *T. ornata*). In searches just before dawn, I have never observed an active turtle. When first encountered early in the morning, turtles are often walking, as if heading in a certain direction for a specific reason. Undoubtedly, early morning activity in warm climates is favored because of moderate temperatures and high humidity. Turtles also may take advantage of morning dew on vegetation, fungi, and fruits. In cooler climates and in the spring and fall, they wait for the sun to warm them before beginning daily activities.

Some box turtles are active throughout any given day during the warmer parts of the year. However, there may be peaks of daily activity as well as times of relative inactivity, at least for southern turtles. In summer, Florida adults show an activity peak in the morning and a lesser activity peak late in the afternoon. During the heat of a clear day, they take shelter and, although alert, do not move much. Patterns also may change somewhat in response to daily weather. On a hot (34–36°C) summer afternoon, box turtles are inactive. If a sudden thunderstorm drops rainfall and temperatures, however, turtles become active. Periods of inactivity during midday heat have likewise been reported for *T. c. major* (Penn and Pottharst, 1940), *T. c. triunguis* (Schwartz and Schwartz, 1974), *T. o. ornata* (Legler, 1960), and *T. o. luteola* (Nieuwolt, 1996). However, Madden (1975) reported no inactivity periods for New York *T. carolina*; perhaps box turtles in cooler climates are less inclined to become inactive either because they rarely experience extended periods of extreme heat or because of the shorter activity season in such climates.

In Florida, morning and late afternoon activity peaks are much less evident in conjunction with the cooler mean ambient temperatures of spring and fall, and by winter, adult box turtles are active only during the warmer parts of the day (fig. 4-1). Although patterns change during the year, adult males and females have similar activity patterns within a season (Dodd et al., 1994). Florida juveniles appear to have the same daily activity pattern regardless of season (fig. 4-2). Perhaps this is because juveniles are largely confined to the cooler, moister parts of the habitat where environmental conditions are more uniform (Dodd et al., 1994; Hamilton, 2000). In more temperate climates, it is likely that juveniles and adults have similar daily activity patterns within any particular season.

Even in the summer during favorable conditions, some box turtles are inactive for a day at a time or longer (Stickel, 1950; Dolbeer, 1969), with periods of activity and inactivity alternating. Inactivity does not mean that turtles are not alert, only that they do not move from a favored resting place. It is likely that they feed during periods of inactivity if potential prey passes within close range. Turtles also remain within resting locations for days or even weeks under unfavorable conditions, especially during periods of cool weather and drought (Stickel, 1950; Dolbeer, 1969; Strang, 1983).

No one knows exactly how box turtles partition their daily activities, although these undoubtedly vary seasonally, especially with regard to feeding and reproduction. On Egmont Key, we noted what 1,360 box turtles were doing when encountered. Most were resting, walking, buried under cover—another form of resting—or feeding, and this left only 5 percent occupied with activities not specified (fig. 4-3; see Dodd et al., 1994).

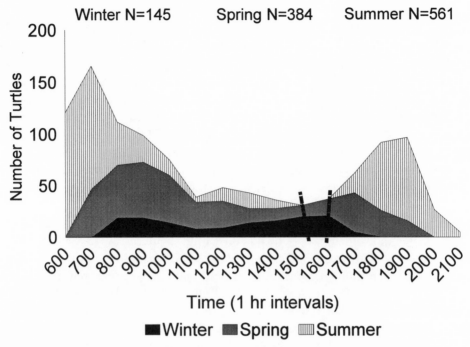

Figure 4-1. Seasonal variation in temporal activity of adult box turtles on Egmont Key, Hillsborough County, Florida. The dashed lines going to 0 indicate that no box turtles were found during the summer between 1500 and 1600 hours (3:00–4:00 P.M.) during this particular study. Data from figure 5 in Dodd et al. (1994).

However, recording what turtles were doing at one random point in time, even for a large sample size, probably provides little indication of the amount of time individuals devote to various activities daily. Missouri *T. c. triunguis* are reported to feed for about an hour in the morning, bask in the sun, and rest for the remainder of the day until it is time to make a form for the night (Schwartz and Schwartz, 1974).

NOCTURNAL ACTIVITY

By all accounts, box turtles, with the exception of some nesting females, are diurnal or crepuscular (active at dawn and dusk). Although *T. coahuila* may be normally active as late as 10:00 P.M. (Brown, 1974), Webb et al. (1963) reported that aquatic box turtles were crepuscular and that they could not be induced to move at night. Drotos (1974) reported that eastern box turtles in Virginia were active as late as 11:30 P.M. but gave no details. In more than thirty trips to Egmont Key over a ten-year period, I have only once seen box turtles active at night. This observation occurred on July 27, 1993, at 9:45 P.M. during a heavy rain shower, when five turtles (both males and females) were seen walking through the undergrowth. Thus although reports of nocturnal activity are rare, some turtles may be active after dark.

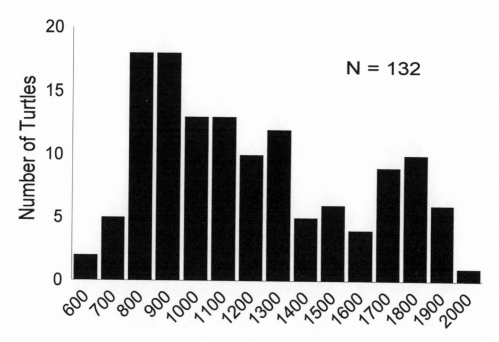

Figure 4-2. Time budget, measured by the number of turtles found active at a particular hour, of juvenile box turtles on Egmont Key, Hillsborough County, Florida. Season had no effect on juvenile temporal activity. Data from figure 6 in Dodd et al. (1994).

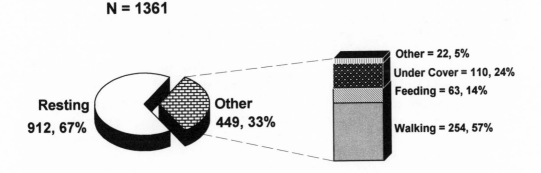

Figure 4-3. Activity of Florida box turtles encountered on Egmont Key, 1991 to 1993. N = 1,361 observations.

Nocturnal activity in box turtles may be associated with nesting, at least in certain instances. Box turtles sometimes nest at night or at least complete nesting after dusk. For example, female *T. coahuila* have been reported nesting after midnight, and both *T. ornata* and captive *T. carolina* deposit eggs after dark (chapter 6; Ewing, 1937). Nesting initiated in late evening or at dusk is completed after sunset, after which a female may return to a favored resting place.

Seasonal Activity

The date on which a turtle first becomes active depends on both air and substrate temperatures, which are variable from year to year. In northern latitudes and at higher elevations, box turtles are active only during the warmer months of the year, generally from March or April to October or November. For example, Missouri and Oklahoma three-toed box turtles emerge from winter retreats from late March to late April and enter retreats in the fall from mid-September to early November (Carpenter, 1957; Schwartz and Schwartz, 1974). The winter retreat entry and emergence dates generally coincide with the first and last killing frosts. However, warm temperatures during the winter allow some turtles to be active (for example, in Washington, D.C., in December and February, Allard, 1935; in Missouri on December 3 at 24°C, Schwartz and Schwartz, 1974; in Texas on December 24 at 15°C, Blair, 1976). Unusually warm temperatures also can lure an overwintering turtle away from a protective retreat with fatal consequences. A Missouri box turtle active on March 3 at 23°C was later found dead after four subsequent weeks of subfreezing temperatures (Schwartz and Schwartz, 1974). Similar mortality has been reported by other researchers (Allard, 1935; Neill, 1948a), although Brisbin (pers. comm.) has not observed such mortality in South Carolina.

At warmer southern latitudes such as in Florida and at Cuatro Ciénegas, Florida and Coahuilan box turtles are active year-round (Brown, 1974; Dodd et al. 1994; Pilgrim et al., 1997). Only during brief periods of cold and drought do they become inactive. Pilgrim et al. (1997) found "peaks" of activity in fall and winter during two years in Florida when flooding concentrated turtles where they were more easily found. In Mexico, seasonal activity patterns of the aquatic box turtle more closely follow spring-fed water temperatures than ambient air temperatures (Brown, 1974). In the warm tropics, activity may be correlated with the wet and dry seasons; as the dry season intensifies, Mexican box turtles become less and less active. Yucatán box turtles (*T. c. yucatana*) are active only during the wet season, June to early November (Buskirk, 1993), and may be nearly impossible to find during the dry season (J. Frazier, pers. comm.).

Activity and Environmental Conditions

Box turtles all favor warm temperatures, and temperature undoubtedly determines the length of the seasonal activity period, especially in temperate climates. Reagan (1974) suggested that box turtles exist within a rather narrow range of microclimatic variables throughout their activity season, and my work on Egmont Key supports his hypothesis. The most favorable conditions for *T. carolina* include warm temperatures, high humidity, and frequent rains (e.g., Stickel, 1950; Dolbeer, 1969). It has long been observed that rainfall stimulates box turtle activity. Rainfall also stimulates terrestrial movement of the otherwise generally aquatic *T. coahuila* (Webb et al., 1963).

In Florida where year-round activity is common, *T. c. bauri* on Egmont Key are active at air temperatures greater than 17°C (fig. 4-4) and at substrate temperatures greater than 16°C (fig. 4-5). For the most part, these temperatures simply reflect the year-round conditions on the island and are not indicative of preference. The mean temperature at which box turtles are found is rather constant regardless of season (Dodd et al., 1994). Cold fronts are rare and usually short-lived, and box turtles are inactive during the few days of cold weather. The temperature extremes shown in figures 4-4 and 4-5, however, probably are important since they reflect both the minimum and maximum temperatures at which activity occurs.

Of the microenvironmental variables best studied, relative humidity (RH) appears to exert the most significant influence on box turtle daily activity, at least during the warmer parts of the year. The thermal and moisture components of the microclimate are extremely important in the location of the form, but relative humidity influences activity independently of the moisture at the form (Reagan, 1974). In effect, forms are located in warm, moist areas, but unless relative humidity is high, turtles will not be active. At low humidity, *T. carolina* become inactive, seeking shelter buried in soil or resting in forms

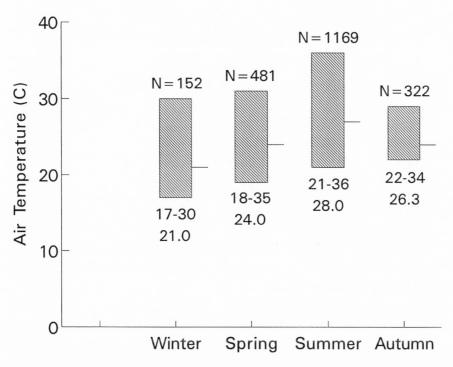

Figure 4-4. Air temperatures at which Florida box turtles were found from 1991 to 1998 on Egmont Key, Hillsborough County, Florida. Data based on 2,124 captures. The bars give the range and the line to the right of the bar shows the mean. The range and standard deviation are given below the bar.

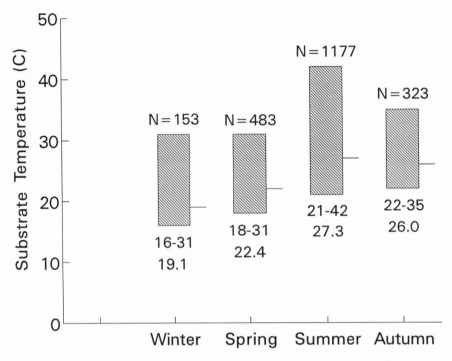

Figure 4-5. Substrate temperatures at which Florida box turtles were found from 1991 to 1998 on Egmont Key, Hillsborough County, Florida. Data based on 2,136 captures. The bars give the range and the line to the right of the bar shows the mean. The range and standard deviation are given below the bar.

(chapter 3) or, in Florida, abandoned gopher tortoise burrows. The mean RH at which box turtles were active on Egmont Key was 67 percent in spring and greater than 72 percent in summer and the warm autumn; nearly all captures occurred when RH was greater than 50 percent (fig. 4-6). The wide range of spring RH values on Egmont derives from weather fronts moving through, drastically lowering humidity in a short period. Otherwise, RH for spring captures probably mirrors those for the other seasons.

The information presented pertains to the mesic-dwelling species and subspecies; the desert-dwelling *T. o. luteola* has slightly different environmental activity correlates. In New Mexico, this turtle is most active at substrate temperatures between 31 and 36°C and much less so below or above these temperatures (Nieuwolt, 1996). Turtles are most active at air temperatures between 13 and 24°C, when solar radiation is low, and when humidity is high (radiation <200 jules/cm^2/h, humidity <20 mbar vapor pressure deficit; Nieuwolt, 1996). Thus, they avoid conditions of high ambient temperatures with intense solar radiation. In the case of the desert box turtle, environmental factors alone are not sufficient to predict activity.

The Mexican aquatic box turtle, a largely wetland-dwelling species, is not as dependent as the more terrestrial species on ambient air or substrate temperatures. This species lives most of its life in spring-fed wetlands where water temperatures fluctuate less than do conditions on land. At the springs, water temperatures are usually above 30°C.

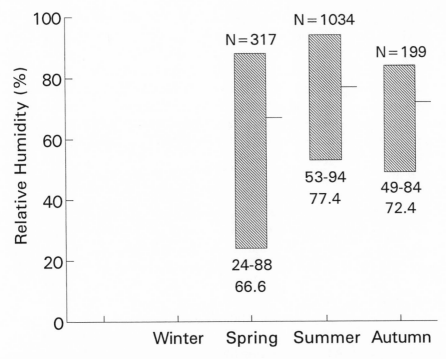

Figure 4-6. Relative humidity at which Florida box turtles were found from 1991 to 1998 on Egmont Key, Hillsborough County, Florida. Data based on 1,550 captures. The bars give the range and the line to the right of the bar shows the mean. The range and standard deviation are given below the bar.

However, water temperature varies both daily and seasonally as dispersing waters cool at night and warm during summer days to near lethal levels, at least in shallow regions. Turtle cloacal temperatures closely track water temperatures, varying only slightly above or below water temperatures depending on season (Brown, 1974). In January, cloacal temperatures averaged 20.7°C (range 14.8–26.7°C), whereas in July, cloacal temperatures averaged 28.1°C (range 20.1–32.7°C). The cloacal temperatures of several turtles caught on land were always greater than 20°C and reached 34.5°C in one individual. Two turtles in a much used terrestrial refuge had a temperature of 29°C when the air temperature was 34°C (Brown, 1974).

Movement

TRACKING TECHNIQUES

Movements of box turtles have been studied using three techniques: mark-recapture, thread trailing, and radiotelemetry. Each technique tells part of the story about how box turtles move through their environment and use various habitats. The least labor-intensive technique involves marking animals and, upon recapture, measuring the distance between capture points. The measured distance tells little about how the turtle uses its environment, although it can provide a rough, probably underestimated measure of home range (Nichols, 1939a; Metcalf and Metcalf, 1970), and it can be used on a casual basis over a long period. The other techniques are more labor intensive.

The turtle's carapace provides an easy base for attaching instruments to monitor movement. The earliest attempts at systematically tracking box turtles involved attaching thread spools to the posterior shell (Breder, 1927). As the turtle walks, string is laid down, which can be followed to map travel routes. The technique can be used only so long as enough string is available; and string breakage can be a problem. However, thread spools can be replaced, allowing tracking for considerable amounts of time. Metcalf and Metcalf (1970) followed adults for up to three months in Kansas, and Stickel (1950) followed turtles for up to 161 days in Maryland.

Instead of spools, thread bobbins have been used successfully to track short-term movements of juveniles for up to five days over a distance of 208 m (110 mm CL) or even 148 m in a single day (105 mm CL; Hamilton, 2000). Thread bobbins are small spools of fine thread used in commercial sewing. Each tightly wound bobbin contains approximately 250 m of thread and weighs just under two grams (6 percent of the body weight of the smallest turtle tracked on Egmont Key). Using duct tape, the bobbin is attached to the rear of the turtle's carapace in such a manner that the thread is let out as the turtle walks through leaf litter. When the thread runs out, the only thing left is the duct tape, which eventually drops off. While monitoring the daily movements of sixty-eight juvenile box turtles on Egmont Key, Hamilton (2000) never saw any indication that the bobbin influenced behavior. If the thread snagged on undergrowth, the fine line broke and the turtle continued on its way.

Thread trailing provides an accurate and extremely detailed profile of how turtles use their habitats. Based on thread-trailing analyses, evidence suggests that vegetation cover affects the sinuosity of trails, that temperature affects the mean distance moved per day, and that ornate box turtles show little directional bias in their day-to-day comings and goings (Claussen et al., 1997, 1998).

The third technique involves putting a radio transmitter on a turtle's carapace and following the animal's movement periodically as time permits. Transmitters are attached in such a manner as not to interfere with normal behavior such as reproduction. In males, transmitters may be placed on the rear or lateral margins of the carapace, depending on transmitter and turtle size. On females, transmitters are placed over vertebral scute 1 so as not to interfere with mating. This technique allows tracking for much longer times than thread trailing, although the exact travel routes between capture points cannot be determined. However, more turtles can be followed and, in time, radio tracking provides a reasonably accurate assessment of long-term habitat use and movement patterns. Schwartz and Schwartz (1974) found that the home range estimate of one radio-tracked turtle was 2.04 times greater than the five-year estimate based on the mark-recapture method.

HOME RANGE

Most box turtles appear to have a well-defined home range that does not vary greatly in size from one year to the next. They do not have territories; that is, they do not defend any particular portion of the home range against intruders, and they are frequently seen in close association with one another (chapter 5). Although the area encompassed by the home range tends to remain constant, there may be slight shifts in habitat use from one year to the next (Stickel, 1950, 1989; Yahner, 1974; Madden, 1975; Strang, 1983). Likewise, slight shifts in the size and shape of the habitat used may occur weekly or monthly within a season. The home range may or may not include appropriate nesting and overwintering sites.

Home range size has been measured using many different computational methods and reported in many different ways, which makes comparisons difficult, especially since field methods and sample sizes vary so much. Box turtles tend to use core areas for day-to-day activities (termed the "utilized home range" by Madden, 1975); but exploratory excursions, feeding forays, and trips to nesting and overwintering sites sometimes far distant from the home range complicate the interpretation of data, particularly when the turtle is not continually tracked or if it is tracked only during a portion of its activity season. Despite these caveats, home range size estimates are reasonably similar in many studies.

Male and female home ranges are similar in size (Stickel, 1950; Legler, 1960; Schwartz and Schwartz, 1974; table 4-1). In some studies, male home ranges are reported as slightly larger than female ranges; in other studies, the reverse is true (table 4-1). Juvenile home ranges are not as large as those of adults, although Stickel (1950) found that there was not much difference between the shortest and longest travel records of juveniles and adults. Missouri juvenile *T. c. triunguis* have home ranges that overlap smaller adult ranges in size, but no juvenile's home range approached the largest size of an adult's home range. One radio-tracked juvenile had a home range of only 0.25 of a hectare over a sixty-six-day period (Schwartz and Schwartz, 1974). Other juvenile *T. c. triunguis* home ranges varied from 0.4 to 3.2 ha (n = 10; Schwartz and Schwartz, 1974) and from 0.3 to 3.7 ha (mean = 1.7; n = 15; Schwartz et al., 1984). Juveniles expand their home range as they get older.

Studies with the largest sample sizes over an extended period suggest that home ranges are fairly small (less than 1 ha to about 5 ha, depending on computational method), and less than 300 m in diameter (table 4-1). As an example, one female had a very small summer home range (52 m in diameter) and appeared quite sedentary over a three-year period (Stickel, 1950). Such small home ranges may not be unusual. In Missouri, 70 percent of the home ranges of 239 *T. c. triunguis* were less than 2 ha, and 15 percent were between 2 and 3.2 ha (Schwartz and Schwartz, 1974). Certainly habitat quality, habitat diversity, and individual preference account for much variation in home range size.

Turtles may reside for a long time, perhaps throughout life, within a particular area. Metcalf and Metcalf (1970) found one Kansas *T. ornata* twenty-eight times over a ten-year period within 7.6 m of his original capture location! Records of box turtles remaining within a home range for long periods are not uncommon: thirteen years for *T. ornata* in Kansas (Metcalf and Metcalf, 1970); fifteen years for *T. c. carolina* in New York (Nichols, 1939a); at least ninety-one *T. c. triunguis* in Missouri were faithful to home ranges over a period of six years (Schwartz and Schwartz, 1974), and twenty-two over a period of

Table 4-1. Comparison of home range size of box turtles, genus *Terrapene*. M/R = mark-recapture.

Location	Method	Computation	Area (ha)	Linear distance (m)	N	Reference
T. carolina						
New York	M/R	Direct measure		generally <228	12	Nichols, 1939a
New York	Telemetry	Bivariate normal	1.4–19.2 (x̄=6.95)		23	Madden, 1975
		Minimum polygon	0.4–6.3 (x̄=2.12)			
		Convex polygon	0.7–9.9 (x̄=4.05)			
Maryland	M/R	Range length		40–174 (x̄=97)	11	Hallgren–Scaffidi, 1986
	Trailing	Convex polygon	0.02–0.5 (x̄=0.2)			
Maryland	M/R	Bivariate normal	♂ x̄=1.20; ♀ x̄=1.13		51, 52	Stickel, 1989
Virginia	Telemetry	Direct measure		55–365 (x̄=213)	6	Bayless, 1984
		Minimum area	0.8–2.6 (x̄=1.25)			
		Ornstein–Uhlenbeck	0.2–3.5 (x̄=2.47)			
Tennessee	M/R	Direct measure		15–183 (x̄=74)	76	Dolbeer, 1969
Tennessee	Telemetry	Convex polygon	0.3–0.6 (x̄=0.38)	89–265 (x̄=190)	4	Davis, 1981
Indiana	M/R	Direct measure		♂ 55–344 (x̄=171)	56	Williams and Parker, 1987
				♀ 52–427 (x̄=176)	53	
Missouri	M/R	Not stated	1.2–4.7 (♂ x̄=1.53; ♀ x̄=1.45)		79, 64	Schwartz and Schwartz, 1974
Missouri	M/R	Not stated	0.6–10.6 (♂ x̄=5.2; ♀ x̄=5.1)		21, 16	Schwartz et al., 1984

Table 4-1 *continued*. Comparison of home range size of box turtles, genus *Terrapene*. M/R = mark-recapture.

Location	Method	Computation	Area (ha)	Linear distance (m)	N	Reference
T. ornata						
Wisconsin	Telemetry	Dixon & Chapman	0.2–58.1		42	Doroff and Keith, 1990
Nebraska	Telemetry	Minimum polygon	9.5–15.8 ($\bar{x}$=13.2), 1993		6	Holy, 1995
			4.6–36.4 ($\bar{x}$=18.8), 1994		15	Holy, 1995
Nebraska	Telemetry	Not stated	2.2–15.8		3	Trail, 1995
Kansas	M/R	Direct measure	2.18	167	1	Fitch, 1958
Kansas	M/R, Trailing	Direct measure		44–556 ($\bar{x}$=170)	44	Legler, 1960
Kansas	Trailing	Direct measure		73–270 ($\bar{x}$=182)	7	Metcalf and Metcalf, 1970
Texas	M/R	Direct measure		♂ 76–137 ($\bar{x}$=111)	6	Blair, 1976
				♀ 67–119 ($\bar{x}$=94)	5	
New Mexico	Telemetry	Direct measure		32–526 ($\bar{x}$=276)	15	Nieuwolt, 1993, 1996
		Minimum polygon	0.03–4.1 ($\bar{x}$=1.64)			
		95% Ellipse	0.08–16.4 ($\bar{x}$=5.03)			
		95% Dixon&Chapman	0.006–4.4 ($\bar{x}$=0.95)			

twenty-four years (Schwartz and Schwartz, 1991). Individuals also remain within their home ranges despite extreme environmental perturbations. After a severe bottomland flood in July 1945, eastern box turtles either stayed within the flooded area or returned to their home ranges after displacement by flood waters; one female returned home from a distance of 204 m (Stickel, 1950). Turtles continued to live within their once flooded ranges in subsequent years.

In contrast, some eastern box turtles seem to have two home ranges and travel back and forth between them at irregular intervals. Stickel (1950) recorded a female dividing her time between a northern range (122 m in diameter) and southern one (of similar diameter) located more than 120 m apart. The northern and southern ranges were occupied for fifty-nine and twenty-eight days, respectively, and neither included nesting or overwintering sites, which took her farther afield. Apparently suitable contiguous habitat separated the home ranges. In other cases, however, reporting of large home ranges may mask the use of two widely separated areas. Missouri *T. c. triunguis* with "large" home ranges actually used woodlots separated by open ridges; the open ridges were unsuitable habitat. Inclusion of the ridge habitat in calculations suggested a much larger home range than was actually used (Schwartz and Schwartz, 1974).

FACTORS AFFECTING HOME RANGE SIZE

Box turtles are not social animals in a behavioral sense, but densities can be high in nature (chapter 8). Therefore, it seems unlikely that the size of a turtle's home range is determined by the spacing of conspecifics. No study yet has demonstrated a correlation between turtle density and the size of the home range (e.g., Madden, 1975). Box turtles need cover for protection from the elements, and they need food, nesting sites, and access to one another. If these factors are in short supply, then home ranges are likely to be larger than they would be under more favorable conditions. In habitats with abundant food resources, the resource quality alone might dictate smaller home range sizes than in habitats where these factors are scarce. This hypothesis seems borne out by Nieuwolt's (1993, 1996) finding that desert-dwelling *T. ornata* in New Mexico had larger home ranges than conspecifics living in more mesic climates. Inasmuch as habitat quality may change seasonally, for example due to drought, it is likely that such changes account for at least some of the variation observed in home range shifts seen in *Terrapene*. Stability in habitat quality may be reflected in the stability of home range size (Stickel, 1950).

In addition to habitat quality, habitat structure may influence the size and spatial distribution of the home range. The presence of walls, fences, ravines, ponds, and tall grasses all influence movements and habitat use (Legler, 1960). Such features direct movements along certain pathways or around obstacles, and their effect is easily seen in figure 4-7. Presumably, turtles living in areas with extensive obstacles to movement would have larger and perhaps differently shaped home ranges than those living in contiguous habitats. In New Mexico, certain *T. o. luteola* used roads and road rights-of-way as movement corridors, and thus had larger home ranges than those turtles that did not (Nieuwolt, 1996). Likewise, Virginia *T. carolina* with home ranges including roads had larger, more elliptical home ranges than did turtles with ranges not including roads (Bayless, 1984).

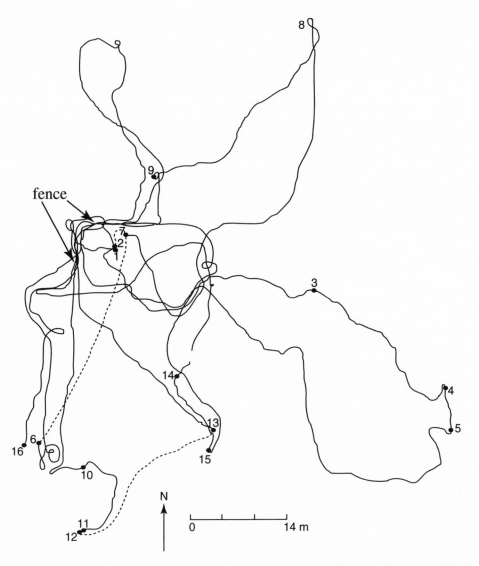

Figure 4-7. Movements of an adult male eastern box turtle during eight days in midsummer (July 7 to July 14), 1945. Note how the turtle follows fence lines (a fence was located at right angles just northwest of locations 1, 2, 7). From Stickel (1950).

Age may also affect the size and location of the home range. During their nineteen-year study, Schwartz et al. (1984) recorded six juveniles that increased their home range size from 0.7 ha to 4.4 ha as the turtles grew larger. However, the home range estimates of all box turtles in the Schwartzes' study area increased from 1974 to 1984 even though the size of the home range was not correlated with the number of captures. In addition to increases in home range size, juveniles sometimes shift the location of the home range as they become adults (fig. 4-8).

DAILY MOVEMENTS

Although some box turtles may remain in one location for days or even weeks, others are active nearly every day and travel considerable distances within a twenty-four-hour period. Many authors using thread trailers have shown that turtles meander through the habitat crisscrossing their own paths, turning often, and wandering around certain objects such as trees (fig. 4-9) (Stickel, 1950; Metcalf and Metcalf, 1970). On Egmont Key, the substrate at the base of many palmetto trees is often worn bare from frequent trampling by turtles. At other times, routes appear direct, as if the turtle was moving to a specific location. Individual turtles use the same pathways repeatedly, and different turtles may use identical pathways.

In terms of daily movement, male desert-dwelling *T. o. luteola* moved 15 m per day (n = 208), females moved 13 m per day (n = 384), and juveniles moved 7.5 m per day (n = 56) (Nieuwolt, 1996). However, these values were derived using mark-recapture locations and therefore do not reflect the actual distance traveled. Turtles may travel a great distance, yet retire near the location from which they started. Strang (1983) measured the distances traveled by *T. c. carolina* in a twenty-four-hour period in Pennsylvania using thread trailers; thirty-three turtles moved a mean distance of 40 m ± 50, but the lengths changed appreciably between rainy (76 m ± 65, n = 12) and dry (19 m ± 20, n = 21) days.

Linear distances traveled may be considerable within a short period, even when the turtle remains within its home range. For example, a Maryland box turtle traveled 139 m in one day without leaving its home range; the straight-line distance between first and last capture was only 52 m, however (Stickel, 1950). Using thread trailers, the two greatest daily movements by *T. c. triunguis* in Missouri were 110 m and 116 m; however, the greatest distances between captures in a twenty-four-hour period using radiotelemetry were 180 m and 229 m (Schwartz and Schwartz, 1974). Collecting records for a male *T. c. carolina* showed his home range diameter over three years to be 81 m, 87 m, and 88 m, yet in only four days he traveled within a 75 m diameter home range. A female traveled a home range with a diameter of 118 m in two weeks in July, whereas a male traveled a home range with a diameter of 56 m during five days in July.

There does not appear to be any correlation between the amount of time since a turtle was last tracked and the distance moved (Stickel, 1950; Nieuwolt, 1996). This suggests that there is no real way to gauge the amount of time a turtle spends in an area without directly observing the turtle. Speeds obviously correlate to motivation, at least up to a point. In that regard, box turtles are fast movers when they want to be. Blair (1976) recorded a *T. ornata* that moved 76 m in one hour.

Finally, nothing is known about how the Coahuilan box turtle (*T. coahuila*) uses its environment or what the extent of its daily aquatic home range might be. However, aquatic box turtles have been observed at least 27 m from water (Webb et al., 1963). The frequency of trails through the thick vegetation surrounding wetlands at Cuatro Ciénegas suggests that terrestrial movements are not uncommon.

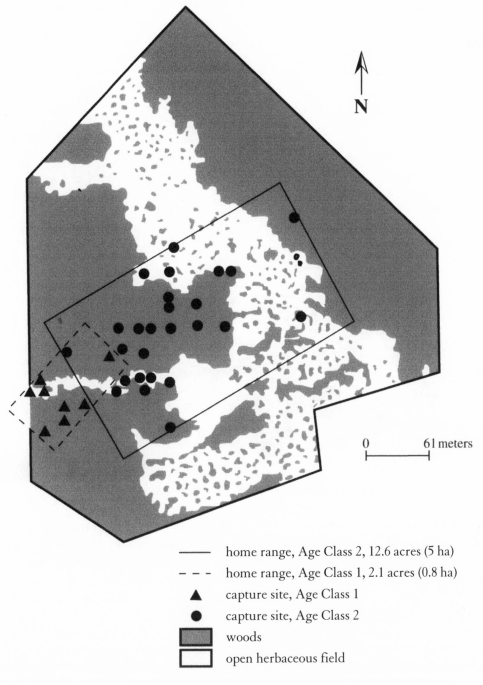

———— home range, Age Class 2, 12.6 acres (5 ha)

- - - - home range, Age Class 1, 2.1 acres (0.8 ha)

▲ capture site, Age Class 1

● capture site, Age Class 2

woods

open herbaceous field

Figure 4-8. An example of the expansion in home range size of a male three-toed box turtle in Missouri as the turtle increased in age and size. The turtle was found from 1965 to 1967 in age class 1 (ca. 97 mm CL, triangles) and from 1968 to 1983 in age class 2 (max. 131 mm CL, circles). From Schwartz et al. (1984).

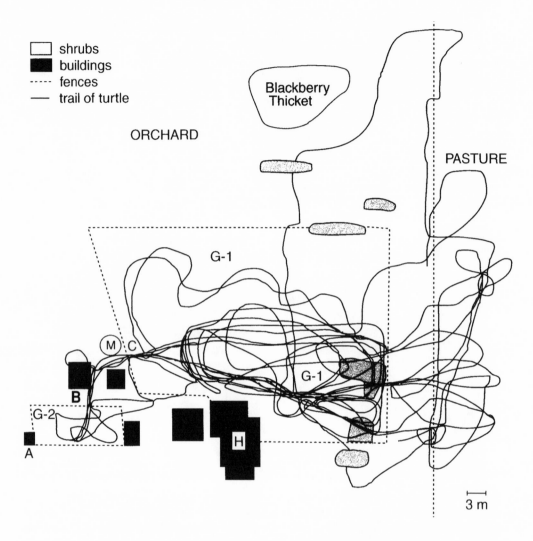

Figure 4-9. Movements, recorded by thread trailing, of a male three-toed box turtle (118 mm CL) in Kansas from July 22 to August 29, 1967. This turtle was recorded sixty-three times from 1957 to 1968 within this area. A, B, C = openings in fences; G-1, G-2 = gardens; H = farmhouse; M = mulberry tree. After Metcalf and Metcalf (1970).

SEASONAL MOVEMENTS

There are two general categories of seasonal movements: for nesting and for overwintering. Many females find appropriate nesting sites within their home ranges, but others travel considerable distances to nesting sites (chapter 6). The same situation holds for turtles seeking refugia (sometimes incorrectly called hibernacula) from harsh winter conditions. A hibernaculum (plural hibernacula) is where an animal hibernates. Turtles do not hibernate in the true physiological sense of the word, hence their place of winter (or summer) dormancy is a refugium (plural refugia). In Missouri (*T. c. triunguis*) and Kansas

(*T. ornata*), turtles used winter retreats within their home ranges (Legler, 1960; Schwartz and Schwartz, 1974). However, *T. ornata* in the Kansas Flint Hills tended to use two specific areas for overwintering, suggesting a seasonal movement to these sites (Metcalf and Metcalf, 1970). Stickel (1950) recorded a Maryland *T. c. carolina* that overwintered 67 m from her normally small home range. In South Carolina, some turtles travel consistently more than 200 m to an overwintering site from a summer home range (I. L. Brisbin, pers. comm.).

Turtles may shift their position during the winter and find new retreats (Claussen et al., 1991). In Tennessee, such winter shifts were common (Dolbeer, 1969), whereas in Ohio and Oklahoma, movements occurred less often. Although remaining within a retreat for an average of sixty-three days, three-toed box turtles moved at least once for an average of 51 m (Carpenter, 1957). The propensity to shift retreat sites is probably correlated with mild winter temperatures. As ambient and soil temperatures increase in the spring, turtles frequently shift their retreat sites, often within a few meters of the previous form.

TRANSIENTS

It has long been suspected that certain adult box turtles do not settle into a home range (Stickel, 1950; Legler, 1960; Williams, 1961; Dolbeer, 1969; Schwartz and Schwartz, 1974) but seem to wander randomly over a pathway known only to themselves. Evidence suggests that such animals do not retrace their routes and hence are true transients rather than animals on a temporary exploratory excursion. For example, an adult male *T. c. triunguis* radio tracked in Missouri traveled 10 km in a straight-line distance over a fourteen-month period. During these wanderings, males will mate with any receptive females that they encounter, and such movement may thus be important for genetic exchange among distant populations (Kiester et al., 1982) and for seed dispersal (Braun and Brooks, 1987).

It is not known what percentage of a population is truly transient, or if one sex is more likely to be transient than the other. Williams and Parker (1987) stated that many, but not all, transient Indiana *T. carolina* were in the smaller size classes, but I know of no published data from other studies. However, even a small number of reproductively successful transients would be capable of maintaining gene flow and evolutionary viability.

Box turtles also occasionally leave their home ranges and temporarily become transients. Perhaps *transient* is not a good term, since it has often been used to indicate only permanent wanderers. However, the turtles certainly are transient in the sense that they do not remain within the new area. Examples of short-term transience are the movements of turtles for considerable distances to a temporary food source, such as fruiting sea grapes, cactus, or mulberries, or a female's nesting foray. Another example is short-term transience because of an environmental perturbation, such as a storm or flood (Stickel, 1950; Dodd et al., 1994). Presumably short-term transients return to their home ranges once the causative factors have ceased to lure turtles away from home. However, even short-term transients may help spread gene flow. Their presence may complicate estimation of home range or population size, but at least they can be identified using newly developed population models in long-term mark-recapture studies (Langtimm et al., 1996).

DISPLACEMENT AND HOMING

When box turtles are displaced from their home range, many if not most animals attempt to return to familiar territory. Immediately upon release, the turtles extend their necks and appear to take stock of their surroundings before beginning their journey home. Homeward treks usually follow a rather direct path (Lemkau, 1970). There may be some initial disorientation, perhaps related to weather conditions, but invariably turtles select the correct compass direction. Most turtles do not linger at a release site. Metcalf and Metcalf (1970) report that displaced *T. ornata* traveled 603 m and 293 m in forty-eight hours, and 956 m in 91.5 hours; in Nebraska, they successfully homed 300 m in three days (Holy, 1995). *Terrapene carolina* displaced less then 780 m in Indiana returned home at an average rate of 75 m per day (10–421 m per day, n = 26; Williams and Parker, 1987). In Maryland, eastern box turtles homed at a rate of 38.4 m per day in 1965 and 20.2 m per day in 1966; differences between years were ascribed to variation in rainfall, with 1965 the wetter year (Lemkau, 1970).

Of 434 different *T. ornata* displaced by Metcalf and Metcalf (1970) in Kansas, eighty-two (18.2 percent) were retaken in the areas from which they had been moved. Thirty turtles displaced twice returned both times; twelve returned three times; six returned four times; and six returned five or more times. The greatest distance a displaced turtle returned to its point of capture was 1.7 km after nearly eleven months. Most turtles that were fitted with thread trailers to record their movements after displacement traveled in relatively straight homeward directions, with occasional stops to investigate cow dung (for insects) or carrion. Only a few turtles (n = 10) remained permanently within the new release site. Some displaced turtles (n = 27 over a three-year period) overwintered at the release site, and five eventually returned home successfully.

In other studies, Legler (1960) reported that two male *T. ornata* returned to their approximate home ranges after displacement of 579 m (using a circuitous route, one turtle took seven days to make the journey); Fitch (1958) recaptured one *T. ornata* after a displacement of 805 m; thirty-eight of forty New York *T. carolina* homed 250–1,150 m (Madden, 1975); Posey (1979) reported that nine of ten Maryland *T. carolina* displaced less than 900 m returned successfully. As in the Kansas study, the propensity to move seems to vary considerably among individuals, with some turtles remaining in the displaced location, some moving part of the way back (e.g., Lemkau, 1970; Metcalf and Metcalf, 1978), and some completing the entire journey. The reasons for such variation are unknown. Adults may show more of a homing tendency than juveniles; only three of seven displaced juvenile *T. carolina* showed a homing tendency on Long Island, New York (Nichols, 1939a), and the lone juvenile in Madden's (1975) release failed to return home.

Homing behavior may have a distance component; that is, displaced box turtles attempt to return home only if displaced at distances not too far from the home range. Based on a limited sample size, Metcalf and Metcalf (1970) suggested that this homing limit was 1.7 to 3.3 km. They noted that one *T. o. ornata* displaced 3 km traveled 305 m in the homeward direction before returning to its displaced release site. However, of a hundred turtles displaced farther than 1.6 km in a later study, eighteen returned to their home ranges successfully; two animals, a male and female, returned after a displacement of 2.8 km (Metcalf and Metcalf, 1978). In addition, one male successfully homed 3.2 km over a period of nine months. Two Nebraska *T. ornata* released in Wisconsin traveled 4 km in thirty-seven days and a total of 8.8 km in forty-one days, respectively (Doroff and Keith, 1990), but it is unclear where they were heading. In New Mexico, an adult female *T. ornata luteola* returned 9.15 km to her presumed home range after accidental displacement, although it is not known how long it took her to complete her travels (Germano and Nieuwolt-Decanay, 1999).

A distance component to homing also seems present in *T. carolina*. In Missouri, Schwartz and Schwartz (1974) displaced forty *T. c. triunguis* 1.6 to 3.3 km into a specific study site. Twenty-three were not recaptured, and only seven, all females, eventually took up residency. Six of the displaced turtles eventually had home ranges comparable in size to those of the residents, and the seventh turtle's home range was only slightly larger. Of the three *T. c. carolina* released by Posey (1979) more than 1.6 km from capture sites, none attempted to home. Turtles not remaining at a release site undoubtedly wander until they find a new appropriate home range. In some studies, however, perhaps turtles recorded as not homing actually did return to their previous home ranges but arrived after the observations were terminated.

Orientation

The most prominent factor aiding box turtles in moving through their environment is their familiarity with physical landmarks. As noted, individuals use the same trails, resting forms, food sources, nesting sites, overwintering sites, and other important areas within their habitats over an extended period, if not their entire life. It should be evident that individual box turtles are well aware of their environment. Movements through home ranges are not random, and box turtles seem to be knowledgeable about and remember the important physical landmarks to which they have become accustomed. Local landmarks are undoubtedly important in refining movements and in assisting in short-term orientation.

Eastern box turtles have been studied extensively as regards their orientation ability after displacement. Tests conducted in open-air arenas demonstrate that the turtles have an internal biological clock that is in tune with the position of the sun (fig. 4-10) (DeRosa and Taylor, 1980, 1982). Box turtles are able to use the position of the sun to choose a homeward direction when displaced to an unfamiliar region (e.g., Gould, 1959; Lemkau, 1970). This type of orientation, termed sun-compass orientation, appears to be used commonly even by aquatic turtles navigating terrestrial environments (DeRosa and Taylor, 1980, 1982; Graham et al., 1996). If the position of the sun is artificially changed, as in laboratory light-dark cycle shifts, box turtles change their orientation accordingly. However, the turtles are unable to choose the correct homeward direction if clouds hide the sun

(Gould, 1957). Likewise, turtles are unable to choose a correct direction on moonless nights, on nights when the moon is visible, or immediately after sunset when the plane of polarized light is directly overhead (DeRosa and Taylor, 1980). Perhaps this explains why box turtles generally are inactive at night.

In addition to celestial orientation, *T. carolina* shows a positive geotaxis; that is, turtles tend to go downslope. At slopes of 0 degrees, 2.5 degrees, and 5 degrees, the homing instinct counteracts the tendency to go downhill, and turtles orient properly to the home direction. However, on a 7.5-degree slope, turtles move downhill in preference to the homeward direction (DeRosa and Taylor, 1980).

Many organisms that migrate or move long distances are known to have the capability to use the earth's geomagnetic field to orient toward a desired location (Gould, 1984). Box turtles can also use geomagnetic cues in orientation, or at least they can detect magnetic fields that may be of use in orientation. Displaced turtles orient toward home under clear skies with normal magnetic fields. If the turtles are transported to the release site under the influence of Helmholtz coils (which produce a 15 percent increase above normal magnetic field strengths), movements become random upon release (Mathis and Moore, 1988). Under laboratory conditions, turtles trained to a certain direction become disoriented when magnets are attached to their shells.

In contrast to findings in the studies described, Holy (1995) was not able to demonstrate that ornate box turtles used sun-compass orientation, although the turtles were able to use magnetic orientation in laboratory trials. She concluded that the mechanism of orientation could not be defined.

Future Directions

MEXICAN TAXA. Absolutely nothing is known about how *T. nelsoni* and *T. c. mexicana* conduct their daily and seasonal activities. Nothing is known concerning their home ranges, movement patterns, orientation, or whether there are transients in their populations. Although this is based on few data, it seems likely that these box turtles are active according to wet/dry tropical seasonal patterns instead of temperate warm/cold seasonal patterns. Likewise, nothing is known concerning the movement patterns, home range, and dispersal of the aquatic *T. coahuila*. These are fundamental questions that must be addressed if the conservation status of these species is as precarious as circumstantial data suggest.

ACTIVITY PATTERNS. Juvenile box turtles are difficult to find, and thus little is known concerning their activities. On Egmont Key, however, juveniles are abundant and readily encountered. Studies are under way to determine their daily and seasonal activities (Hamilton, pers. comm.). However, these juveniles live on an island free of mammalian predators, which undoubtedly influence activity elsewhere, and it is unclear how far the results of Hamilton's (2000) study can be extrapolated to other populations of juveniles. Simply stated, we need to know more about the activity of juveniles. Perhaps juveniles are not rare but simply extremely difficult to find because they move little and are

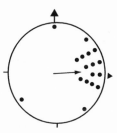

A. CLEAR SKIES
   TERRESTRIAL ARENA

B. CLEAR SKIES
   AQUATIC ARENA

C. CLOUDY SKIES
   TERRESTRIAL ARENA

D. CLEAR SKIES
   TERRESTRIAL ARENA
   6 HR. PHASE DELAY

◄─ **Homeward direction**

•   **One individual**

◄─ **Mean vector**

◄   **Predicted direction**

Figure 4-10. Experimental results demonstrating the ability of eastern box turtles to use celestial cues in orientation. Closed circles = males; open circles = females. Under cloudy skies, turtles were unable to orient in a homeward direction. After DeRosa and Taylor (1980).

cryptic. Incorporating field enclosures and innovative tracking techniques—such as using aluminum tags and following movement with a metal detector (Smith, 1992) or using passive integrated transponders or harmonic radar—may lead to important insights (Engelstoft et al., 1999).

Hatchling box turtles apparently are rather plastic in their temperature preferences, at least during the first four months or so of life (Curtin, 1998). After this time, the young adopt the thermal preferences that they will have as adults. According to Curtin (1998), the initial environmental temperatures experienced by young box turtles may have a profound influence on their activity patterns later in life. Although seasonal shifts in temperature preferences in reptiles are not uncommon, the potential for early experience to influence later activity patterns, habitat selection, and temperature preferences offers a potentially exciting field of investigation.

DISPERSAL. As a correlate of our lack of knowledge concerning the biology of juvenile *Terrapene*, no one knows how they disperse through their environment. If juvenile dispersal occurs within relatively short distances of the nest, local populations may have a high degree of genetic similarity. If dispersal distances are greater, how long does it take for a juvenile to set up a home range? Perhaps greater movements by some nesting females away from their home ranges ensure that local populations will not be too closely related.

HOME RANGE. The wide range of figures for the home range of box turtles calls into question the techniques used to track turtles and to compute the sizes of home ranges. It seems clear that many factors influence home range size, particularly habitat quality. Studies of home ranges need to incorporate a variety of tracking techniques in addition to rigorously quantifying habitat variables. Does resource quality really influence home range size and activity, as some tantalizing data suggest?

Turtles must be tracked for extended periods, and the types of terrain available must be taken into account in mapping home ranges. A variety of new computer programs (e.g., Ranges IV) that can analyze differences in habitat use among individuals on daily and seasonal scales, and that can discriminate between core areas and areas used less frequently, should provide a better picture of how and why *some* turtles move and what activities they undertake. There is no a priori reason to believe that there will ever be a consensus as to what the home range of a box turtle should be, nor should there be. Understanding the sources of variation that influence home range size will prove a difficult but rewarding field of study, especially given the range of habitats used by box turtles.

TRANSIENTS. A large number of turtles caught in mark-recapture studies are never seen again (chapter 8). It is likely that these turtles are either true transients that never settle down or temporary transients moving through a study area. Even multiple recaptures do not mean residency, as these turtles may have been captured while moving between one home range and another or from a home range to nesting or overwintering sites. Separating these categories has important implications for the analysis of demography and population structure. Unfortunately, no studies have yet attempted this. What percentage of a "population" is composed of true transients? Are transients more likely to be males or females? Are young rather than older turtles more likely to be transients? Do transients ever settle down?

DISPLACEMENT AND HOMING. It seems somewhat odd that box turtles should have such well-developed abilities to determine compass direction upon human-mediated displacement and to be able to find their way home from considerable distances. Box turtles, at least most of them, are, after all, relative homebodies. Whereas returning from displacement due to environmental perturbation has been documented, such naturally occurring displacement would seem to be rare. However, if excursions to seasonally available food sources, looking for mates or nesting and overwintering sites, or simply short-term explorations of surrounding habitat are common, then it is not surprising that *Terrapene* should have good navigational abilities. I suggest that the orientation and homing abilities of box turtles likely evolved in conjunction with the propensity for short-term movements outside the home range rather than as a result of the need to home following displacement. Testing this hypothesis could prove interesting.

5 | Behavior and the Senses

While the turtle is a slow and awkward creature owing to the rigidity of its queer, bony, and box-like construction, it is not lifeless nor dumb, but alert and responsive and possesses, unquestionably, some degree of an inner or psychic life.

H. A. Allard, 1949

 Box turtles are not exactly exciting to observe. As have other researchers studying them in the wild, I have spent many hours watching sitting turtles. They usually just sit there and, if you are lucky, one might stretch a leg or snap at an annoying fly. Box turtle watching will never replace bird watching, but there is still much to learn of their psychic and seemingly stoical approach to life. In this short chapter, I review the temperament and behavior of box turtles and summarize the little that is known of their senses. Readers will note that I do not mention taste among the senses. After watching box turtles eat and after reviewing their diets as summarized in the literature (chapter 7), I have concluded that they must not have any taste buds.

Behavior

INDIVIDUAL RECOGNITION

The presence of a great variety of shell patterns, sizes, and shapes, as well as variation in head and limb patterns and coloration, suggest a mechanism of individual recognition among box turtles. In addition to visual cues, box turtles may be able to discriminate individuals by odor, certainly between the sexes. However, most authors ascribe no social behavior to box turtles, calling them asocial or even solitary. Although the degree to which individuals recognize one another is debatable, it seems likely that they are able to identify neighbors or at least to recognize intruders. Latham's (1917) observation of one turtle's aggression toward an intruder could be an example of this.

In a series of trials with eastern box turtles, Davis (1981) tested the potential for individual recognition. She measured aggression, particularly associated with feeding, using both naive hatchlings in captivity and adults from populations adjacent to and far away from one another. Not surprisingly, eastern box turtles were less aggressive toward neighbors than they were to turtles from far distant populations. In addition, hatchlings raised together were less aggressive toward members of their own group than they were to members of a different group. In both experiments, strangers were approached and "nosed" more often than were familiar conspecifics (nosing involves lowering the head with the neck bent, and facing the other turtle at a distance of 1 cm or less); "head-duck-ing" (retracting the head with a sudden jerk) occurred more often among strangers than neighbors; and more biting and snapping were directed toward strangers than neighbors.

Davis (1981) recorded an interesting behavior termed gaping, whereby a stranger opened its mouth in an exaggerated threat display toward an approaching turtle. As with the other agonistic behaviors, gaping was directed more often at strangers than at neigh-bors. On the other hand, a behavior termed "neck-arching," whereby the neck is extended fully and arched forward, was directed more toward neighbors than strangers and was seen more often among wild-caught turtles than captive-reared hatchlings. Clearly, these postural displays convey recognition that box turtles distinguish known from unknown conspecifics and react accordingly.

In captivity, certain box turtles tend to pair together; that is, they are often found together with shells touching. Davis (1981) could not discount the possibility that some turtles select location over company, but it seems likely that certain bonds form among individuals, at least on a short-term basis. Many authors have noted that box turtles some-times can be found in close association with one another, even outside the mating season and for no other easily discernible reason. Perhaps neighbors keep in touch, and certain individuals prefer the occasional company (or presence) of conspecifics. Other turtles may be entirely solitary. Thus, it may not be possible to rule out some degree of sociality among individual box turtles.

TEMPERAMENT

Although they are not used in today's behavioral descriptions, anthropomorphic terms are used often in some of the older literature to describe the behavior of box turtles. For example, Allard (1949) records what he termed selfish behavior by feeding box turtles. He noted that some turtles did not seem interested in a piece of food until another turtle expressed interest in the item. Once that occurred, the first might fight for the morsel even though the food previously was ignored. Indeed, the first turtle might gulp the food regardless of whether it appeared already satiated. Although one might call box turtles single-minded or determined, it would be hard to attribute this behavior to conscious selfishness.

Box turtles are normally rather placid animals, but on occasion they can be aggres-sive. Accounts of "vicious" fights and "savage ferocity " in encounters are not uncommon. Aggression occurs in male-male, female-female, and intersexual encounters. Aggression has been reported both in the wild and in captivity (e.g., Boice, 1970; Harless and Lambiotte, 1971; Davis, 1981), suggesting that the confined quarters of captivity alone do not trigger aggression, except perhaps when turtles are fed in close proximity to one another. Instead, aggressive tendencies seem associated with certain individuals. Some turtles are meek and mild mannered, whereas others are continually ready to fight.

Box turtle fights usually include a good deal of posturing and biting. Opponents square off facing each other, raise themselves up on all four legs, and sway back and forth. Individuals lunge at their opponents, and biting can result in injury. Turtles may push, shove, or attempt to roll a rival onto its carapace. Fights usually end when one turtle either walks away or withdraws into its shell, although some turtles may continue to attack a well-boxed and inert rival. Some descriptions of victors include the word *smug*; although it seems odd, the winners of box turtle fights do show a strutting demeanor that gives an impression of smugness. But then again, sometimes it is difficult to tell fights from courtship (chapter 6).

As noted, box turtles are not territorial (chapter 3), and there is no indication that aggressive encounters are fought over rights to space. However, a few accounts in the literature make one wonder. For example, Latham (1917) tells of observing a box turtle at the edge of a clearing. The turtle was alert and had its neck outstretched as if looking for something. After Latham sat back and observed this turtle for a while, a second turtle emerged from the other side of the clearing 4 m away. At this point, the first turtle, which had been watching intently, charged across the clearing and attacked the second. The attacker lunged at and bit the second animal, flipping it over on its side. After releasing its grip, the attacker crawled over its foe and slowly walked away. Strangely, the second turtle slowly followed the first until it disappeared in the brush. At that point, the second turtle turned and walked back across the clearing. Latham whistled, shouted, and talked loudly, but the turtle ignored him; only when he moved his arms did turtle number two draw into its shell.

In captive situations, some evidence points to a dominance hierarchy, but whether this occurs in the wild is unknown. For example, a captive group of *T. coahuila* (three males and three females) was dominated by one male that apparently prevented the other males from mating. Fights among the males occurred, but that male was able to exclude the others from associating with the females (Tonge, 1987). I have noted fights between males over females in captivity to the point where weaker (or smaller) males had to be removed from the pen of an aggressive tyrant.

Fighting over food is commonly reported in the literature on captive box turtles. Two turtles vying for the same mealworm may bite and lunge at each other or even steal a mouthful from the jaws of a rival (Boice, 1970). Certain domineering box turtles may hold a more submissive turtle at bay by simply placing a foot on the rival's head and holding the second animal down until the mouthful is eaten. Bites may be directed at the head, neck, or limbs of a competitor. While it is unknown if such intense rivalry occurs in natural settings where food may not be as restricted spatially, I suspect that two turtles vying for a single blackberry would exhibit these same aggressive characteristics.

LEARNING

We know little concerning the ability of box turtles to learn in the wild. However, individuals easily recognize landmarks within their home ranges, and they seem to remember the location of particularly favorable sites, such as those with food or access to water. On Egmont Key, the aggregation of turtles around a site with garbage cans certainly reflects well on their ability to learn where food might be located. Such learning may occur as the turtles mature within a habitat, or perhaps the turtles learn new situations as they explore their environment. Learning the location of critical resources and the position of geographic features would seem selectively advantageous. Inasmuch as box turtles do not have large home ranges and live relatively long lives, the ability to remember locations should come as no surprise.

A number of authors have noted that in captivity, box turtles recognize people and come to associate them with food. Allard (1949) tells of walking into a nearly deserted pen and, within seconds, having numerous turtles come out of their hiding places and approach for food. It seems unlikely that they recognized Allard himself; more likely, they associated the vision of a large bipedal animal with the provision of food. As soon as one turtle spotted the human visitor, it was as if all the turtles suddenly became alert and crawled from their hiding places. The association of humans with feeding (associative memory) persisted from one year to the next.

Locomotion

Walking and sprinting are important characteristics of the behavior of box turtles. Although small and close to the ground, box turtles can move considerable distances over a relatively short time (chapter 4). In bursts, sprinting aids in escape and minimizes exposure to predation or human-induced threats, such as when crossing highways. Although walking and sprinting are used for different purposes, the fusion of the backbone to the shell and the resulting limitations on limb movement make the mechanics rather similar. This is because the shell imposes restrictions on stride length. In order to increase speed, a turtle must therefore increase its stride frequency.

In general, larger box turtles have greater strides and, as might be expected, stride length is greater for adults than for juveniles. Large size simply allows for greater stride length. Juveniles compensate for their small size by increasing their stride frequency at a greater rate than might be expected by size alone. Another important consideration is temperature. Since box turtles are strictly ectothermic (see glossary), a turtle's locomotor ability is temperature-dependent. For example, for *T. carolina* in Ohio, voluntary locomotion occurs most efficiently at 24–32°C, although this may not be a truly optimal temperature (Adams et al., 1989). At both higher and lower temperatures, box turtles have less of a tendency to move. It seems likely that box turtles at different latitudes might have different optimal temperatures for locomotion.

A box turtle carrying a load shortens its stride length, just as humans do, but it does not decrease its stride frequency. Of course a box turtle's load is really its shell, so one may assume that the ancestors of turtles moved much faster than their present-day counterparts. Loading weights on a turtle's shell, and then experimentally testing the turtle's locomotor performance, suggests that terrestrial turtles are better able to manage weight during terrestrial locomotion than can aquatic turtles; the weight of a shell is not a burden to a terrestrial turtle. Likewise, locomotor speed is not affected by body mass, sex of the turtle, or sexual maturity.

How fast can a box turtle move? Adult *T. carolina* can move a maximum of about 0.05 m per second (180 m per hour) during voluntary locomotion (Adams et al., 1989), but increase their speed 72 percent when prodded or poked ("forced" locomotion; Marvin and Lutterschmidt, 1997). Maximum speeds increase with body mass. For example, an ornate box turtle weighing nearly 500 g was clocked at 0.4 m/sec, whereas 100 g turtles only attained speeds of less than 0.2 m/sec (Wren et al., 1998). In addition, ornate box turtles are about 2.9 times faster than comparably sized eastern box turtles, with stride lengths 1.3 times longer and stride frequencies 2.3 times greater than those of eastern box turtles (Wren et al., 1998). As Wren and colleagues (1998) suggest, these differences may be related to the different types of habitats in which these turtles are found. Turtles of the open grasslands (e.g., *T. ornata*) tend to run from intruders and bite when handled; turtles of the woodlands (e.g., *T. carolina*) tend to retreat into their shells. Of course, there are exceptions. Florida box turtles living in open grasslands are adept at running.

The Senses

SIGHT

As they traverse their environment or peer from hiding places under brush, box turtles seem to be able to recognize the world around them and perceive space accurately. Unlike freshwater turtles, box turtles recognize and respond to the visual cue of a cliff: they can detect a sudden drop-off in elevation in their path (Yerkes, 1904). This might be particularly important to a terrestrial animal, and box turtles take extra care when maneuvering around ledges and escarpments in order to avoid falling. On the other hand, I have observed box turtles trapped or dead in wells left by decayed palm tree trunks on Egmont Key. These wells act as pitfall traps, and many turtles, especially small ones, are unable to escape. Aquatic turtles, of course, might never encounter such problems, except for females on nesting forays or when wandering between ponds. Freshwater turtles are likely to proceed right over the edge of a cliff.

Box turtles are able to see color, with red and orange their favorites. They pay little attention to greens and blues. Allard (1949) noted that eastern box turtles can use color to distinguish ripe from unripe fruits, although it might be impossible to rule out the influence of odor. Inasmuch as a few females nest after dark, this suggests that they have some ability to see in low light, at least to find their way back to a protective form. The few that I have seen active after dark were alert and walking in such a manner as to suggest that they could easily see where they were going.

Although their visual acuity is unknown, box turtles are able to see things from many meters away, especially if food or a potential predator is involved. For example, a beetle or worm will be chased and attacked even if it is well in front of a turtle. Likewise, the fact that most of the box turtles we encounter on Egmont Key are "resting" (Dodd et al., 1994) may reflect more on their ability to detect a walking human than on an inherent and continual resting state. In an open field, Florida box turtles easily perceive an approaching human and run as fast as they can to shelter. Such recognition occurs when the intruder is at least 20–25 m away from the turtle and in some cases allows the turtle to escape into dense underbrush. Legler (1960) suggested that ornate box turtles could detect an approaching human from a distance of 60 m. The background (or lack of it) may assist turtles in detecting motion.

Motion seems to be important in a box turtle's feeding behavior. Although turtles will eat nonmoving objects, they are much more inclined to snap at moving prey. Ornate box turtles readily snapped at grasshoppers moving in a glass jar, but they snapped at live grasshoppers (66.7 percent of thirty trials) far more than at dead grasshoppers (11.7 percent of seventeen trials; Fitch, 1965). Turtles also chased moving prey regardless of the prey's color. These results, as well as others reported by Fitch (1965), suggest that smell is not as important as movement in prey detection and/or choice.

HEARING

The ear of the box turtle consists of a tympanic membrane system involving a cartilaginous disk lying underneath undifferentiated skin on the side of the head. Displacement of the membrane causes the disk to move, a rotational motion that is transmitted to the inner ear. Box turtles can hear sounds, but whether they hear in the same manner as humans is conjectural. As Latham (1917) noted, it is possible to yell at turtles and have them totally ignore you, but whether they do not hear you or are simply not interested is another matter.

Hearing ability is measured by the response of the auditory nerve to sounds of various wavelengths. It is unknown what the turtles actually hear. Perhaps they are better able to detect low-level vibrations through the substrate, such as those coming from prey or an approaching predator, rather than airborne sounds. As with other turtles, box turtles respond best to sounds in the range of 100–600 cycles per second. Response declines and tapers off at about 3,000 cycles per second and at tones less than 100 (Wever and Vernon, 1956). Turtles suffering from an inner ear infection hear at 20–40 decibels less than healthy turtles. In that regard, the presence of caseous cysts in the inner ear could substantially interfere with a turtle's hearing acuity.

SMELL

Undoubtedly, box turtles can smell. Often when approaching food or some other object within its environment, a box turtle stops and touches its nose to the item. Exactly what kind of cues are recorded is unknown, but turtles do not appear to have the chemical sensitivity of lizards and snakes. Indeed, the function of their sense of smell is uncertain. When an individual touches its nose to the ground as if smelling the substrate while moving through the environment, is it obtaining cues about food sources or moisture, or can it detect that another box turtle has walked through the area? Perhaps all of the above. Experiments have shown that box turtles have olfactory receptors, located in the olfactory epithelium, that are sensitive to various odors (Tonosaki, 1993).

Several authors have conducted experiments to determine if box turtles use the sense of smell in food recognition. Allard (1949) wrapped an old fish and a stone in separate burlap coverings and placed them with his captive colony of eastern box turtles. All the turtles ignored the wrapped stone, but only one turtle explored the sack-wrapped fish. After nose touching and some halfhearted pawing, the turtle abandoned the investigation. Was the animal merely curious, or did it smell the old fish? Likewise, Fitch (1965) tested the olfactory discrimination of ornate box turtles in a series of experiments employing odorous prey and prey rendered odorless. For example, she offered ornate box turtles liver and stones, both wrapped in burlap. In 40.9 percent of twenty-two trials, the turtles attempted to open the burlap sacks containing liver. Only one stone bundle was examined with interest. In most cases, the turtles nosed the bundles before tearing at them, although there was a great deal of individual variation in behavior. These and other experiments (using lacquered and unlacquered grasshoppers, scented and unscented glass beads, and various other items) suggest that box turtles are able to discriminate odors, but that olfaction may not be as important as visual cues in locating and pursuing prey.

Future Directions

BEHAVIOR. The experiments of Davis (1981) suggest that box turtles may be able to recognize conspecifics and that neighbors may be more readily tolerated than strangers. Previous observations also suggest that individual recognition occurs early in life. A wealth of information could be gained by a thorough examination of intraspecific interactions. If patterns of recognition are set during the first few months of life, this could affect spacing behavior and subsequent habitat use. One result might be that individuals within a localized area are kin-related and are recognized as such, a recognition that minimizes local aggressive encounters. On the other hand, individual recognition might cause some animals to disperse and thus avoid the genetic consequences of inbreeding. The potential for individual recognition leads directly to questions concerning the genetic structuring of populations (chapter 8).

THE SENSES. As even a brief review of the literature reveals, little is known of the ways in which box turtles use their senses in daily activities. The experiments performed by Fitch (1965) set the stage for experiments that might be conducted to discern color, pattern, odor, prey, and conspecific recognition. It is somewhat surprising that no one has expanded upon these observations to develop a better understanding of the cues that box turtles use to sense their environment. Experiments might also be able to evaluate the importance of taste in the box turtle's choice of foods.

6 | Courtship and Reproduction

There is no sense in suppressing the comment that a pair of copulating box turtles is ludicrous to behold.

ARCHIE CARR, 1952

One could easily imagine an expression on his face depicting a mixture of pride and astonishment at the acrobatic feat he was successfully performing.

ALVIN CAHN AND EVERT CONDER, 1932

 The literature on box turtles is replete with descriptions of mating and egg production. There are a few important studies of *T. ornata* and *T. coahuila*, but most such information is based on observations of *T. carolina*. Although often overlooked in favor of their more easily observed terrestrial and aquatic relatives, box turtles have much to offer as model organisms for field investigations on how reproductive traits affect the life histories of long-lived organisms.

The Reproductive Cycle

The best general descriptions of the reproductive cycles of box turtles are provided in the works of Altland (1951) for *T. carolina* and Legler (1960) for *T. ornata*. It is likely that most temperate box turtles follow somewhat similar patterns, although the timing of specific events can be expected to change with latitude or perhaps from year to year based on local environmental conditions. Little is known about the reproductive cycles of the Mexican species, but evidence from other tropical turtles suggests that the cycles do not differ much from those of the more temperate species, at least in terms of spermatogenesis (sperm formation). Brown (1974) suggested that reproductive events of *T. coahuila* might be extended longer into the winter season than those of their northern relatives. For *T. nelsoni, T. carolina mexicana* and *T. c. yucatana*, the reproductive cycles may be synchronized with the wet-dry tropical seasons rather than with the warm-cold seasons characteristic of temperate climates.

THE MALE CYCLE

In turtles, as in other reptiles (Zug, 1993), a series of changes in the development of the sex cells eventually leads to the production of sperm. These changes occur in the testes, paired organs, which in ornate box turtles are pale yellow and oblong, with a dark brown or black epididymis. Testicular cells that will eventually become sperm are called spermatogonia. Differentiation occurs in a progressive sequence, termed spermatogenesis, and the places where differentiation occurs vary slightly within the testis depending on the stage of spermatogenesis. Each spermatogonium will eventually give rise to four spermatozoa through a series of cellular divisions.

Spermatogonia differentiate to primary spermatocytes, primary spermatocytes to secondary spermatocytes, secondary spermatocytes to spermatids, and spermatids to mature sperm, or spermatozoa. Each cellular stage has its own physical characteristics, and the different types of cells are readily identifiable. Most of the stages of spermatogenesis occur within the seminiferous tubules of the testis, with the spermatozoa eventually located in the lumen of the tubules awaiting transport to the epididymides. Mature sperm may be found in the epididymides at all times of the year, although Brown (1974) noted two adult male *T. coahuila* in the last week of July in which he found no sperm in the epididymides.

When ornate box turtles emerge from winter dormancy in Kansas, their testes are the smallest they will be during the year (Legler, 1960). During the summer activity season, testis size both increases and decreases slightly, depending on the stage of spermatogenesis; the largest testes are observed in males in mid-September, which corresponds to the initial appearance of spermatids and sperm, the peak of the spermatogenic cycle. From emergence until early June, testis size increases during the initiation of spermatogenesis and the development of the primary spermatocytes. This is normally the time when most mating occurs in Kansas ornate box turtles.

Testis size decreases in June with the continued development of primary spermatocytes and the appearance of secondary spermatocytes. By July, however, the testes again increase in size shortly after the appearance of spermatids. Testes continue to increase in size until their growth eventually levels off during the late summer. With the onset of winter dormancy in October, however, the testes are once again shrinking. By dormancy, most of the spermatazoa have migrated to the epididymides. A general schematic of the male reproductive cycle is shown in figure 6-1.

THE FEMALE CYCLE

The female reproductive cycle also follows a sequential progression, termed oogenesis (egg formation). The primordial sex cells, the oogonia, are located in the wall of the ovary. Each oogonium is surrounded by a group of cells that eventually forms the follicle, a structure that becomes important in the control of reproduction through its endocrine function. During development, the oogonia differentiate into primary oocytes, which in turn become secondary oocytes. Secondary oocytes grow substantially through the accumulation of lipids, a process termed vitellogenesis. These lipids are stored by the female in various areas of her body, in part for use in reproduction. Lipids are converted into a substance called vitellogenin, which is transformed into lipoprotein, the yolk of the egg.

Unlike males, in which each primordial sex cell becomes four mature sex cells, only one mature ovum results from the process of oogenesis. The other three cells, the polar bodies, eventually disintegrate. Mature ova are shed directly into the body cavity at ovulation after the ovum ruptures through the walls of the follicle and ovary. The ovum usu-

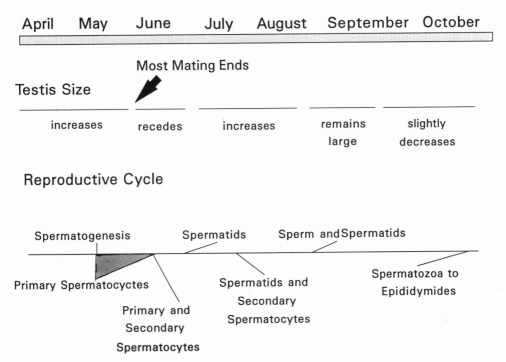

Figure 6-1. Schematic representation of the male reproductive cycle of *Terrapene ornata* in Kansas. Based on data in Legler (1960).

ally then migrates to the nearest ostium, or opening to the oviduct. Ova from the right ovary usually find their way to the right oviduct, and those from left ovary to left oviduct, but cases in which the ova crossed over the body cavity to the alternate oviduct have been reported in box turtles (Legler, 1958, 1960). After ovulation, the follicle transforms into a structure called the corpus luteum (illustrated by Altland, 1951) and continues its important endocrine functions.

Technically, the ovum does not become a mature egg until it is fertilized. This is because differentiation usually stops during the second oocyte stage and does not continue until fertilization. Fertilization normally occurs in the oviduct, after which the egg's protective membranes, albumen, and shell are laid down. Although the process has not been described for box turtles, Lou Guillette (pers. comm.) of the University of Florida suggests that eggshell fibers are deposited about 24–36 hours after ovulation, and calcium at 36–48 hours after ovulation. Using radiographs, eggs should thus be visible three to four days after ovulation. Shelled eggs are probably retained in the oviducts for an additional period of 14–21 days, depending on clutch size and nesting conditions.

Again using Legler's (1960) data for *T. ornata,* the female reproductive cycle appears as in figure 6-2. The ovarian cycle begins in July or August after ovulation is completed. During this time, the ova are undergoing primary oogenesis, and ovary weights are correspondingly low. Corpora lutea are observed from late June into July. Enlarged follicles (to 2.5 cm diameter in *T. carolina*) are not present until October and persist through April and May. As a result, ovary weights are greatest from the late fall through early spring. After ovulation in May or June, the cycle begins again. Thus, oogenesis initiated in one year results in an egg clutch the following year.

The number and size of follicles can vary even as winter dormancy approaches. Brown (1974) found a total of thirty-four follicles (range 2.5–9.1 mm in diameter) in seven different female *T. coahuila* in the fall. Nearly one third of the follicles were greater than 5–9 mm in diameter, and they occurred in five of the seven females.

Of course the timing of this sequence is modified depending on the number of clutches a female deposits and on environmental influences such as latitude, weather, and resource availability. For example, Brown (1974) noted that ovulation might begin as early as the first week of April in *T. coahuila* and extend to the end of that month; enlarged follicles were found as early as late August.

Resource acquisition may play an important role in the timing of the female's reproductive cycle. If resources are scarce as she yolks up her clutch, perhaps clutch size or frequency could be affected in the following year. She may even skip reproduction altogether in a year that follows a year of scarce resources. Differential resource availability or acquisition may be responsible for observations of box turtles that vary clutch size annually or skip reproduction in some years (e.g., Dodd, 1997a).

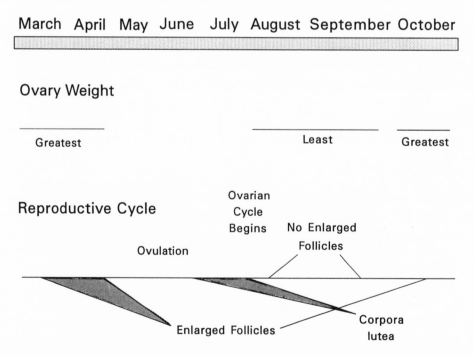

Figure 6-2. Schematic representation of the female reproductive cycle of *Terrapene ornata* in Kansas. Based on data in Legler (1960).

Ovaries within individual box turtles are known to function alternately from one year to the next—that is, one ovary is more likely to be responsible for ovulation in one season; in the next season, the other ovary is more active. According to Legler (1960), newly mature *T. ornata* may use only one ovary to produce eggs in their first nesting season; likewise, old females also may have only one functional ovary.

DELAYED FERTILITY IN BOX TURTLES

As already noted, male box turtles have viable sperm in their epididymides throughout the activity season. Mating also occurs throughout the activity season (see later discussion). Along with the potential for nearly continuous mating, female box turtles are known to store sperm within their oviducts for a considerable period of time. For example, Ewing (1943) reported that female *T. c. carolina* in his captive colony could produce fertile offspring up to four years after their last contact with males. Apparently, box turtles are able to store sperm in seminal receptacles, structures modified from tubular albumen-secreting glands in the oviducts (Hattan and Gist, 1975).

The function of sperm storage is unknown, but it is tempting to hypothesize that in areas where turtles are sparsely distributed, sperm storage would ensure successful long-term fertilization despite the limited possibilities of chance encounters between males and females. Many, if not most, temperate box turtle populations were quite dense in recent times, however, making the necessity of sperm storage less significant; perhaps Miocene to Pleistocene populations were not as dense. An alternative suggestion is that sperm storage might ensure that a female can take full advantage of a successful mating with a robust, fit male and ignore suitors of lesser quality even if it means passing up mating opportunities. Sperm storage also may intensify sperm competition. If such occurs in box turtles, sperm storage may be an important trait leading to the evolution of female-mediated sexual selection; that is, it is the female that ultimately makes the decision to mate. Anyone who has watched a male box turtle frantically trying to mount an unreceptive female can see the potential merits of this argument.

Finding Mates

The mechanism by which adult turtles find each other is unknown. Box turtles have rather extensive overlapping home ranges (chapter 3) and populations can be dense (chapter 8). As such, finding mates may simply involve bumping into a neighbor or a transient (chapter 4) progressing through the neighborhood. As discussed later, box turtles appear to be ready to mate at almost any daylight hour during their respective activity seasons. Chance encounters likely result in some reproductive activity.

Box turtles also seem to possess a degree of individual neighbor recognition (Davis, 1981), but there is no pair bonding. Neighbors seem less antagonistic toward each other than to strangers, at least under captive circumstances. Perhaps individuals are aware of the nearby presence of members of the opposite sex based on previous contacts. When the desire to mate occurs, a male turtle might travel to the region inhabited by the neighbor and then use visual or chemoreceptive cues to locate her. Ernst (1981) observed wild male *T. c. carolina* smelling the ground as they walked through the woods. Males are more likely to undertake travels in search of mates than are females.

Once located, a female may or may not be physiologically or behaviorally receptive to courtship. Box turtles are well-known for ignoring unreceptive potential mates. A too enthusiastic male that skips or rushes through some of the courtship phases may find himself ignored (the female may simply close her shell) or, as his rear feet become trapped when she closes her plastron, dragged about by an uninterested female to the point that his legs become twisted and bruised (Evans, 1953). Males have also been observed courting and mounting other males (Ewing, 1935; Harless and Lambiotte, 1971; Madden, 1975) and even other species of turtles (Ernst, 1981); it is difficult to discourage a male box turtle that is intent on mating.

Courtship and Mating

Courtship in box turtles may occur at virtually any time during the seasonal activity period. For example, Dolbeer (1969) observed mating twelve times during his seven-month study in eastern Tennessee; eight observations were in September, whereas the others were in May, June, August, and October. I have observed mating attempts among captive *T. c. bauri* in late November in northern Florida. In central Texas, *T. ornata* has been seen mating from early April to October (Blair, 1976). Reports of matings in the fall are common, although both Ewing (1933) and Legler (1960) suggested that peaks in mating activity occur both immediately after winter dormancy and immediately before winter dormancy. Other researchers (e.g., Allard, 1949 [although he previously reported that most mating occurred in the spring shortly after winter dormancy, Allard (1935)]; Madden, 1975) have not reported peaks in mating activity while observing mating throughout the entire activity season. Courtship occurs at any time during daylight hours (pers. obs.; Cerda and Waugh, 1992).

For the Mexican species, few data are available. Captive *T. coahuila* mate year-round (Cerda and Waugh, 1992). In the Cuatro Ciénegas basin, copulation has been recorded in April, October, and late December (Brown, 1974), so it might be possible that the aquatic box turtle mates year-round in natural habitats. Unlike most terrestrial box turtles elsewhere in Mexico and to the north, the aquatic box turtle normally mates in the water (Brown, 1974; Cerda and Waugh, 1992). *Terrapene carolina major* also has been reported to mate in water (Penn and Pottharst, 1940; Evans, 1968)

The best descriptions of the courtship sequence in box turtles are those of Cahn and Conder (1932) and Evans (1953) for *T. c. carolina*. Based on seventy-two observations of mating, Evans (1953) suggested that the behavior could be divided into three phases but that there was considerable variation among the phases in the courtship sequence. The entire process may last six hours. In phase 1, the male moves toward the female but stops about 10 cm away from her. He keeps his legs straightened and his head held high, although one leg may be raised above the ground. The female watches the male and may retract her head, legs, and tail into her shell (Rosenberger, 1936). The male then approaches the female, circles her, and at the same time bites at her shell. He may push her shell as he bites at it, a movement that can be repeated many times, or he may bite her shell, seize it, and drag her toward him as he moves backward. He may or may not lunge at her shell. If he does, he retracts his head before he hits her and pokes it out after ramming her. He then may repeat the charge. The female seems to hunker down to await the next charge or attempts to walk away, usually without success. Ernst (1981) reported that the male "smells" his perspective mate, especially in the inguinal region, around the tail, and at the head. This part of phase 1 can last from several minutes to an hour.

During the second part of phase 1, the male mounts the female. The posterior part of her plastron may or may not be open during initial mounting. If it is not, he attempts to induce her to open it, sometimes after considerable pushing and shoving (Levell, 1985). As the male mounts the female, he tries to hook his rear claws into the inner surface of her plastron. Initially, he might be too high on her carapace, which causes his claws to scrape across the posterior portion of her shell. This causes a scratching vibration, which may help to stimulate her and make her receptive to his intentions. Eventually he finds the right height, where he again uses his claws, this time to scratch the plastron as he gropes for a foothold. Evans (1953) suggested that the scratching from his claws as they explore for the opening between her plastron and carapace serves as the mechanism that induces the female to open the rear part of the plastron. When she relaxes and opens the posterior portion of the plastron, phase 2 begins.

As the female relaxes her plastron, the male slides his rear feet apart, keeping the claws in the space between the plastron and carapace. As the claws touch the bridge, the female's plastron closes on his rear toes, thus anchoring the male firmly to the back of the female. The widely spaced rear limbs serve to stabilize the male in this rather awkward position. His head is kept extended and arched out over her shell, and his front legs seem to be left hanging in midair. Once secure, however, the male leans forward over the female's carapace and bites in the direction of her head. The front claws may be used to grip the front edge of her carapace. During this time, the male seems to the human eye to be showing fierce determination; the female hardly pays attention. A combination of gripping, biting, stimulation from his locked rear claws, and the grinding of his plastron onto her carapace induces phase 3 of courtship.

In phase 3, the male abandons his biting and grasping and leans back, thus resting on his rear ankles and carapace. His imprisoned rear claws hold him firmly to the female. At this point he is almost vertical in relation to the ground. Meanwhile the female rocks back on her ankles, bringing their tails into parallel position and their cloacae into apposition. After a few more seconds, the male rocks back as far as possible so that his carapace is at about a 45-degree angle, with him nearly upside down, after which he returns to a vertical position. The penis is extruded and brought into position to be inserted into the female's cloaca. With each rearward fallback, the male thrusts his penis forward until intromission is effected.

Phase 3 may last two hours, but Ewing (1935) noted that males and females separate rather easily if disturbed during this phase of copulation. Cerda and Waugh (1992) reported that copulation lasts an average of 61.3 minutes (n = 58, SD = 42.2) in captive

T. coahuila, but the mating sequence was not described in terms of phases. In a seminatural outdoor enclosure, copulation has been observed to last as long as two hours and twenty minutes in *T. coahuila* (Brown, 1974).

During phase 3, the female *T. carolina* uses her legs to brace the male (Cahn and Conder, 1932). His feet are pressed firmly into the inguinal region of her body, just posterior to the inguinal regions of her shell, whereas the female's legs are outside the male's. She presses her legs inward against the outer portion of his legs, thus holding the male's legs in a vice grip (Cahn and Conder, 1932; see figure 6-3, this volume). Although Legler (1960) noted that female *T. ornata* exert considerable pressure on the rear legs of males during copulation, he stated that the position of the legs as illustrated by Cahn and Conder (1932) was impossible for the ornate box turtle. Instead, the female simply hooks her legs around those of the male. Legler (1960) speculated that the well-developed rear leg musculature of males was an adaptation to the pressure exerted by females during copulation.

Copulation ends as the female relaxes her plastron, thus causing the male's rear claws to break free of their hold. He slides off her carapace onto the ground. Cloacal apposition is thus broken, and copulation ceases. At this time the male may tumble onto his back and must right himself. Because of his intense exertions, fatigue may cause him to be unable to turn over easily. Cahn and Conder (1932) and Evans (1953) noted that rear leg strength in males seems to decrease substantially after copulation, and Allard (1939) speculated that male *T. carolina* are prone to mortality after copulation because of their inability to right themselves if they land in soft leafy debris. On the other hand, male

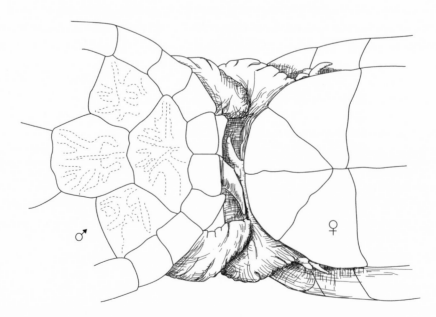

Figure 6-3. Position of the hind legs of *Terrapene carolina* during copulation. After Cahn and Conder (1932).

T. coahuila have drowned females during copulation in captivity (Webb et al., 1963), but whether this occurs in nature is unknown. In any case, the male may remain in the vicinity for some time (two hours, Cahn and Conder, 1932), whereas the female usually wanders off immediately.

Precise descriptions of the courtship and mating sequence of the aquatic box turtle and the other Mexican taxa are not available. The male *T. coahuila* has been observed to "butt" the female with his shell as they court in shallow water, to push the rear part of a female's carapace with his head, and to make "rapid movements" above a submerged female (Brown, 1974). Audible sounds are produced as the male's shell strikes the female. In several instances, males have been seen in a vertical posture while mating, reminiscent of the vertical posture of the more terrestrial species.

During the courtship sequence, male box turtles are oblivious to food and observers —to everything except the mating process (Rosenberger, 1936). Indeed, males may not be particularly attentive to the sex, species, or subspecific status of a partner. Lin (1958) described a courtship sequence between a captive *T. c. bauri* male and a *T. c. triunguis* female. At 3:30 P.M., the turtles first were observed mating. The male was in the vertical position with his front limbs hanging limp. The hind feet were wedged behind the female's thighs and inner rear lateral parts of her carapace as already described, and their tails were in juxtaposition. Periodically, the male would pull his shell away from the female by extending his hind limbs. As he relaxed, the shells of the turtles snapped back together. The male also withdrew his head and front legs into his shell, shut his eyes, and extended his hind legs. When his head then extended and his hind limbs relaxed, their shells again came together.

Unlike in other observations of box turtle mating, the female *T. c. triunguis* was not passive in this courtship. Instead, she jerked her body strongly, causing the male to shake, and she dragged him around. The male jerked from side to side and backward, causing her to walk even more. At 6:20 P.M., the male withdrew his tail and fell on his carapace, although he was still joined to her. By 9:00 P.M., he finally extracted his penis from her cloaca. Lin (1958) reported that the male's penis was extruded for thirty minutes following another courtship bout.

Mating between different subspecies occurs readily in captivity, and occasionally intergrades (or presumed intergrades) are found in the wild. The mating sequences are obviously similar among the subspecies of *T. carolina*, as related, but how much intraspecific intergradation is successful in zones of contact between subspecies is unknown. True hybrids between *T. carolina* and *T. ornata* have also been reported (Clark, 1935; Shannon and Smith, 1949; Smith, 1955; Blaney, 1968; Ward, 1968), but the exact nature of the isolating mechanisms between the species is unknown. Perhaps contact is minimized solely by differences in habitat preferences and activity patterns (chapters 3 and 4).

One unusual feature of mating in ornate box turtles is the report by Brumwell (1940) that a male squirted water ("a stream of fluid from each nostril which sprayed over the female's back") on the female as he mounted her. I can find no other reports in the literature of similar behavior. Although Brumwell (1940) thought that this behavior was analogous to the "boiling" of water reported for snapping turtles (*Chelydra*), it is more likely a reflection of the male's having recently been in water prior to spotting the female and making sexual advances toward her.

Nesting

One of the most important activities in the life cycle of a female box turtle is the selection of the site where she will deposit her eggs. Nest site selection is extremely important because it will influence both the temperature at which the eggs develop and the likelihood of predation of both nest and hatchlings. Temperature affects developmental rate, the sex of offspring, and perhaps fitness characteristics of hatchlings, such as their size and growth rate (St. Clair, 1995) and their ability to avoid predators. In addition, good nesting sites should be free of catastrophic disturbances, such as periodic flooding, and should contain substrates that are friable and will allow proper gas exchange.

Although a great deal depends on the selection of the nesting site, the female does not choose the site with a recognition of the outcome of her choice. Nest site selection is a product of natural selection for certain physical parameters, such as nest substrate, and of the availability of these parameters within her environment. If the female cannot find an ideal location, she may settle for one less optimal. In captivity, females even deposit eggs on the substrate surface.

Box turtles do not nest synchronously, as do certain sea turtles (for example, the ridleys, genus *Lepidochelys*). However, many females may nest at the same time as a result of similar environmental conditions, most notably rain. In this sense, their mating pattern is associative but not socially mediated. Whereas many turtles may choose to nest on one particularly favorable night, other turtles may nest on subsequent nights, according to their own predilection. For eastern box turtles, the nesting process consists of four phases: site selection, digging, egg deposition, and concealment (Congello, 1978). These phases are similar to those observed in *T. ornata* (Legler, 1960) and probably for the other species as well.

SITE SELECTION

The exact criteria by which females select nesting sites is unknown. Box turtles may return to the same general area to lay their eggs (Stickel, 1950; Madden, 1975). Exactly why a female would travel long distances from her home range, almost certainly bypassing at least a few favorable nesting sites, is unknown. However, other turtles tend to return to the same general areas from which they hatched (wood turtles, Blanding's turtles, sea turtles), so it is possible that female box turtles are returning to their own natal region. Considering that turtle nests are subject to generally high levels of predation, returning to an area where eggs have hatched successfully in the past makes evolutionary sense. Presumably such areas possess the proper mixture of favorable substrate, temperature, and concealment to boost the probability of hatching success. Females may travel distances of up to 774 m from home ranges to nesting sites in Maryland (Stickel, 1950); Legler (1960) reports that female *T. ornata* sometimes also travel long distances from their home ranges to nest.

Box turtles seek areas free of surface debris that may inhibit digging. *T. ornata* prefers bare, well-drained, sloping areas protected from erosion by upslope clumps of rocks or sod (Legler, 1960). In captivity, *T. coahuila* prefers hard substrates over soft substrates (Cerda and Waugh, 1992). A box turtle may test the substrate numerous times before digging the chamber in which she will deposit her eggs. No substrate "sniffing" has been observed, however, and all tests are conducted using the back feet. Legler (1960) observed a female *T. ornata* that dug six times before settling on a nesting site; the tests consisted of merely scratching the soil surface to the completion of a nearly perfect nest chamber. Extensive scratching prior to nest digging has also been seen in captive *T. coahuila* (Cerda and Waugh, 1992).

Congello (1978) suggests that preferred nest sites may be the sunnier areas on an otherwise shaded forest floor, although this is not always the case. Although the nesting site may not be selected specifically for sunny conditions, the result may be to increase temperature, which in turn may increase developmental rates. As such, certain life history parameters (e.g., sex ratios) may be the product, in part, of nest site selection and availability. Nests deposited in cleared shady areas are likely to produce male hatchlings, whereas sunny locations will produce females. If shady nesting areas are more prevalent than sunny ones, the population may have a skewed sex ratio. The skewed sex ratio of the Florida box turtle population on Egmont Key likely resulted from this differential in nest site availability (Dodd, 1997a).

Despite the impression in the literature that box turtles always choose optimum sites, this is not always the case. In North Carolina, eastern box turtles have been found laying eggs on a sandy area in the bend of a very small stream, in cleared areas along road rights-of-way, and in the middle of the road in a deep woodlot (J. Sealy, pers. comm.). Dirt roads in relatively untraveled areas might provide good nest sites, and the sandy, open nature of some of these sites may have appeared optimum to the female, but whether successful hatching could have occurred is another matter.

DIGGING

Once a site is selected, the female uses her rear claws to scrape away debris such as leaf litter or small gravel. Legler (1960) reported that the *T. ornata* female makes a shallow depression up to 5 cm deep, large enough to support her body, prior to digging the cavity itself. During digging, the plastron rests at the posterior of the depression at an angle of 20 to 30 degrees; perhaps a shallow body pit allows the female to dig a deeper nest than she could without it. Such a body pit has not been noted in the other box turtles (e.g., the observations of Allard, 1935, and Congello, 1978) that have longer mean body lengths. However, if this were selectively advantageous, small females of the other species might be expected to construct similar shallow depressions prior to nesting.

The method of digging a nest among turtle species is strikingly similar, and box turtles offer no innovations to the stereotypical pattern. The following account is based on the observations of Allard (1935, 1948) and Congello (1978) on eastern box turtles in Washington, D.C., and Pennsylvania, respectively. The female extends her forelegs in order to elevate the anterior portion of her body slightly and to brace it as she digs. The nest is dug using only the hind legs, and the body is held at an angle of about 10 degrees, with the rear of the plastron resting upon the ground. The cavity is cleared and the chamber is dug by alternating movements of the hind limbs; both limbs are never used simultaneously.

The rear feet dig using a semicircular motion. Both the claws and the soles of the feet are used to remove dirt or sand from the nest cavity. The turtle curls the toes of its feet and uses the foot as a scoop, depositing the excavated material in piles on either side of the cavity. She may then tamp down the discarded dirt as she continues to dig. As a result of her efforts, a flask-shaped cavity is formed with a narrow neck. The depth of the cavity depends on the size of the female and on her ability to dig effectively. Turtles with missing claws or those that have foot problems dig imperfect or shallower cavities.

Box turtles may abandon nesting for a variety of reasons, including nest obstruction or disturbance. Some turtles abandon even advanced nest cavities for no obvious reason (Legler, 1960). As with sea turtles, the degree to which a nesting box turtle may be disturbed during nesting depends on the portion of the sequence she is carrying out. During site selection, ground scraping, and the initial phases of digging, the female can be disturbed easily by movements or noise. If disturbed or if impediments to nesting are encountered (such as root limbs, rocks, or excessively compacted soil), she may relocate to a new nesting site or abandon the area completely in favor of nesting later. However, once the cavity is about half completed or egg laying commences, the female usually will not be disturbed, even if handled. She will complete egg deposition and begin nest covering activities. Again in parallel with sea turtles, there is a degree of individual variation in the responsiveness of nesting females to disturbance; some are easily disturbed whereas others are not.

The flasked-shaped nest cavity (see figure 1 in Allard, 1948) is usually as deep as the female can reach with her hind limbs while the posterior part of her plastron rests on the lip of the cavity. In Congello's (1978) series of observations, this was between 6 and 10 cm. In Legler's (1960) study of *T. ornata*, the cavity of one female measured 5.5 cm deep, 8 cm wide at the bottom, and 6 cm wide at the opening. Cavities were usually symmetrical, but the shape depended on the physical digging capabilities of the female. Some captive *T. coahuila* dig a nest chamber in less than forty minutes (Cerda and Waugh, 1992), but Allard (1935) noted that digging may require three to four hours if the substrate is hard.

About thirty minutes prior to egg deposition, the cloaca becomes dilated, although in rare instances this does not occur. If cloacal dilation does not occur, egg deposition takes longer than normal. Legler (1960) thought that the presence of thick mud around the opening of the nest cavity indicated that the female had voided her bladder in order to soften the soil and make digging easier, but Allard (1948) never observed urination around the egg cavity in more than twenty years of observing captive *T. carolina*. Still, there are reliable records that box turtles "emptied a surprisingly large quantity of water from their bladders into the excavation" (n = 3 in Ohio; Conant, 1938:140), and I have seen photographs of recently completed nests over which females had obviously eliminated copious quantities of water. The prevalence of this behavior needs further examination.

Egmont Key, gravid female Florida box turtles have been observed from late March
arly August, suggesting an extended nesting period (Dodd, 1997a). Oviductal eggs
e been found in female eastern box turtles as late as October (Mitchell and de Sá,
4), but it is unknown how often such late egg clutches occur in nature. Infertile eggs
e been deposited by Florida box turtles within an outdoor enclosure as late as the last
k of August.

In northern latitudes, the nesting season may be shorter. Legler (1960) observed nest-
by *T. ornata* from early May to mid-July, although oviductal eggs were present as
ly as April 25. Legler (1960) suggests that *T. ornata* may be able to retain eggs until
orable conditions are found, but this has not been reported for the other species.
ptive *T. coahuila* in Jersey, United Kingdom, also nested primarily from May to July
rda and Waugh, 1992). Based on an examination of reproductive tracts in wild
atic box turtles, Brown (1974) suggested that nesting might occur into September.

Eastern box turtles often nest just before, during, or after rainfall. According to
ngello (1978), the turtles may be able to detect favorable nesting times several hours
ore a storm by the presence of cloud cover or rising humidity levels. At other times,
tles may nest after a prolonged period of rain. Attempts to simulate rainfall in order
stimulate nesting activities were not successful (Congello, 1978). In Pennsylvania, 65
cent of box turtle nestings were recorded during the last quarter of the new moon,
hough all nestings occurred on days with high humidity or rainfall. As a result,
ngello (1978) suggested that a photic stimulus or lunar cue might be involved in stim-
ting nesting activity. Temperature seems to play less of a role in nesting, at least as long
the temperatures are sufficient for activity. Congello (1978) noted a box turtle in
nnsylvania nesting at 13°C.

Nesting has most often been reported to occur late in the afternoon toward dusk for
st box turtles, although it does not occur until late at night (after midnight) in
coahuila (Brown, 1974). Actual egg deposition usually took place after dark for Kansas
ornata (Legler, 1960) and for captive *T. carolina* in Washington, D.C. (Allard, 1935). On
mont Key, however, I observed a female Florida box turtle finishing the covering of
r nest at 8:00 P.M. as night was falling, and Ewing (1935) recorded nesting by eastern
x turtles as early as 3:45 P.M. with completion by 5:30 P.M. Madden (1975) recorded
nale *T. carolina* completing nests both before dark and as late as 12:40 A.M. Stickel
50) reported a female digging an egg cavity in gravelly clay on the shoulder of a little-
ed road at 6:45 P.M. on July 6; by 7:45 P.M., the egg cavity was covered. In Kansas, a
nale *T. ornata* was observed scraping the earth at 6:00 P.M. on July 22, digging from 7:30
10:00 P.M., and depositing her eggs for the next half hour (Legler, 1960). It is likely that
e variation in observed times that nests are started and completed reflects the local envi-
nmental (weather and substrate) conditions under which nests are constructed.

ggs

here are three general categories of turtle eggshells: pliable eggshells, eggshells that are
gid and rather calcareous (termed brittle), and eggshells that are hard but expandable.

Depositing Eggs

Eggs are deposited singly, usually about two to five minutes apart. Dep
size (four eggs in Congello's 1978 study), egg laying takes thirty minute
a considerable amount of variation in deposition time, at least in ea:
Congello (1978) recorded one female depositing five eggs in ten minutes,
turtle deposited four eggs in twenty minutes. Allard (1935) recorded a
eggs in ten minutes to four eggs in twenty-five minutes. However, act
takes only about five or six seconds per egg. As the cloaca swells, eggs
muscular contraction. The female remains motionless throughout
although in between eggs, she may hiss and move her head in and out
eggs are positioned carefully in the cavity by the hind feet, and each eg
separately into position. Allard (1935) noted that the eggs are moved :
possible. Covering the nest begins either immediately after the last eg
after a short rest.

Covering the Nest

After egg deposition is completed, the female begins to cover the nest
that can take up to one hour to complete (Congello, 1978). As in nest dig
ing comprises a series of stereotypical movements of the hind legs. Shot
disturbed while covering (for example, if she is picked up), she resumes
as soon as she is allowed to do so, at the same point in the sequence :
disturbed.

The female anchors herself with her front feet and raises herself at a
angle. She appears to try to move softer material, such as grasses if avail:
cavity, and immediately covers her eggs by using her hind legs to so
toward the anterior portion of her carapace. Her hind feet then direct th
ward. Once the softer material is in place, she begins to push the prev
dirt directly into the cavity. Again, she alternates movements of the hind
ing down the dirt before putting more into the hole. During this proce
self up somewhat on her forefeet, presumably to gain leverage.

The female uses as much of the previously excavated dirt and deb
cavity as possible. Leftover mud or dirt is scattered over the nest area ar
She then brushes debris, grass, or small pebbles over the nesting site in
it (Congello, 1978). Allard (1935) states that the female painstakingly
"treading" and "tramping" the covered nest site using her toes, feet, kn
Indeed, it is often very difficult to discern the position of the nest (Legler
if rainfall should occur during or immediately following nest covering.

The Timing of Nesting

In temperate species of box turtles, the peak in nesting generally occurs i
peak periods probably vary to some degree latitudinally. Undoubtedly,
from one year to the next, depending on local environmental condition

Thus, there is almost a continuum of possible shell types, at least in terms of their resistance to outside pressure. Box turtle eggs are pliable at oviposition; as they swell during development, they come to feel somewhat harder and more rigid. The eggshells of *T. ornata* resist flexing to some degree; if you push onto the eggshell of an ornate box turtle, for example, the shell resists the push at first but will give way eventually. Rather than break outright, it indents. As it does so, the mineral layer forming part of the shell flakes off, forming crusty indentations, with some minor loss of the egg's outer mineral layer (Ewert, 1985). Thus, the eggshell resists outside forces by bending rather than by cracking or breaking. All eggshells tend to lose their integrity as hatching nears, probably as a result of calcium uptake by the developing embryo.

The eggshell is composed of a series of layers. The outermost layers are mineralized with calcium carbonate (as aragonite crystals), whereas the innermost layers are composed of fibers of various carbohydrates and proteins, possibly collagens. The eggshell provides rigidity; encapsulates the developing embryo and yolk; protects them from external environmental influences such as small predators (for example, ants), pathogens, and fungi; and possibly provides calcium for shell and bone growth. The tough fibrous material holds the various internal membranes together and provides support. At the same time, all layers must allow the passage of respiratory gases and waste products. Pliable-shelled eggs respond rapidly to environmental influences, such as hydration or dehydration.

The freshly deposited eggs of box turtles are translucent, pigmentless, and oblong in shape. The white color normally associated with turtle eggs develops soon after deposition. This occurs as the vitelline sac (the fluid-filled sac containing both embryo and yolk) ceases movement and the eggshell membrane changes from translucent white to a chalky white, hence the term *chalking*. The embryo develops on a disk floating on the surface of the yolk mass. As with other turtles, eggs are deposited in the gastrula stage. Completion of development within the egg occurs outside the female's body in the nest chamber. Initially the embryo is located at the upper pole of the egg. It develops on its side on a flat disk in such a manner that its left side usually faces the massive amount of yolk and albumin toward the center of the egg and its right side is adjacent to and parallel with the eggshell. Shortly thereafter it moves, head pointed down, to near the egg's equator. The hatchling breaks through the eggshell (termed *pipping*) at what becomes, by definition, the right end of the egg (Ewert, 1985). Embryos are responsive to touch at about 6 mm in length (Tuge, 1931).

Twinning has been reported on rare occasions (Crooks and Smith, 1958; Tucker and Funk, 1976; R. Zappalorti, pers. comm.), as have occasional developmental abnormalities (Tucker and Funk, 1977) and albinism (Arndt, 1980).

Nest Environment

After box turtle eggs are laid and covered within the nest cavity, the physical environment becomes extremely important to further development. If the ground becomes flooded or if the soil inhibits gas exchange, normal development cannot take place and the eggs will die. Box turtle eggs can tolerate a wide range of moisture levels as they develop, however. Under laboratory conditions, eggs of *T. ornata* incubated in a moist environment increased their weight by 6 percent as they absorbed water. On a dry medium, they lost as much as 17 percent of their water compared with their weight at oviposition. In neither case did moisture content influence hatching success, although the moister eggs took longer to develop (Packard et al., 1985). These eggs were larger than the dry-incubated eggs, and a larger size at hatching may be associated with increased fitness (e.g., Janzen, 1993).

During development, a box turtle egg may increase in weight as much as 18.5 percent because of moisture uptake (Lynn and von Brand, 1945). Moisture uptake causes the width rather than the length of the egg to expand (Tucker et al., 1978a). The embryo consumes a maximum of approximately 450 cubic millimeters of oxygen per hour per egg during the latter stages of development. Hence the placement of the eggs within the nest cavity must allow for sufficient oxygen exchange.

Within the egg, ammonia is detoxified by converting it to urea and storing it within the egg. As urea accumulates during development, it may increase to levels that can inhibit further development. In dry environments, this inhibitory effect may be more pronounced (Packard et al., 1985). In turn, this could affect growth, which influences the size and vigor of the hatchling.

Packard et al. (1985) suggested that the relatively large eggs of *T. ornata* may be of particular advantage to this terrestrial emydid in an arid environment. Large eggs might be better adapted to survive the variety of stressful hydric conditions found within the nests of this species, especially when compared to the smaller eggs of eastern species that favor mesic habitats. While the argument seems physiologically sound, I know of no data demonstrating differences between the nesting environments of the various species and subspecies of *Terrapene*. In any case, the moisture conditions within the nest may have a profound influence on future survival.

INCUBATION

Literature records show a wide range of times needed for box turtle eggs to complete development (e.g., 69–136 days, Allard, 1948), but the temperature of the nest during incubation is not generally reported. The length of time that box turtle eggs take to complete development and hatch is certainly temperature dependent. Simply stated, the warmer the temperature during incubation, the shorter incubation duration will be—up to a point, beyond which the eggs will die. Under laboratory conditions, *T. carolina* eggs take a mean of 73.6 days (range 68–81) to pip at 25°C, and 50.7 days (range 46–53) at 30°C (Ewert, 1985). Similar values were recorded by Dodge et al. (1978), who also noted that hatching failed to occur at 34°C. For *T. ornata*, the corresponding values are a mean of 74.4 days (range 73–76) at 25°C, and 51.0 days (range 50–52 days) at 30°C (Ewert, 1985). Values reported from field data are included with the species accounts.

Mitchell and de Sá's (1994) finding of a gravid female *T. c. carolina* in southeastern Virginia in early October raises the interesting possibility that some box turtles possess a mechanism to retain eggs during the winter (arrested development within the female's oviducts) or to deposit eggs that would undergo embryonic diapause within the nest (see glossary). Although several turtles in at least four families have been reported to retain eggs for a period of several weeks (Ewert, 1985), egg retention has not been reported in *Terrapene*. In addition, no turtles have been proven definitely to retain eggs throughout a prolonged winter period.

A number of turtles are known to deposit eggs that then undergo embryonic diapause within the nest, but not *Terrapene* (Ewert, 1985). Cold temperatures may also temporarily arrest development, but this cannot explain the presence of eggs in a female in October. Hampering explanation of this observation is the fact that captive turtles sometimes retain eggs within their body cavities as a result of an inability to find suitable nesting sites. Mitchell and de Sá (1994) could not determine whether their road-killed specimen had been in captivity, so the question remains open.

With regard to this question, a brief note by Myers (1952) seems to have been overlooked by several researchers. Myers found well-developed hatchlings of *T. c. triunguis* within a nest in mid-October in Missouri. The late hatching dates suggested that the hatchlings might have overwintered in the nest if they had not been disturbed. More intriguing was the finding of one nest in which an egg with a 25.6 mm hatchling hatched on April 9. Myers (1952) suggested that a small percentage of box turtle hatchlings might overwinter within the egg. Field biologists should be alert for either very late nesting activity or gravid females in the fall, especially within populations of box turtles that undergo dormancy during unfavorable environmental conditions.

TEMPERATURE-DEPENDENT SEX DETERMINATION (TSD)

In box turtles, as in many species of turtles and tortoises, the temperature during incubation determines the sex of the resulting offspring. Unlike mammals and birds and even a few other turtles such as softshells (Trionychidae), box turtles do not have sex chromosomes. In general, hatchlings from warm nests become females, whereas hatchlings from cooler nests become males. Variation in nest site selection thus influences the nest's temperature, which in turn determines the sex of the hatchling. It is not surprising, therefore, that many box turtle populations appear to have skewed sex ratios (chapter 8).

Under laboratory conditions where *T. carolina* eggs were incubated at a constant temperature, males were produced in 73 percent of the eggs incubated at 22.5°C, in 96 percent of eggs incubated at 25°C, and in 81 percent of the eggs incubated at 27°C; no males were produced at 30°C (Ewert and Nelson, 1991). For *T. ornata*, 100 percent males have been produced at temperatures of 22.5°C and 25°C (Ewert and Nelson, 1991), whereas 100 percent females were produced at 29°C (Packard et al., 1985). Although temperature clearly influences the sex of the hatchling, the specifics of TSD differ somewhat between these species.

Terrapene ornata appears to follow what Ewert and Nelson (1991) describe as a Type Ia pattern. In this pattern, there is a single clearly defined transition temperature, above which females will be produced and below which males will result. This temperature has been termed the pivotal temperature, and it varies among turtle species with TSD. A second pattern (Type II) is found in snapping turtles and a few other species. In this pattern, males are produced at both the upper and lower ends of the incubation temperature spectrum, but females are produced in the median zone; thus, there appear to be two transition temperatures. *Terrapene carolina* fits neither of these patterns, although it may operate on some variation of pattern Type Ia (Ewert and Nelson, 1991). The exact pivotal temperature for either species remains unknown.

EGG SIZE AND SHAPE

There are two major constraints to the size of eggs within a female box turtle: the pelvic opening and the distance between the plastron and carapace as the eggs are laid. Eggs must be able to pass freely through the pelvic opening, and the female's shell must allow sufficient room for the eggs to pass from her body. Box turtle eggs are oblong and flexible, hence their length is not nearly as important as their width in terms of the pelvic opening and shell aperture. Female body size could exert an influence on the size of the egg (assuming larger females have larger pelvic openings), but it is not her volume in itself that is important. Egg size (measured as width, length, shape, or volume) does not show a relationship with either female body size or clutch size (Nieuwolt, 1993; Nieuwolt-Dacanay, 1997) in *T. ornata*, but egg width and weight are positively correlated with female plastral size in *T. c. major* (Tucker et al., 1978a).

Intraspecific variation in egg size and number are given in the individual species accounts. However, average egg sizes are about 33.2 mm in length × 16.9 mm in width for *T. coahuila* (Brown, 1974), 36.1 mm in length × 21.7 mm in width for *T. ornata* (Legler, 1960), and 47 mm in length × 17 mm in width for *T. n. nelsoni* (Milstead and Tinkle, 1967). Because of the variation in average female body size among the subspecies of *T. carolina*, average egg size also varies considerably. Carr (1952) gives ranges of 32.0 mm length × 19.5 mm width for *T. c. carolina* to 38.4 mm length × 22.4 mm width for *T. c. major*, the largest of the modern box turtles. Average egg weights are approximately 5.66 g for *T. coahuila* (Brown, 1974), 8.4–9.2 g for *T. carolina* (Cunningham and Huene, 1938; Allard, 1949), and 10.09 g for *T. ornata* (Legler, 1960). Lynn and von Brand (1945) reported the average volume for 12 *T. c. trianguis* eggs as 8.1 cc (range 7.1–9.0 cc).

NUMBERS OF EGGS AND REPRODUCTIVE POTENTIAL

Although the female's pelvic opening may restrict egg size, it does not restrict egg number. Theoretically at least, the number of eggs in a clutch should be restricted only by the space available within her shell after subtracting the space required for her internal organs. In box turtles, as in many other turtles, the clutch size may (Nieuwolt, 1993; Nieuwolt-Dacanay, 1997; Dodd, 1997a) or may not (St. Clair, 1995) increase positively with female carapace length. However, the biological importance of this relationship is obscure since measures of variance sometimes are quite small even for significant relationships (Dodd, 1997a).

Box turtles normally lay from one to about seven eggs per clutch, but there are two literature reports of eleven eggs per clutch for *T. carolina* (Zieller, 1969; Warner, 1982). However, the average clutch size is much smaller and varies considerably among species and subspecies (see species accounts). In northern populations of *T. carolina*, females routinely deposit four or more eggs per clutch (Warner, 1982; Ernst et al., 1994; Palmer and Braswell, 1995; Messinger and Patton, 1995; St. Clair, 1995), whereas in southern populations clutch sizes are smaller, generally from one to three eggs (Milstead and Tinkle, 1967; Brown, 1974; Dodd, 1997a).

Mean clutch size also can vary among years and between geographic regions. For example, mean clutch size ranged between 3.8 and 5.0 over a six-year period in captive *T. coahuila* (Cerda and Waugh, 1992). Dodd (1997a) also found some variation among years in mean clutch size of *T. c. bauri* (2.36–2.5 eggs), but the difference was not statistically significant. In addition to normal eggs, box turtles occasionally produce what have been somewhat inaccurately termed "yolkless" eggs in sea turtles; that is, abnormally small or malformed eggs with or without a small quantity of yolk (Madden, 1975).

One must be careful when using literature reports of both clutch size and clutch frequency. For example, Iverson (1977) suggested that *T. c. bauri* laid only one clutch per year (based on dissections), whereas new data based on radiographs show that they can lay up to three clutches per season (Dodd, 1997a). In another case, Milstead and Tinkle (1967) reported that *T. n. nelsoni* in Nayarit, Mexico, only laid one clutch per season (= 2.7 eggs per clutch), although they admitted that the data might be faulty. Still, these authors used their data to suggest that southern box turtles have smaller reproductive potentials than northern box turtles, which is clearly not always the case (see later discussion).

Box turtles may produce more than one clutch per year, especially in captivity (Cerda and Waugh, 1992) and in the more southerly latitudes. Even eastern box turtles in New Jersey have been reported to deposit more than one clutch in a season (Riemer, 1981). Florida box turtles lay from zero to three clutches per year (Dodd, 1997a); three-toed box turtles in an outdoor enclosure in Louisiana deposited from two to six clutches per year (Messinger and Patton, 1995); 33 percent of the ornate box turtles in Legler's (1960) Kansas study laid two clutches in a year; and aquatic box turtles may deposit from one to three clutches (Brown, 1974). Multiple clutches also have been reported in *T. c. major* (Tucker et al., 1978b; Jackson, 1991), although sample sizes were small or not based on records for individual females.

There has been some discussion in the scientific literature concerning the effects of latitude on clutch size and frequency (Iverson, 1992a; Iverson et al., 1993). In general, southern turtles lay more clutches of fewer, but larger, eggs than northern conspecifics, even after taking body size into consideration, and this relationship appears to hold for box turtles. Thus, southern box turtles may or may not have a greater reproductive potential than northern box turtles, despite the assertions of Milstead and Tinkle (1967) to the contrary. For reasons discussed later and in chapter 10, this is not as simple a relationship as it initially appears.

Individual reproductive potential is defined as the total number of eggs produced per female per year. In terms of the population, it factors in the mean clutch size × the mean clutch frequency × the percentage of the population reproducing in any one year. Maximum individual reproductive potential per year is about eleven eggs in *T. c. carolina* and *T. coahuila*, about nine eggs in *T. c. major* (Tucker et al., 1978b), and about eight eggs in *T. c. bauri*. Average individual reproductive potentials are often much lower, however. About a third of the *T. coahuila* examined by Brown (1974) had a reproductive potential of approximately 6.8 eggs per female per season, whereas *T. ornata* had a mean reproductive potential of 8.2 eggs per female per season for a similar proportion of the population (Legler, 1960). For most turtles, the realized reproductive potentials are lower than these values.

It is difficult to determine reproductive potential for an entire population because so little is known about the percentage of the population reproducing or about individual variation in reproductive output. For example, between 2 percent and 54 percent of the Florida box turtles I radiographed on Egmont Key were gravid in any sampling period, but there was a great deal of variation among sampling periods and years (Dodd, 1997a). Similar results were obtained for *T. ornata* in New Mexico (Nieuwolt, 1993; Nieuwolt-Dacanay, 1997). From 0 percent (in two of three years in August) to 90 percent (n = 10 in May of one year) of the females she radiographed were gravid. On Egmont Key, we know little about *average* clutch frequency among individuals. Clutch frequency may vary among individuals and years. A female may deposit several clutches one year, one the next, and skip the third year altogether.

The number of eggs per clutch may vary among individuals within a year. For example, on Egmont Key, I have seen females lay successive clutches of three, two, and two or three, three, and two eggs within a season. Mean clutch sizes appear to decrease with successive clutches in some species and subspecies (*T. coahuila*: Brown, 1974; *T. ornata*: Legler, 1960). However, these studies were conducted only over a two- to three-year period on single populations, so it is unknown how universal this trend might be.

Not all wild box turtles reproduce in any one year, a phenomenon reported in a number of other turtle species. Again on Egmont Key, I have seen a few females over a four-year period that have never been gravid, although inconsistencies in sampling may be responsible for these somewhat anomalous results. Indeed, I never saw more than 42 percent of the females on Egmont Key gravid in any one year (fig. 6-4). In any case, there is a great degree of variation in both individual and population-level reproductive output in box turtles. Simply determining the mean clutch size or frequency may obscure important life history information. The important questions to ask are why such variation occurs and how widespread the variation is.

At present, we have only vague clues as to what may account for the variation in clutch size and frequency in box turtles. It seems clear that these reproductive parameters are plastic in nature, suggesting that they might be under the influence of resource-based energy allocation in a variable environment (Nieuwolt, 1993; Nieuwolt-Dacanay, 1997). Simply stated, in "good" years (or in the reproductive seasons following good years), resources may be abundant enough for turtles to store energy that can then be used for reproduction. If resources are not available, reproduction may be reduced (in terms of fewer or smaller eggs) or prevented altogether.

On Egmont Key, a dry island, my subjective impressions are that food resources (fruiting plants, leaf-litter invertebrates) are abundant in years following good winter rains. Rainy winters are succeeded by periods of higher than average reproductive output; dry winters are followed by low individual reproductive output. In New Mexico,

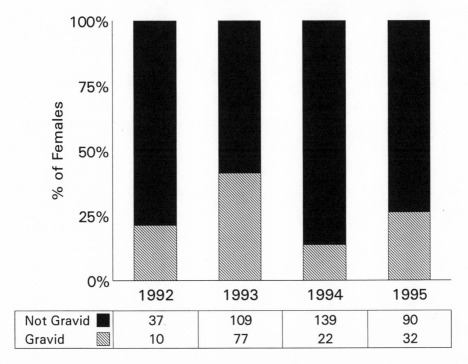

		1992	1993	1994	1995
Not Gravid	■	37	109	139	90
Gravid	▨	10	77	22	32

Figure 6-4. Minimum percentage of female *T. c. bauri* that were gravid in any one year on Egmont Key, Florida, 1992 to 1995. Total number sampled = 516; total gravid = 141. After Dodd (1997a).

Nieuwolt (1993) and Nieuwolt-Dacanay (1997) found a similar correlation, although spring rains appeared to be most important for the arid-dwelling *T. o. luteola.* However our sample sizes are rather small, and more data are required to confirm this speculation.

If reproductive output is tied directly to the availability of energy resources in variable environments, as predicted, then there should be a great deal of intraspecific variation in reproductive parameters, such as clutch size, clutch frequency, egg size, and the percentage of the population reproducing each year. This appears to be the case for box turtles, although questions of female body size and phylogeny must be taken into consideration.

FERTILITY

For some reason, box turtle eggs sometimes seem to have low fertility rates. In clutches of two or three eggs, it is not uncommon to have one or two of the eggs infertile. In some cases, this may be due to lack of access to males (e.g., Ewing, 1943), but even in wild populations or in captive populations with free access to courting males, fertility rates can be low. For example, 27.1 percent (n = 156) of the eggs of captive *T. coahuila* were infertile at the Jersey Wildlife Preservation Trust (Cerda and Waugh, 1992). In his large colony of captive female *T. carolina,* Allard (1935) noted that up to 18 percent of the eggs that escaped predation were infertile. In contrast, Tucker et al. (1978b) recorded a 90 percent fertility rate for eggs (n = 32) of wild-caught *T. c. major.*

Hatching

Hatching is first heralded by the appearance of a longitudinal slit at the narrow end of the egg. As the time for hatching approaches, the hatchlings may use the caruncle on the tip of the nose to break through the eggshell, although Allard (1935) noted that the front limbs frequently break through the soft eggshell prior to the emergence of the head. The caruncle is reported to disappear over a wide range of times: seven days in *T. c. carolina* (Ernst and Barbour, 1972), a mean of eighty-three days in five captive *T. c. major* (Tucker and Funk, 1977), and up to thirty days in *T. ornata* (Legler, 1960). Undoubtedly the amount of time the caruncle is retained depends on the environment and activity of the hatchlings.

Box turtle hatchlings retain a large amount of unused yolk contained in external yolk sacs (Ewert, 1985). Hence, they are not ready to leave the confines of the egg immediately upon pipping, unlike some other turtles, such as the mud and musk turtles. Pipping may require from several hours to several days. It takes from one to five days for the external yolk to be resorbed. Yolk resorption may start prior to abandoning the eggshell, but it usually is completed shortly thereafter.

Frothingham (1936) provides the following account of the hatching of *T. carolina*. When first uncovered, the hatchlings had already pipped and had their heads and one or both front feet protruding from the broken eggshell. Their eyes were closed, their mouths were open, and the front limbs were struggling to extract the rest of the body from the shell. The entire hatching process took from some unspecified time during the day until as late as 1:30 A.M. for at least two of the five turtles. However, the last turtle was not completely free of the egg until three days later. When the young turtles were free of the eggshells, the yolk sacs had still not been absorbed completely and were the size of a large pea. The eyes did not open in the first hatchling until five days after the hatchlings were discovered.

The yolk sac is completely absorbed by the hatchling usually within a week. As the yolk is absorbed, the carapace tends to straighten out, thus getting rid of curvature resulting from development within the confines of the egg. Within two to three days after the yolk has been absorbed, the shells are much firmer (Tucker and Funk, 1977). The yolk appears to be forced into the hatchling through the action of smooth muscles acting on the yolk sac (Ewert, 1985). Yolk provides the hatchling with nourishment during its first days of life and through the oncoming winter. It is an important source of parental investment that the female provides to her offspring. The umbilical scar persists for about two to three weeks (Tucker and Funk, 1977).

Future Directions

MEXICAN TAXA. One of the most glaring omissions in the discussion so far is the almost complete absence of information on four taxa of box turtles: both subspecies of *T. nelsoni* and both tropical subspecies of *T. carolina* (*mexicana* and *yucatana*). For example, Lee's (1996) exhaustive treatment of the herpetofauna of Yucatán barely mentions *T. c. yucatana* and provides no information on its reproductive biology. This is not Lee's omission. Little is known about any aspect of these species' biology. Obtaining life history data on these species should be a priority for future research on Mexican chelonians. It would be important to know, from an evolutionary perspective, how these species compare with their northern conspecifics in terms of reproductive output and in other aspects of reproductive ecology. Do reproductive cycles mirror those of the more temperate species, or are they more in synchrony with the wet-dry seasonality of the tropics?

THE ROLE OF OLFACTION. There are many behaviors involving mate finding and courtship that have not yet been examined. One of these, the role of olfaction in mate finding, mate attraction, and mate selection, certainly deserves more attention. Box turtles clearly have a sense of smell, although they may not perceive odors in the environment as we do. They appear to sniff the ground as they wander through their habitat, and they certainly sniff one another during encounters. Several researchers have noted olfactory behavior during mate finding and courtship and have speculated on its function (Davis, 1981; Ernst, 1981). If olfaction plays a role in courtship, it could have important implications for mate choice (sexual selection) and as a pre-mating isolating mechanism in areas where individuals of more than one species or subspecies come into contact.

NEST TEMPERATURE. The importance of nest site selection by female box turtles cannot be overstated, for reasons already outlined. Whereas we know the gross effects of temperature on developing eggs fairly well (effects on incubation duration, TSD, physiological processes), we know little about the temperature of actual nests. Can Congello's hypothesis about the placement of nests in sunny locations be corroborated by field data? Are nests placed in sunny locations on a forest floor warmer than nests in shade? To date, no data are available. Fluctuations in nest temperatures undoubtedly occurs. Do these fluctuations affect TSD and how? What are the pivotal temperatures for box turtle eggs, and do they vary taxonomically or with latitude? Why do some females hatch from nests at lower temperatures?

NESTING BEHAVIOR. Even though seemingly well described, certain aspects of the nesting process remain sketchy. For example, some authors have reported that females release their bladder contents when faced with digging in hard-packed soils. It would be interesting to see if this behavior is widespread, under what conditions it is employed, and whether it really facilitates nest construction. Variation in nesting behavior deserves more study, especially using quantitative methods.

REPRODUCTIVE CYCLES AND CLUTCH PARAMETERS. General outlines of the timing of reproduction in box turtles seem fairly consistent among species. However, more data are needed on the variation that occurs, especially in terms of the nesting season. Are seasons prolonged in the southern and tropical species, as preliminary data suggest? What effect does resource allocation play on the duration and timing of the nesting season, as well as on clutch size, clutch frequency, and egg size? How much variation occurs from one year to the next in these parameters, and how does this variation affect population structure and survivorship? Do years of high resource availability result in the subsequent production of larger hatchlings than in years of resource scarcity?

EGGS. Packard et al. (1985) speculate that *T. ornata* has larger eggs than its eastern relative *T. carolina* because larger eggs are better adapted to withstand fluctuations in nest moisture than are smaller eggs. These authors suggest that a greater variation in moisture content of nest chambers may be expected in the arid environment in which the ornate box turtle lives than in the nest chambers of the eastern box turtle. Are *T. ornata* eggs any larger than those of the other species or subspecies of box turtle that also live in arid environments? Do nests in fact vary much in moisture content? In turn, what role does egg size play in the fitness of hatchlings? Some authors (e.g., Janzen, 1993) have suggested that larger hatchlings have a better chance of survival than smaller hatchlings. Do larger eggs produce larger hatchlings? St. Clair (1995, 1998) could not demonstrate a relationship between incubation temperature and hatchling growth, although it did affect hatching size, energetic costs, and metabolic rate. Therefore, does initial egg size really make a difference, or can its effects be enhanced or overruled by the developmental environment?

REPRODUCTIVE OUTPUT. Little is known about the variation surrounding most parameters involved in reproductive output. In a box turtle population, how many females are reproducing in any one year? Do clutch size and frequency change? How many hatchlings actually result from the eggs that are produced? Why does fertility appear low in some populations (individuals?) but not in others? If reproductive output does indeed vary annually among both individuals and populations, why? In addition, some studies appear to suggest that female body size influences various reproductive characteristics, such as egg or clutch size, whereas others do not. What is the source of this variation—that is, is it a result of natural selection acting differently in different parts of the range, or is it a reflection of procedural (analytical) differences among human researchers?

OVERWINTERING OF EGGS AND HATCHLINGS. The finding of adult turtles late in the season with shelled eggs suggests that some females deposit eggs very late in the season or somehow carry the eggs through the winter. Although the latter has not been reported, there is a possibility of the former. Do young box turtles simply overwinter in the nests, as they do in some painted turtle (*Chrysemys picta*) populations, or is there some mechanism for developmental diapause? How common is this phenomenon, if indeed it occurs at all?

Most of the questions outlined can only be addressed through a coordinated field and laboratory approach. Inasmuch as it is difficult to separate environmental influences from natural variation in reproductive parameters of even short-lived species, it will be difficult to obtain convincing data addressing questions of reproductive variation without long-term studies. Although intensive in labor and perhaps cost, carefully planned long-term studies are the only solution to the natural variation vs. environmental influence conundrum. Fortunately, box turtles would appear to be excellent candidates for such studies on reproductive ecology.

1. Terrapene carolina. Plate by Georges Cuvier from the so-called Disciples Edition of *La Règne Animal.* See Duvernoy (1836). Photo courtesy Kraig Adler.

2. Terrapene carolina. Plate from Sowerby and Lear (1872). Photo courtesy Kraig Adler.

3. Terrapene carolina. Watercolor by Charles-Alexandre Lesueur (see Bonnemains and Bour, 1996). Photo courtesy of the Muséum d'Histoire Naturelle–Le Havre, No. 78027. Reprinted with permission.

4. Terrapene carolina. Plate from Holbrook (1842). Reproduced courtesy of the Society for the Study of Amphibians and Reptiles.

5. Terrapene carolina. Plate from Babcock (1919). Artist: Henry Blake.

6. Terrapene carolina. Commemorative print by David Dennis for the First World Congress of Herpetology, Canterbury, England, 1989. Reproduced with artist's permission.

7. Box turtle leg rattles. Creek, Seminole, Cherokee, or Yuchi. Ca. 1940; 27.5 × 27.5 × 17.5 cm. Gilcrease Museum, No. 9327.43. Photo courtesy of Gilcrease Museum, Tulsa, Oklahoma.

8. Pottery box turtle by Sara Ayers, Catawba Nation. Author's collection.

9. Hatchling box turtles by Tom McFarland. Author's collection

10. Box turtle necklace. Artist: Barbara Bell, Philadelphia. Photo courtesy of B. Bell. Author's collection.

11. Stamps featuring box turtles. Clockwise from upper left, Staffa Scotland (60 p); United States; National Wildlife Federation (1972); National Wildlife Federation (1996); Tortuga Local Post (Miami); Kampuchea; Dagestan (2,500 kpks).

12. Box Turtle Beer, Old North State Brewing Company, Youngsville, North Carolina.

13. *Terrapene carolina carolina*. Winston County, Alabama.

14. *Terrapene carolina carolina*. Indiana.

15. *Terrapene carolina carolina*. Black plastron; note concavity (male) of plastron. Huntingdon County, Pennsylvania.

16. *Terrapene carolina carolina*. Hatchling; note the egg caruncle on the tip of the snout. Winston County, Alabama.

17. *Terrapene carolina bauri*. Adult. Egmont Key, Hillsborough County, Florida.

18. *Terrapene carolina bauri*. Plastrons; the female (right) has a flat plastron, whereas the plastron of the male (left) is concave. Egmont Key, Hillsborough County, Florida.

19. Terrapene carolina bauri. Hatchling, 27 mm carapace length. Egmont Key, Hillsborough County, Florida

20. Terrapene carolina major. Adult. Photo by Richard Bartlett.

21. Terrapene carolina major. Plastron, male. Photo by Richard Bartlett.

22. Terrapene carolina triunguis. Adult male. Photo by Richard Bartlett.

23. Terrapene carolina mexicana. Adult female. Photo by Richard Bartlett.

24. Terrapene carolina mexicana. Yearling. Photo by Richard Bartlett

25. *Terrapene carolina yucatana*. Adult. Campeche, near Candelaria. Photo by Julian C. Lee.

26. *Terrapene coahuila*. Adult.

27. *Terrapene coahuila*. Yearling. Photo by Richard Bartlett.

28. *Terrapene ornata ornata*. Adult female. Kansas.

29. *Terrapene ornata ornata*. Adult male plastron. Photo by Robert Zappalorti.

30. *Terrapene ornata luteola*. Adult male. Near Sierra Vista, Arizona. Photo by Martin A. Tuegel.

31. Terrapene nelsoni nelsoni. Adult female. Photo by John Iverson.

32. Terrapene nelsoni klauberi. Adult male. Sonora, Mexico. Photo by Peter J. Mayne.

33. Egmont Key, Florida: habitat of *Terrapene carolina bauri.*

34. Cuatro Ciénegas, Coahuila, Mexico: habitat of *Terrapene coahuila.* Photo by John Iverson.

35. Konza Prairie, Kansas: habitat of *Terrapene ornata ornata.*

36. East side of Huachuca Mountains near Sierra Vista, Arizona: habitat of *Terrapene ornata luteola.* Photo by Martin A. Tuegel.

37. *Terrapene carolina bauri* yearling attacking a worm. Alachua County, Florida.

38. *Terrapene carolina bauri* adult male (140 mm CL) eating a sea grape. Egmont Key, Hillsborough County, Florida.

39. *Terrapene carolina bauri* adult resting in form. Egmont Key, Hillsborough County, Florida.

40. *Terrapene carolina bauri*, Volusia County, Florida. This turtle carries a radio transmitter for study of its movements. Note the huge numbers of mosquitoes feeding at the seams between its carapace scutes. Photo by Peter G. May.

41. *Terrapene carolina bauri*, Egmont Key, Hillsborough County, Florida. One form of thread-trailing device using a commercially obtained bobbin.

42. *Terrapene carolina carolina* attempting copulation; May, 1997. Photo by James Harding.

43. *Terrapene carolina triunguis* egg deposition. Louisiana. Photo by Martha Messinger.

44. *Terrapene coahuila* swimming. Cuatro Ciénegas, Coahuila, Mexico. Photo by James Buskirk.

45. *Terrapene carolina bauri* fire-scarred shell. Alachua County, Florida.

46. *Terrapene carolina carolina* with flesh fly (*Sarcophaga latisterna*) on eye. Photo by Robert Zappalorti.

47. *Terrapene carolina bauri*, Egmont Key, Hillsborough County, Florida. Caseous cyst after removal from right side of the head of a 142 mm CL female Florida box turtle. This turtle had a similar-sized cyst on the left side of her head and was unable to withdraw the head into the shell. She was later recaptured healthy with no signs of the previous trauma.

48. *Terrapene carolina triunguis*. Female. Louisiana. Healed shell after severe trauma to the carapace. Box turtles have a remarkable capacity to recover from intense trauma. Photo by Martha Messinger.

7 | Food and Feeding Behavior

Generally speaking, a box turtle is about as omnivorous as any organism could be expected to be.

JOHN MURPHY, 1976

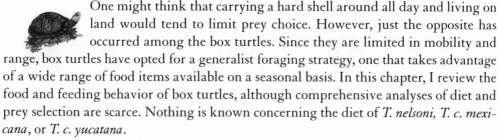

One might think that carrying a hard shell around all day and living on land would tend to limit prey choice. However, just the opposite has occurred among the box turtles. Since they are limited in mobility and range, box turtles have opted for a generalist foraging strategy, one that takes advantage of a wide range of food items available on a seasonal basis. In this chapter, I review the food and feeding behavior of box turtles, although comprehensive analyses of diet and prey selection are scarce. Nothing is known concerning the diet of *T. nelsoni, T. c. mexicana*, or *T. c. yucatana*.

The *Terrapene* digestive system consists of (a) an esophagus with wide, fused, and branching folds; (b) a stomach with a typical turtle pattern of large, broad, unbranched, and parallel longitudinal folds; (c) a duodenum consisting of a zigzag fold-on-fold pattern, which disappears in the first part of the small intestine and is replaced by a single layer through the colon; and (d) a distensible colon, which empties into the cloaca (Parsons and Cameron, 1977). As far as is known, the digestive tract of box turtles does not have any unique morphological modifications or contain unusual symbioses, such as the presence of celluolytic bacteria which assist in digestion of plant material.

The Box Turtle Diet

FOODS OF WILD TURTLES

By all accounts, box turtles are omnivores, eating a wide range of plant and animal material. Most summaries of the diets of box turtles are based on casual observations rather than detailed analyses. The most comprehensive data on the foods of box turtles are reported by Surface (1908) for 40 Pennsylvania *T. carolina* (fig. 7-1); Klimstra and Newsome (1960) for 117 Illinois *T. carolina*; Legler (1960) for 25 Kansas *T. ornata*; and Brown (1974) for 45 *T. coahuila*. Surprisingly, the percentage of plant and animal foods in the diet of *T. coahuila* is similar to that of their terrestrial counterparts, although the precise composition reflects this species' aquatic habits (fig. 7-2). Although nothing is known about prey selection, box turtles probably eat whatever strikes their fancy, whatever they can catch.

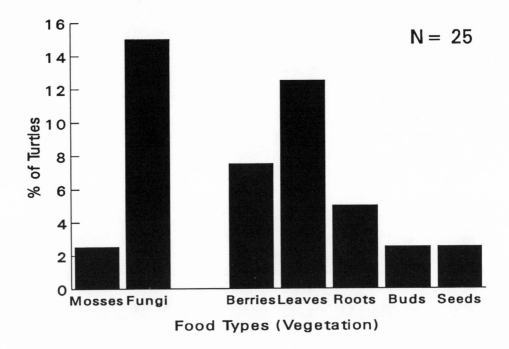

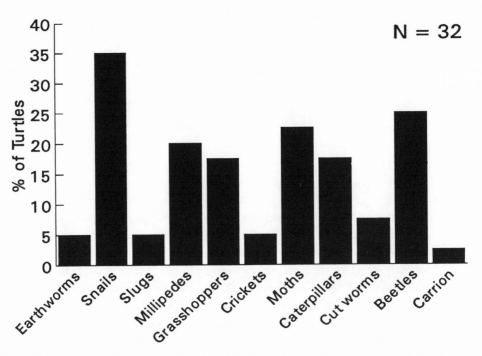

Figure 7-1. Frequency of occurrence of various food items in the diet of *Terrapene carolina* in Pennsylvania. Data from Surface (1908).

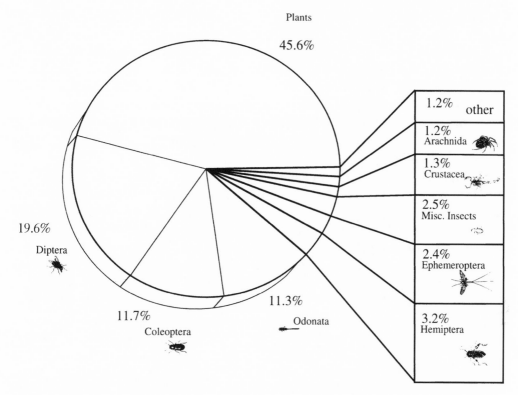

Figure 7-2. Frequency of occurrence of various food items in the diet of *Terrapene coahuila*. Diagram modified from Brown (1974).

In various analyses, vegetation (including fungi) makes up a considerable portion of the diet. For example, 62.5 percent of Pennsylvania eastern box turtles had plant material in their digestive tracts (fig. 7-1; see Surface, 1908). Comparative values are available at other locations and for other species: 89 percent (51.6 percent by volume) for Illinois eastern box turtles; 32 percent for North Carolina eastern box turtles (Stuart and Miller, 1987); 91 percent for Kansas ornate box turtles; and 45.6 percent (by volume) for aquatic box turtles. Box turtles eat leaves and shoots, buds, roots, fruits, seeds, and mosses. Seeds reported in the diet may be all that is left after the sweet pulp has been digested. There is even an observation of a box turtle eating a green oak gall (Latham, 1972).

Fruits of cacti (*Opuntia*), may apples (*Podophyllum*), grapes (*Vitis*), blackberries (*Rubus*), ground cherries (*Physalis*), elderberries (*Sambucus*), strawberries (*Fragaria*), half-flower (*Scaevola*), sea grapes (*Coccoloba*), Brazilian pepper (*Schinus*), wild plum (*Prunus*), smartweed (*Polygonum*), red mulberry (*Morus*), apples (*Pyrus*), and persimmons (*Diospryos*) are known to be a part of the diets of box turtles, and many other species likely are eaten when and where available. Box turtles have a well-known penchant for raiding fruit and vegetable gardens, especially for cantaloupes and tomatoes, and at one time some farmers deliberately killed box turtles in the mistaken belief that the turtles could cause serious economic harm.

Plants are often difficult to identify in stomach contents, and few authors have made the effort beyond noting the presence of unidentified plant material. In addition to seeds, Surface (1908) reported that eastern box turtles ate grass blades (Graminae), wintergreen (*Gaultheria*) leaves, and sweet cicely (*Osmorhiza*). In Mexico, the aquatic box turtle forages among and bites into the tender stems of both spike rush (*Eleocharis*) and stonewort (*Chara*) (Brown, 1974). Fruits, pads, and flowers of cacti (*Coryphantha*; *Opuntia*) are eaten by box turtles (Thomasson, 1980; Trail, 1995).

In addition to flowering plants and mosses, box turtles eat a variety of fungi when available, including *Amanitopsis vaginata* (Creaser, 1940), *Cyathus striatus* (Legler, 1960), and red *Russula* (Brown, 1992). In Pennsylvania, fungi constituted between 15 percent and 55 percent of the diet of eastern box turtles (Surface, 1908; Strang, 1983); in Kentucky, they comprised 10 percent by volume in the stomachs of ten eastern box turtles (Bush, 1959). Mushrooms may be seasonally available, especially after spring and summer rains. In Maryland, most of Stickel's (1950) forty-three records of box turtles feeding on mushrooms occurred during the first two weeks of July when mushrooms were plentiful. Some species eaten by box turtles are quite poisonous to humans, and there are cases of human poisoning from eating a box turtle (Carr, 1952). Babcock (1919:418) reports that "during the coal miner's strike of 1902, in the vicinity of Scranton, Pennsylvania, many miners roamed over the hills and captured and ate turtles which made them sick. It is probable that these were box turtles, and the flesh may have been rendered temporarily poisonous to man from a diet of toadstools, of which the turtles are very fond and which does not seem to poison them."

Certain other foods may be available seasonally, and box turtles are always ready to take advantage of an abundant food source. Several authors have noted them congregating under fruiting plants, particularly cacti, mulberries, and blackberries (Legler, 1960; Dolbeer, 1969; Metcalf and Metcalf, 1970; Dodd et al., 1994; Trail, 1995), and even under a kite nest (Parker, 1982). Legler (1960) saw twenty ornate box turtles under a fruiting mulberry tree, and afterward began looking specifically under fruiting trees to find turtles. Likewise, I have observed *T. c. bauri* eating half-flower berries, cactus fruits, and sea grapes on Egmont Key. In October when the sea grapes are heavy with fruit, turtles come from various parts of the island to gorge themselves. They may spend several days under or near a fruiting tree, or they may travel back and forth daily between a favored cover site and a fruit-laden tree. On a few memorable occasions, I have seen between forty and fifty turtles under a single tree, all with mouths stained purple (Dodd et al., 1994). Undoubtedly, these long-lived turtles remember the locations of particularly favorable fruiting plants and make an effort to return during fruiting season.

The principal food of box turtles throughout their range consists of invertebrates, primarily earthworms, millipedes, insects (larvae, pupae, and adults), and gastropods (snails and slugs). Invertebrates are found in more than 80 percent of the stomachs of box turtles containing prey (Surface, 1908; Klimstra and Newsome, 1960; Legler, 1960; Stuart and Miller, 1987) and constitute 46–89 percent by volume (Klimstra and Newsome, 1960; Legler, 1960; Brown, 1974; see fig. 7-2). Gastropods in the diet of box turtles include *Heliosoma*, *Succinia*, *Polygyra*, and *Retinella*. Bush (1959) found that snails and slugs comprised 52.5 percent by volume of the diet of ten eastern box turtles in Kentucky. Other specific prey items include robber flies, insect larvae (caterpillars, grubs, maggots), cicadas, crickets, stink bugs and other true bugs, ants, beetles, wood roaches, termites, spiders, dragonfly larvae, sowbugs (e.g., *Armadillidium*), amphipods, ostracods, isopods, and crayfish. Basically, a box turtle will eat anything it can catch. Indeed, the only prey I have seen reported as being rejected was a newly transformed spadefoot toad (*Scaphiopus*), a frog known to be highly distasteful. Because of their invertebrate diet preferences, box turtles should be considered beneficial to have around the garden despite their vegetarian forays.

Prey are sought out by the turtles as they forage and are actively chased. Although not known for their sprinting speed, hungry box turtles can move surprisingly fast. They are quite agile when tracking prey; several anecdotes remark upon the speed at which ornate box turtles chase and snap at insects, particularly grasshoppers (e.g., Ortenburger and Freeman, 1930; Burt and Hoyle, 1934). In addition to surface foraging, box turtles tunnel through the leaf litter in their pursuit of invertebrate prey. I have found box turtles on Egmont Key working their way through a tunnel munching contentedly on cockroaches found in the palm leaf litter. Box turtles must not have any taste buds. There appears to be some degree of regional variation in the types of invertebrates eaten, but this more likely reflects prey availability than active selection for favorite prey types. For example, grasshoppers are a favorite food of the grassland *T. ornata* (Ortenburger and Freeman, 1930; Legler, 1960), whereas cockroaches figure heavily in the diet of Egmont Key *T. c. bauri*. Both insects are extremely abundant in their respective habitats.

Ornate box turtles, in particular, have learned to exploit an important ecological attribute of the Great Plains: dung piles dropped now by cattle but presumably by bison in the distant past (Legler, 1960; Metcalf and Metcalf, 1970; Trail, 1995). Because such piles retain moisture and provide a rich source of nutrients, many invertebrates inhabit the piles and lay eggs there. Box turtles frequently tear open such piles to feed on this ephemeral community, and they detour from their forays to visit dung piles otherwise distant from their path of travel. Even displaced box turtles take time on their homeward journeys to rip through dung piles with their powerful forelegs (chapter 4).

In a drying pool in New Mexico, Norris and Zweifel (1950) observed *T. ornata luteola* foraging for and consuming large numbers of tadpoles of spadefoot toads. These authors thought that box turtles could have significant impacts on local spadefoot reproduction because of the turtles' penchant for sitting in water coupled with their large appetites. Tadpoles confined to puddles or other small water bodies could be at risk in the presence of a predatory turtle. Legler (1960) hypothesized that box turtles probably were able to catch metamorphosing leopard frogs and bullfrogs as they left their natal ponds, although he did not actually observe this occurring. With regard to other vertebrates, R. J. Donahue (in Legler, 1960) saw a box turtle capture and eat a hatchling bobwhite quail, and there is a report of a box turtle eating a house sparrow (Anton, 1990). Box turtles also rarely eat small bird eggs and minnows. However, Brown (1974) noted that *T. coahuila* did not pay much attention to minnows swimming close by as the turtles foraged in shallow water.

Box turtles are quite adept as scavengers. Carrion is commonly reported in the diet, including horned lizards (*Phrynosoma*; Eaton, 1947), a collard lizard (*Crotaphytus*; Norris and Zweifel, 1950), a cottontail rabbit (*Sylvilagus*; Legler, 1960), a roof rat (*Rattus*; Blair, 1976), chickens, ducks, and a cow (Ernst et al., 1994), cichlid fishes (*Cichlosoma*; Brown, 1974), a green heron (*Butorides*; Brown, 1992), a garter snake (*Thamnophis sirtalis*; Kolbe, 1998), a copperhead (*Agkistrodon contortrix*; Jensen, 1999), and even a road-killed *Terrapene* (Norris and Zweifel, 1950). Ornate box turtles frequently dine on small mammals captured in traps (in Legler, 1960; Metcalf and Metcalf, 1970). Woodrats (*Neotoma*) and water snakes (*Nerodia*) also may be scavenged.

Stones (up to 7 mm diameter) and even sandy soil are consumed by *T. ornata* (Legler, 1960; Skorepa, 1966; Kramer, 1973). Legler (1960) reported that stones were found in many stomachs and constituted up to half the stomach contents. Stones presumably aid digestion through assisting maceration or perhaps are eaten for their mineral content. Legler (1960) suggested that stones were picked up merely by accident, but active stone eating seems more likely. It is hard to imagine a box turtle "accidentally" eating a 7 mm stone.

DIET DIFFERENCES BY AGE AND SEX

Data comparing the diets of juveniles and adult males and females are scarce. However, there are no reports of differences between the diets of males and females (e.g., Stuart and Miller, 1987). This seems reasonable since males and females use the same habitats at the same times (chapters 3 and 4). Ernst and Barbour (1972) reported that juveniles were primarily carnivorous and became more herbivorous with age. Two juvenile ornate box turtles did indeed have a wide variety of invertebrates in their stomachs (Legler, 1960). However, juvenile eastern box turtles only had grass fragments in their guts (Surface, 1908), and Stuart and Miller (1987) found no differences between the diets of adult and juvenile eastern box turtles. Given the many accounts of adult box turtle diets, there seems to be no basis for a generalized statement concerning changes in diet as turtles mature. Both adults and juveniles consume what food is available; if differences exist, they likely reflect the presence of seasonally available resources.

DIETS IN CAPTIVITY

There is a great deal of information on what box turtles eat in captivity, both in the popular and in the older scientific literature. Because little is known of the nutritional requirements of any box turtle species, some of what has been written is wrong and much is based on "what works." Box turtles, like all creatures, have individual tastes. If given the opportunity, some eat foods that are not good for them (e.g., hamburger) to their detriment, some eat just about anything, and others do not eat at all. Given this variation, box turtles held in captivity should be fed a wide variety of foods, both animal and vegetable, to mirror as much as possible their diet in the wild. If a box turtle will not feed within a week or so, it should be released as near as possible to where it was found. If it is under medical care, specialized feeding will be required.

Vegetables and fruits should be mixed and of high nutrient content. Excellent choices include tomatoes, bananas, cantaloupes and other melons, berries, prickly pear fruits, grapes, corn, yams, mustard greens, collards, endive, dandelions, and mushrooms. Vegetables in particular can be mixed together in a salad, and rice can be mixed with both plant and animal foods. Spinach, beets, brussels sprouts, cauliflower, kale, and broccoli should be avoided or given sparingly because they contain oxalic acids or bind iodine (Lowe, 1996). Oxalic acids bind calcium and are detrimental to bone and shell development, and iodine is important in thyroid function.

It is readily apparent that box turtles have strong insectivorous and carnivorous dietary preferences. They love insects, earthworms, snails and slugs, and many other types of invertebrates. In addition, they can be fed fish, commercial trout chow, and very lean meat, but not chicken or hamburger. Many keepers supplement their turtles' diets with commercially prepared dog and cat foods. However, these foods may contain too much fat. If using commercial pet foods, always make sure that the dietary content is low in fat. Another thing to avoid is monotonous feeding; that is, a singular food type or the same series of foods, such as mealworms. As an occasional snack, mealworms are fine; by themselves, they are nutrient poor for long-term care. Always avoid overfeeding. I have found that by using a wide variety of animal and vegetable foods, captive box turtles can be kept healthy. Of course, box turtles should never be given foods exposed to pesticides or herbicides.

As a precaution, most keepers recommend using commercially available calcium and vitamin supplements. These can be dusted on plant foods and even on live foods, such as crickets. Supplements should be given once a week for adults and up to three times a week for active growing juveniles.

Feeding Behavior

When a wild box turtle on land approaches a potential stationary food item, such as a piece of fruit, it extends its neck, often with gular pumping, and looks at the item intently. It may then touch the item with its nose and pull back (e.g., Allard, 1949; Webb et al., 1963). Olfaction appears to play some role in prey identification, at least initially, although several experiments have cast doubt on the overall importance of smell in food preference (Allard, 1949; Fitch, 1965). Box turtles have different categories of receptor cells in their olfactory epithelium (Tonosaki, 1993), but whether these are involved with feeding, mate selection, or some other chemosensory function is unknown.

Once food is identified, the turtle uses its fore claws to hold or to tear the item apart, using the right and left forefeet simultaneously or in alternate sequence. The box turtle often extends its neck to get a better angle and turns its head as it eats to get a better grip or mouthful of food. While eating, the turtle seems intent and preoccupied. Of course with no teeth, box turtles bite and tear their food, and then gulp and swallow; they are not known for their finesse. From a human perspective, each time a turtle eats, it looks as if it had been starved for months, so focused is it on the task at hand. And indeed box turtles may go days or weeks without feeding.

Olfaction may play a role in the identification of prey, but sight seems to be the most important sense. Box turtles apparently can see color, since they have many cone cells in the retina, and they seem to have a preference for orange and red (chapter 5). Movement also is important, however, for attracting a turtle's attention. For example, immobile grasshoppers in glass jars (to eliminate scent) were ignored, but as soon as the prey moved or was moved by an experimenter, the turtle showed immediate interest (Fitch, 1965). Given the very small size of some of the prey, such as terrestrial isopods and small adult and larval beetles, box turtles must have good visual discriminatory ability, at least to detect movement. They quickly chase slow-moving animals, biting and snapping as they hold the victim down with the front feet. Even while feeding on fruit or carrion, a box turtle readily snaps at flies and insect larvae found at the food source.

Coahuilan box turtles forage underwater, using their forelimbs to pry apart vegetation; they extend their necks horizontally and search intently among the shallow-water benthos and vegetation for food (Brown, 1974). Underwater foraging is interspersed with occasional breaks to raise their heads above water and survey their surroundings. Terrestrial box turtles often likewise raise their heads as they rest in their forms or as they move about their environment.

If a box turtle found many moving prey simultaneously, it might have difficulty in determining which victim to attack first. One captive eastern box turtle solved the dilemma by biting each mealworm presented, thus rendering them helpless until they could be consumed at leisure (Myers, 1956). Whether such encounters occur in nature and whether wild box turtles use similar methods to manage multiple prey is unknown.

Because they are solitary, most box turtles probably feed alone, thus avoiding intraspecific conflict over food items. However, congregation under fruiting plants at least offers the possibility for competition or conflict. I can find no reported instances of aggressive interactions while feeding under natural circumstances, and I have never seen aggressive interactions among box turtles on Egmont Key as they associated under a bush ripe with sea grapes. In captive circumstances, however, aggressive interactions while feeding are common. These have been documented by Boice (1970) for *T. carolina* and are discussed in chapter 5.

Box Turtles and Seed Dispersal

Because of their vegetarian diet, many turtles are known to disperse seeds of the plants they consume (Rick and Bowman, 1961; Hnatiuk, 1978). Certain rare plants, now on the verge of extinction, even may have depended on abrasion in a tortoise's gut in order to germinate successfully (Iverson, 1987). Whereas most reports refer to seed dispersal by tortoises, Braun and Brooks (1987) found that eastern box turtles are also important agents of seed dispersal. These authors noted that seeds remained in the digestive tract for periods ranging from two days for pokeweed (*Phytolacca*) to twenty days for huckleberry (*Gaylussacia*). During that time, a box turtle can move a considerable distance and thus assist in plant seed dispersal (chapter 4).

In addition to dispersing seeds, passage through a box turtle's digestive tract may increase germination rates, at least for some seeds. For example, seeds of jack-in-the-pul-pit (*Arisaema*), mayapple, pokeweed, black cherry (*Prunus serotina*), and summer grape (*Vitis aestivalis*) ingested by box turtles had a significantly higher rate of germination than seeds that did not pass through turtles (Braun and Brooks, 1987). Mayapples also had a shorter germination time. Many other species were unaffected, and a few even had reduced rates of germination. These authors suggested that seed length might be impor-tant. Since smaller seeds remained in the gut longer, they were more prone to digestive action and thus had decreased germination rates.

Energy Budget

Although the impact that box turtles have on local community ecology is largely unknown, they undoubtedly affect their environment. They eat, maintain a standing-crop biomass, and defecate. In doing so, they are intimately associated with community energy flow and nutrient cycling. Only one study has attempted to document the box turtle's energetic relationship to its environment, and this study remains unpublished (Russo, 1972). The information that follows is derived from this dissertation on *T. carolina* in New Jersey.

When developing a model of energy flow, it is necessary to understand the caloric content of what a turtle eats; how much of the resulting energy is assimilated and used by the turtle for growth, maintenance, and reproduction; and how much energy is returned to the environment when the turtle defecates. The latter includes both unused food and the metabolic by-products of daily life. To determine energy budgets, Russo (1972) fed captive box turtles a diet of meat, the caloric content of which was determined in the lab-oratory. He then determined the caloric content of the feces. Individual differences were noted in both ingestion and defecation, but there was no difference between the sexes in these values. The food took a mean of 11.75 days (SD = 2.4 days) to pass through the digestive system, but the lack of freely available water may have retarded food passage through the gut. Russo (1972) estimated that 72 percent of the protein was assimilated and that most of the solid defecated material constituted lipids. The laboratory analyses showed that the caloric value of the meat diet was 8 kcal/g, whereas an analysis of the caloric value of prey based on stomach contents was only about 5.8 kcal/g.

Determining how the turtles use energy is a little more complicated, but various physiological variables can be measured. A box turtle's energy use can be measured in terms of its respiration, production (measured as calories/gram/day), energy content of its eggs (when present), and urinary output. The last is tricky since box turtles can excrete urea, uric acid, ammonia, or various combinations of these, depending on the amount of water ingested. About 37 percent of the ingested material can be accounted for by meas-uring metabolic waste, egestion, and production, leaving 63 percent accounted for by total respiration. Russo (1972) found that neither size nor sex influenced respiration rate. Further analysis showed that about 44 percent of the ingested food is used for body main-tenance, producing about 2.5 kcal of heat per turtle. This is considered a relatively low rate of heat production, but it is comparable to that of other turtles studied thus far.

At the community level, each box turtle produces about 930 kcal per season, or about 3,783 kcal/ha/summer, given literature reports of density (chapter 8). These values are estimates based on laboratory trials conducted at 25°C, a slightly suboptimal temperature for box turtle activity (chapter 4). Russo (1972) extrapolated his energy budget to suggest that box turtles comprise only about 0.04 percent of the fixed energy within their community and are thus "insignificant" in terms of community energy flow. A more ectothermal perspective might suggest that importance in community dynamics is not necessarily derived from energy consumption alone.

Future Directions

Many of the suggestions that follow relate to the need for better diet information put into the context of the environment in which box turtles are found. This information might be gathered using both field techniques (e.g., stomach flushing) and laboratory experimental procedures (e.g., choice experiments combined with photographic analysis of feeding), or by detailed microhistological analyses of feces. Under no circumstances do I justify killing a box turtle merely to find out what it has eaten at a particular point in its life.

FOOD AVAILABILITY AND DIET PREFERENCE. As we have seen, box turtles are generalist feeders, and there are no apparent diet preferences reported in the literature, at least on a population level. However, little is known concerning the choices available to foraging turtles. It would be interesting to conduct a comprehensive survey of insects and plants available to box turtles on a seasonal basis and to relate the results to actual food choice. In conjunction with such a survey, feeding choice trials could be carried out using wild individuals. Given a choice between invertebrates and fruit, which would a turtle prefer? If fruit is preferred, why do all turtles not congregate under fruiting trees?

FORAGING AT SPECIFIC LOCATIONS. The seasonality and stationary nature of fruiting plants suggests that box turtles could learn the locations of such plants and return at the appropriate season. Although I think this occurs, it has not been demonstrated. In this regard, the presence of transients at certain times of the year can be detected through population models (Langtimm et al., 1996). It seems unlikely that transients show up coincidentally at a time when plants are heavy with fruit. How far will a box turtle travel to reach a seasonally fruiting tree or bush? How would a turtle learn the location of a fruiting tree if the tree were outside the turtle's home range?

FOOD AND THE SENSES. As already indicated in the discussion of the senses, both taste and smell may have bearing on prey choice, once the food is found by sight. Box turtles appear to smell potential food items, but experiments have provided mixed results concerning the influence of smell on actual selection, attention holding, and consumption. As noted in chapter 5, no one has built upon Fitch's (1965) work to explore more fully the sensory cues turtles use in food capture, selection, and consumption.

CHANGES IN FOOD CHOICE. Given the small size of juveniles and the fact that they sometimes are found in greater abundance in some habitats than adults, it seems reasonable that they have different dietary needs and preferences. This has not been demonstrated, however.

ENERGY ALLOCATION. Determination of an energy budget for the eastern box turtle was an important step in understanding its role within its environment. However, further studies are required, both on *T. carolina* and the other species, to corroborate Russo's (1972) results and to compare them with work on turtles in other habitats. An energy budget might shed light on resource allocation and how box turtles partition yearly energy reserves for growth and reproduction in various parts of their range. If the caloric intake varies among regions, this might explain why box turtles deposit different egg clutch sizes in different geographic regions. On the other hand, if caloric intakes are similar, other explanations (e.g., genetics, differences in assimilation rates, metabolic efficiency) would be required to explain variation in reproductive parameters (clutch size and frequency, egg size) and growth rates.

8 | Population Structure and Demography

The dilemma of long-lived species: A general conclusion . . . is that the suite of life-history traits that coevolve with longevity results in populations that are severely limited in their ability to respond to chronic increases in mortality of neonates and even less so to increased mortality of juveniles or adults.

JUSTIN CONGDON, ARTHUR DUNHAM, AND RICHARD VAN LOBEN SELS, 1993

 Describing the home ranges, habitat preferences, foods, morphology and evolutionary history of box turtles is relatively straightforward. Assessing population dynamics is more intricate, requiring treatment of a series of variables and of how these factors change over time, either through the long span of geologic time or in response to ecological conditions, such as changes in habitat structure or predator biology. Life is always in motion, never stagnant.

In the latter part of this chapter, I examine several critical variables in the life history of box turtles—population descriptors, if you will. These variables are always in flux; that is, there is no way to talk about them without putting them into an immediate context. For example, whereas one may cite life history theory to discuss why sex ratios should be of a certain proportion in a box turtle population, there is no such thing as "a box turtle population's sex ratio." Sex ratio is a description of the proportion of males to females within a population *at a particular point in time*; the figures will likely change temporally within a population, will certainly be different across species, and will probably be different even in other populations of the same species. All too often, we forget that finding differences between studies does not necessarily mean one author was "wrong" or used improper techniques. Variation happens!

Techniques do matter, however, perhaps in population biology more than in any other topic covered by this book. Every technique involving counting animals has explicit assumptions that make the use of the technique rigorous and valid or totally unacceptable. Many authors have ignored these assumptions and, as such, some information in the biological literature may be cited often but have questionable validity or applicability. In these days of laptop computers and readily available statistical programs, it is not acceptable to count animals without putting the results into a temporal and spatial framework and without examining the assumptions associated with the models used. Without knowing these factors, estimates of population size, density, sex ratios, biomass, and survivorship are of limited value.

Box Turtle Sizes and Ages

BODY SIZE

The largest living box turtle ever recorded was a *T. c. major* from St. Vincent's Island, Florida, measured at a carapace length of 216 mm (Auffenberg, 1958). If *T. c. putnami* was really an ancient version of *T. c. major*, as some authors have suggested (chapter 2), then this subspecies often reached a size of well over 200 mm CL. The largest known fossil shell is thought to have been nearly 320 mm CL (Auffenberg, 1967; Milstead, 1969). Of the smaller subspecies, there are few records of *T. c. carolina* in excess of 165 mm CL. The maximum size appears to have been attained by a female (198 mm CL, 1,395 g) found in 1970 at Ossining, New York (Cook et al., 1972). Other size records are as follows (from Conant and Collins, 1991, except as indicated): *T. c. bauri* 166 mm CL (Dodd, 1997b); *T. c. triunguis* 179 mm CL; *T. c. yucatana* 159 mm CL (Buskirk, 1993); *T. c. mexicana* 155 mm CL (Smith and Smith, 1979); *T. o. ornata* 154 mm CL; *T. o. luteola* 149 mm CL; *T. coahuila* 168 mm CL (Iverson, 1982a); *T. nelsoni* 151 mm CL (Iverson, 1982b). Additional data on body size are included in individual species accounts.

Members of the Carolina species group of box turtles (*carolina*, *coahuila*) show a definite sexual size dimorphism (SSD): males are on average larger than females and grow to greater maximum sizes (Brown, 1971; Stickel and Bunck, 1989; Ernst et al., 1994; Dodd, 1997b; Pilgrim et al., 1997). In the Ornata species group, females seem to be the larger sex or perhaps the sexes are equal in size (Legler, 1960; St. Clair, 1995), although surprisingly few data are available. However, SSD is dependent on which measure is used—some measure of carapace size (usually carapace or plastron length) as opposed to body mass. The size differences already indicated are based on carapace and plastron lengths. If body mass is used as a measure of body size, SSD is not as apparent. Mean body masses are often similar between adult males and females, and in smaller size classes females may actually outweigh similar-sized males. This is undoubtedly due to the presence of eggs. Smaller females produce eggs, which add to body mass; similar-sized males, of course, do not increase in mass during the reproductive season. Body mass differences might also result from seasonal or even daily variation in feeding and defecation, especially since only a fraction of the female population is gravid at any one time (Dodd, 1997a, 1997b). In Tennessee, eastern box turtles generally attain their greatest weight in late summer (Dolbeer, 1969). On the other hand, no seasonal variation in body mass attributable to sex was observed in a captive colony in South Carolina (Brisbin, 1972).

There have been a number of explanations suggested for the presence of male-biased sexual size dimorphism, among them aggression between courting males, predation avoidance, and increased traveling ability. These explanations do not seem to hold for Florida box turtles because females exhibit aggression, both sexes need to avoid predators, and both sexes wander on occasion. A fourth explanation, mechanical advantage, may be the key. Simply stated, large males have a better chance of successful mating than do small males because the plastron concavity of larger males allows a better fit during copulation. Large males are better able to hold onto a female, to grasp the front margin of her carapace during courtship, and to lean down and stimulate her with his courtship bites. In this regard, female *T. c. bauri* have a greater shell depth than males, regardless of body mass (Dodd, 1997b). Although the greater depth of females probably evolved in response to selection to maximize reproduction (a large body cavity allows greater reproductive effort), it results in the necessity for larger males to effect intromission. Females have greater shell depths than males in other species and subspecies within the Carolina group (Brown, 1971; Stickel and Bunck, 1989; Ernst et al., 1994) and may be responding to similar selection tradeoffs. In species with a less domed and more flattened carapace (e.g., *T. ornata*), perhaps larger size is less important to holding on, and thus females are equivalent in body size to males or slightly larger.

GROWTH

Although it is often said that reptiles have indeterminate growth—that is, that they can continue to grow throughout their life span—this does not appear to occur in *Terrapene*. Box turtles grow rather rapidly during their first years, attaining sexual maturity, at least in Florida, at about five to six years for males and from seven to eight years for females (Dodd, 1997b). Growth then slows considerably until some point at which it nearly stops. On Egmont Key, we have a number of turtles that have been followed for up to eight years but that have not added any measurable increase to their carapace length, and Nichols (1939b) recorded six turtles that showed no appreciable increase in plastron length ten to fifteen years after the first measurement. Whereas the specifics of growth parameters (rates, maximum size, size at sexual maturity) undoubtedly vary considerably among species and geographic regions, the overall growth trajectories probably are similar (Legler, 1960; Blair, 1976; Stickel and Bunck, 1989; Ernst et al., 1998b). Of course, adults still put on weight, which results in turtles of a certain size showing considerable variation in body mass, regardless of sex.

There appears to be some variation between the sexes in growth rates. On Egmont Key where males reach larger sizes than females, they reach maturity a year or two sooner than females (Dodd, 1997b). This may or may not reflect differing growth rates, since males and females probably do not attain maturity at similar carapace lengths. On the other hand, if males reach maturity at smaller carapace lengths, then their growth rates may be considerably faster. This is unusual for species with sexual size dimorphism; usually the smaller sex grows faster and attains sexual maturity sooner than the larger sex. However, we do not know how universal these results might be for *Terrapene*. Until more data are available, generalizations should be advanced with caution.

There are some interesting growth data available for Stickel's Maryland population of *T. c. carolina* gathered from 1944 to 1981 (Stickel and Bunck, 1989). Small turtles were estimated to grow at about 22.8 percent per year in carapace length during the first few years. In the eight- to thirteen-year age classes (based on scute ring counts and direct measurement through the years), males grew at an average rate of 6.7 percent per year in carapace length compared with the female rate of 5.3 percent per year. Older turtles (fourteen to nineteen years) grew more slowly, with males at 2.3 percent per year in carapace length and females at 3.4 percent per year. As turtles aged beyond twenty, growth slowed still further until it became negligible (also reported for *T. c. bauri* by Ernst et al.,

1998b, but using a less precise approach). Somewhat similar results were found in Kansas *T. ornata*; very young turtles grew at a rate of 17.5 percent per year in plastron length, a rate that slowed as the teen years approached. Older turtles had considerably slower growth until their twenties, when growth effectively ceased (Legler, 1960).

These rates seem reasonable. Both sexes of *Terrapene* grow rapidly when young, but as maturity approaches, males grow more rapidly in *T. carolina*, whereupon growth slows and energy can be allocated toward reproduction. Females grow somewhat faster in their late teens, presumably to reach as large a size as possible prior to the onset of reproductive maturity. Once the animals are fully mature, growth slows in both sexes, and ingested energy can be allocated toward reproduction. In *T. ornata*, growth is rapid during the early years, but growth trajectories are probably more similar between the sexes until sexual maturity is reached. As with eastern box turtles, older turtles probably grow little if at all. In neither species is subsequent growth rate dependent on environmental conditions during embryonic development (St. Clair, 1995).

LONGEVITY

Turtles are among the longest-lived of vertebrates (Gibbons, 1987), but a few provisos are in order. Turtle longevity is difficult to measure because the life span of a turtle may equal or exceed that of the human observer. Many reports of chelonian longevity come from animals held in captivity and, as such, are biased by that captivity. Long-term captive animals are usually well fed, may have had access to health care, and are normally not subject to predation or to environmental disasters. That an animal can live a long time in captivity does not mean it does so in nature.

Still, there are many reports of wild box turtles living to great age. Some people simply cannot resist the urge to carve initials and dates into the shell. Turtles with old dates have been found in many locations; often such finds are duly reported in newspaper accounts, and while some are surely hoaxes (such as one marked "G. W. 1776"), it seems unlikely that all would be. One box turtle from Rhode Island, with the dates 1844 and 1860 and two sets of initials on its plastron, was thought to have been at least 138 years old (Graham and Hutchison, 1969). Although a few *Terrapene* of exceptional longevity have been found in the northeastern United States, most "dated" turtles are younger. The following are some examples: a turtle found in 1826 (or 1827?) in Newton, Pennsylvania, with the date 1761 carved in its shell (Harlan, 1827); a very old turtle found in 1926 on Long Island, New York, with the date 1878 carved in its shell (Townsend, 1926); another turtle found on Long Island in 1926 that carried the date 1884 (Nichols, 1939b); a box turtle found repeatedly from at least 1932 to 1951 in Ohio County, Kentucky, with the date 1887 carved into it (Edney and Allen, 1951); a turtle bearing the date 1905 carved into its shell found in 1951 in Erie County, Ohio (Price, 1951); a three-toed box turtle found in Fayetteville, Arkansas, in 1959 with the date 1923 carved into it (James, 1961); an eastern box turtle from Friendsville, Tennessee, found in 1988 with the date 1941 (Avent, 1988). Assuming such turtles were marked as adults, ages of more than fifty years seem readily attainable by box turtles.

Biologists use three methods to age turtles: recapture of individuals marked at a known point in time, counting scute rings, or using skeletochronology of the long bones. Long-term studies involving marked individuals seem to bear out the anecdotal accounts above. Of the 366 turtles originally marked by Elizabeth and Charles Schwartz in Missouri in 1965, twenty-two persisted at least until 1989 (Schwartz and Schwartz, 1991). Hall and colleagues (1999) captured seven *T. carolina* in 1995 originally marked by Lucille Stickel in the 1940s at the Patuxent Wildlife Research Center in Laurel, Maryland. Stickel (1978) reported that 15 percent of the adult males and 11 percent of the adult females marked in 1945 were still present in 1975. Likewise, many turtles initially marked in 1958 by E. C. Williams in Indiana were resident in the population in 1983 (Williams and Parker, 1987). Williams and Parker (1987) noted that a turtle with the date 1911 carved on its carapace was still present in the population in the 1970s. Ornate box turtles also live well into their twenties and thirties (Legler, 1960). Blair (1976) and Metcalf and Metcalf (1985) record *T. ornata* from twenty-eight to at least thirty-two years old.

A method frequently used to age turtles involves counting the rings on the scutes of the carapace or plastron. It has often been assumed that one ring is added during each growing season, much the same as tree rings are added each spring and summer. Indeed, these scute (or laminar) rings have sometimes been called annuli or annular rings, reflecting this idea. By carefully counting the rings at first capture, then recounting the rings in subsequent captures, a partial age might be estimated. However, recent research has shed doubt on the reliability of the technique (reviewed by Germano and Bury, 1998); even some early box turtle researchers noted that the number of rings did not necessarily reflect the exact age (Nichols, 1939b). For some individual turtles, the technique works well; for others, rings may or may not be added in direct relationship with the number of years between captures. In addition, wear that invariably accompanies aging makes it nearly impossible to count more than twenty rings. Thus, some age estimates using scute rings undoubtedly are in error, some are accurate, and others can be used only to gauge relative age.

A third method of aging turtles, termed skeletochronology, is to count the number of rings in the long bones of the limbs, especially the humerus (Zug, 1991). At least with the bones, wear should not be a problem, although bone resorption may obscure direct correlations. As with scute rings, however, there is the problem of verifying that ring number correlates with actual age. Of course, the turtle would have to be dead. No one has yet attempted to use skeletochronology to estimate the age of box turtles.

So how long do box turtles live in the wild? Most box turtles probably follow a survivorship curve similar to that of other long-lived turtles (Gibbons, 1987; Congdon et al., 1993, 1994). Once maturity is attained, it seems as though the probability of mortality does not increase with age. A few turtles are lucky enough to live long lives, whereas the majority live fifty years or less. An elderly box turtle lives sixty or more years. As with humans, box turtles with ages approaching or exceeding one hundred years are probably not especially unusual and, as Graham and Hutchison (1969) note, a few may attain great age.

Population Structure

SIZE-CLASS STRUCTURE

Literature reports on the size-class structure of turtle populations tend to favor adults. This may be due to the scarcity of juveniles in a population or perhaps to the difficulty investigators have had in finding juveniles. There is little doubt that juvenile box turtles are difficult to find, but in some populations, they are truly scarce (Pilgrim et al., 1997). An example of a population size-class structure for Florida box turtles is presented in figure 8-1. In this population (from Egmont Key), the number of turtles in various size classes gradually increases from hatching (~27 mm CL) to about 120 mm CL (size at maturity), and most of the population is in the 130–150 mm CL adult size classes. Very large turtles make up a very small percentage of the population. Thus there tends to be a curve with a skewed distribution, a moderate tail to the curve (representing juveniles and subadults), and a sharp drop-off (representing very large turtles). A nearly identical size-class histogram was presented by Legler (1960) for his population of *T. o. ornata* in Kansas, and a somewhat similar size-class structure was shown by Brown (1974) for *T. coahuila*. In Brown's study, there were few small turtles; both males and females were most common in the small to medium adult size classes; and the numbers of large females declined abruptly whereas the number of large males tapered off more gradually.

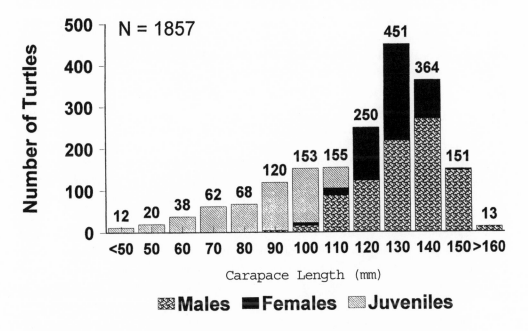

Figure 8-1. Population size-class structure of Florida box turtles on Egmont Key, Hillsborough County, Florida. Data collected from 1991 to 1998. N = 1,857 turtles.

AGE-CLASS STRUCTURE

Little information is available on the age-class structure of box turtle populations because it is difficult to determine the age of adult turtles accurately. Both very small (presumably young) and very large (presumably old) turtles make up a small percentage of most populations.

Few good age-structure data presently available reflect the variable proportion of juveniles within a population, although sampling biases in some cases may obscure the value of the results. Small box turtles, after all, are difficult to find in almost all areas. For example, juveniles made up 25 percent of the population of *T. c. bauri* on Egmont Key. Slightly smaller percentages have been reported for a few other well-studied box turtle populations: 19.4 percent in New York *T. c. carolina* (Nichols, 1939b), 18–25 percent in Missouri *T. c. triunguis* (Schwartz and Schwartz, 1974), and 15.4 percent for *T. ornata* in Kansas (Legler, 1960). These percentages are much greater than the less than 10 percent reported by Stickel (1950) for her Maryland *T. c. carolina* and the less than 4 percent reported by Pilgrim et al. (1997) for *T. c. bauri* in central Florida. Not surprisingly, such percentages may change through time. In a long-term study in Maryland, the proportion of juveniles (5–10 lamellar rings) changed dramatically: from 4.2 percent in 1945 to 6.2 percent in 1955, 4.8 percent in 1965, and 15.7 percent in 1995 (Hall et al., 1999). Fewer adults in the population in 1995 may reflect the lingering effects of a catastrophic flood in 1972, which was thought to have wiped out much of the population. The Maryland population is still rebuilding, even twenty-three years after a catastrophic decline.

SEX RATIOS

For most iteroparous species (i.e., those with overlapping generations) with genotypic sex determination (see glossary), a sex ratio of one male to one female (1:1) would seem to be the norm. The reason for this is simple: if sex ratios were skewed toward one sex, the rarer sex would become more valuable and selection should favor its increase, all other things—survivorship, growth, longevity, etc.—being equal. As with much in biology, however, all things are not equal, and certainly not for turtles. Random environmentally induced fluctuations in population size, random demographic events, isolation, and differential mortality all may alter the expected 1:1 balance, at least on a short-term basis. In addition, temperature-dependent sex determination may alter hatchling sex ratios from one year to the next as a result of different ambient nest incubation temperatures (chapter 6). Thus, the sex ratio tends to fluctuate around 1:1 through time for some turtle populations, although at any particular moment it may be quite different from 1:1.

The best long-term data sets on the sex ratios of *T. carolina* are those of Lucille Stickel in Maryland and for the Florida box turtles of Egmont Key. In Stickel's population, the sex ratio has been variously reported as male-biased (Stickel, 1989; Hall et al., 1999) or nearly equal (Stickel, 1950, 1989), depending on the year sampled. Population declines from 1945 to 1995 were accompanied by an imbalanced male-biased sex ratio. On Egmont Key from 1991 to 1995 (eighteen collecting trips), the sex ratio was always 1.6 males:1 female, regardless of year, month, or sampling season (Dodd, 1997b). Several studies have reported male-biased sex ratios in wild populations (Nichols, 1939b; Dolbeer, 1969; Schwartz and Schwartz, 1974; Strass et al., 1982), whereas others have reported nearly 1:1 or slightly skewed female-biased ratios (Williams and Parker, 1987; Pilgrim et al., 1997). Likewise, female-biased sex ratios have been reported for *T. ornata* in Kansas (1:1.7; Legler, 1960) and Wisconsin (1:1.6; Doroff and Keith, 1990) and for *T. coahuila* (1:1.3; Brown, 1974). In some populations the sex ratio appears to shift from male-biased to equality or female-biased from one year to the next. The shift can be of such a magnitude as to cause occasional statistically significant deviations from 1:1, although long-term deviations are not statistically significant (Williams and Parker, 1987).

Variation in reports of sex ratios may reflect biases in sampling design or scale, or they may represent true long-term population sex ratios. If the sampling regime is such that the probability of capture of one sex exceeds the probability of capture of the other (for example, sampling when males are more likely to be active than females), then the results will not mirror the true population structure. Likewise, the results of studies conducted on populations for only a few years might be rather different than if studies covered a much longer period or if a single population were sampled many years apart. Short-term shifts may occur in the sex ratio, and the sex ratio of a population would shift through time. This is why there is no such thing as a "true" sex ratio for a species; sex ratio is a demographic character reflecting a particular set of conditions at a particular point in time, even assuming unbiased data collection.

What *is* known is that the temperature of incubation influences the sex ratio of the hatchlings. Biased sex ratios in an adult population could reflect variation in the thermal regimes of nest sites. If only cool areas were available to nesting females (for example, as a result of shading of most of the available nest sites), then a male-biased adult sex ratio might result if survivorship of the sexes were equal through development to sexual maturity—a big if. On Egmont Key, most of the available nesting sites, until recently, were in the shaded interior of the island, which should have lower temperatures at egg depth than at the more exposed, but fewer, sunny sites. Differential temperatures of nesting sites could result in the biased adult sex ratios we observe on Egmont, especially since capture and survival probabilities are not significantly different for males than for females. Certainly, other explanations are possible. It should be evident, however, that the determination of sex ratio is far more complicated than simply counting the number of males and females.

POPULATION SIZE AND DENSITY

Estimation of population size is as much art as it is science. Most methods involve marking a number of animals, then recapturing them weeks, months, years, or even decades from the date of original marking. Sampling animals at regular intervals and recording the number of animals marked in relation to the number of animals unmarked is termed a "mark-recapture" study. Mathematical models can be used to estimate population size based on the capture history of individuals through time. If enough data can be gathered, mathematical models can also be used to estimate population parameters, such as recruitment, population growth rate, and survivorship (Lebreton et al., 1992; Pradel, 1996).

The size of a population is usually given for a prescribed sampling area (e.g., the number of box turtles in a state park), although "population" is often undefined. More useful perhaps is knowing the density of individuals within a prescribed area; that is, how many box turtles there are within a state park of a certain number of hectares. As with sex ratio determination, estimating population size or density is a much more complicated matter than simply counting individuals. Sampling considerations are paramount: Are there differences in capture probabilities between males, females, and juveniles? Does behavior change daily, seasonally, or annually, which might in turn affect capture? Can animals be marked reliably for future recognition? Do transients occur in a population? What are the rates of mortality and natality? Answers to these questions determine which population models can be used, which in turn affects the accuracy of the estimate (Langtimm et al., 1996; Thompson et al., 1998). Until recently, the statistical procedures necessary to determine many population parameters were too difficult to carry out easily. Computer technology and the introduction of innovative software, such as the program "MARK" developed by Gary White of Colorado State University, have changed all that.

For our studies on Egmont Key, we have been able to estimate many important population parameters. Using the Jolley-Seber open population model, we first tested for the accuracy of the mark-recapture model assumptions using goodness-of-fit procedures. The best model estimator suggested that Egmont's box turtles have rather constant survival probabilities but that capture probabilities are variable. Further, males and females had an equal probability of capture, but juveniles were less likely to be captured than adults. Thus, our estimate of adult population size was more accurate than our estimate of total population size. The overall estimate of 544 adult box turtles on the southern 36.4 ha of Egmont Key (95 percent confidence range of 415–672 adults) is statistically quite rigorous, with a low coefficient of variation (Langtimm et al., 1996). This translated to a crude estimate of 14.9 adults per hectare. The estimate was crude because it assumed that the turtles used all habitats within this area equally, which we know is not the case (Dodd et al., 1994).

Other studies in which population size or density have been reported either did not have access to or have not used the statistical tests needed to validate their estimates. Still, some of these estimates have been remarkably similar to our estimates for Egmont Key. Density values as reported in the literature are as follows: *T. c. carolina* in Indiana 4.4–5.7/ha in 1960–67; 3.7/ha in 1970; 2.7/ha in 1983 (Williams and Parker, 1987); *T. c. carolina* in Maryland 9.9–12.4/ha (Stickel, 1950); *T. c. carolina* in Tennessee 18.8–22.7/ha (Dolbeer, 1969); *T. c. triunguis* in Missouri 18.4–26.9/ha (Schwartz et al., 1984); *T. c. bauri* in central Florida 16.3/ha (Pilgrim et al., 1997); *T. ornata* in Kansas up to 13.9/ha (Legler, 1960). These values represent box turtle populations in a range of habitats, from hardwood hammocks in Florida to Kansas prairies.

Unfortunately, we have no idea how representative the estimates given above might be, either for undisturbed populations or for populations affected by many generations of human-induced disturbances. There are reports in the literature of huge numbers of box turtles found within certain habitats, particularly in Florida, Georgia, and the prairies of the American Midwest (Cragin, 1885; Ortenburger and Freeman, 1930; Neill, 1948a;

Carr, 1952). These vast populations may represent an important biological phenomenon that passed away almost unnoticed when it had scarcely yet been recognized. Perhaps it still exists in some protected areas.

On Egmont Key, we are finding large numbers of adult unmarked box turtles even after eight years of intensive survey (fig. 8-2). Because Egmont Key is a spatially enclosed population, we constantly speculate on how many turtles are really there. Given that one of the most important assumptions of mark-recapture studies is that animals must be marked in such a manner as to be unmistakably recognized upon recapture, and that turtles do not regenerate shell so as to hide our carapace marks, why are so many turtles unmarked after such a long sampling time? Either box turtle population sizes can be truly immense, or perhaps there is a cleverer explanation (fig. 8-3)!

BIOMASS

Data on standing crop biomass (the total weight of all the target organisms in a population at a given time) may be an important factor in helping biologists understand the role animals play in overall community ecology, including energy flow and ecosystem productivity (Congdon and Gibbons, 1989; Dodd, 1998). It provides an index of how much energy is tied up in turtles and how turtles help move that energy through the community. Data on biomass, in conjunction with other ecological data, help put box turtles into a community context in order to answer the question: Why are they important? For

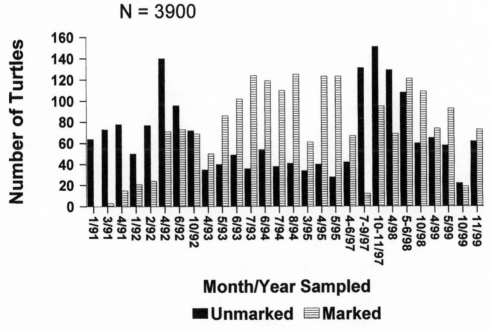

Figure 8-2. Relationship between the numbers of unmarked and marked Florida box turtles found on three- to five-day collecting trips to Egmont Key, Hillsborough County, Florida, from 1991 to 1998. N = 3,900 captures.

The _Real_ Reason there are so many unmarked box turtles on Egmont Key!

Figure 8-3. Suspicions confirmed . . .

example, if box turtles are a major factor in energy flow and nutrient cycling, then a reduction in population size may have significant impacts for the overall community. For this reason, biomass may be a more important population parameter in some contexts than number of animals alone.

Whereas a large number of researchers have reported data on individual mass, or weight, of box turtles, these data are not often put into a population context. Accurate measurements of total biomass based on rigorous population estimates, data on population structure, and direct measures of individual body mass are rare (Iverson, 1982c; Dodd, 1998). The reason for this is not hard to understand. Biomass estimates are difficult to obtain because they require a great deal of accurate data on sometimes complicated population parameters. They are subject to error as a result of differential susceptibility of animals to capture and of variation in movement, activity patterns, and habitat use, even among age classes and between seasons and years. Indeed, the biases influencing population estimates are the same ones that may result in incorrect estimates of biomass.

Data collected through the years on Egmont Key lend themselves well to obtaining a reasonable estimate of standing crop biomass for Florida box turtles, at least on that island. Inasmuch as data were available on population size, sex ratio, the percentage of juveniles, and individual body mass over a relatively long time, it was possible to derive a biomass estimate of from 5 to 8 kg of box turtles per ha (Dodd, 1998). These results approach or surpass Iverson's (1982c) estimates for mainland *T. carolina* and *T. ornata*.

Given the similarity among several population density estimates (in Langtimm et al., 1996; Pilgrim et al., 1997), it might seem that a range of from 5 to 8 kg/ha would be reasonable, at least for *T. carolina*. However, similar density estimates could involve differently sized adults in populations structured quite differently. For example, both Langtimm et al. (1996) and Pilgrim et al. (1997) arrived at similar density estimates for *T. carolina bauri*, but the differences in size-   and age-class structure between populations suggest differences in biomass, which in turn might reflect differences in the relative importance of this species within the respective communities.

Since Egmont's terrestrial box turtles occupy an environment that is physically rather harsh, they may play a more important role in this ecosystem than an equivalent biomass of turtles would in a freshwater ecosystem. However, these data must be used with caution since other box turtle habitats may be more productive than on this xeric island, and particularly since Egmont Key is relatively predator free. Population and individual parameters also may vary considerably, and it is by no means clear how universal an estimate of from 5 to 8 kg/ha may be among box turtle populations. Still, it is about the only good estimate available and provides other researchers with a value for comparison.

Demography

NATALITY AND MORTALITY

Natality is simply the number of new turtles born into a population within a year, and mortality is the number dying. Females may or may not produce successful clutches each year, this being affected by both physiological processes (mating, oogenesis) and ecological factors (sufficient nutrients, predation). There are no good data available on box turtle natality at the population level. In terms of mortality, Williams and Parker (1987) estimated that males were lost at a rate of 6.6 percent per year and that females were lost at a rate of 6.8 percent per year (for *T. c. carolina* in Indiana). As with natality, mortality rates probably vary depending on a host of ecological considerations, particularly catastrophic disasters, disease, food availability, environmental conditions, and, above all these days, human-caused factors.

SURVIVORSHIP

Survivorship is related to longevity, but the two are very different demographic parameters. Survivorship is simply the mathematical probability that an animal will survive from one sampling period, whether that be a week or year, to the next; most figures on survivorship refer to annual survivorship. There are many possible survivorship scenarios in a box turtle population and, as with other demographic variables, there is every reason to suspect that survivorship rates are different among populations. For example, survivorship rates may be low at hatching and increase through life at a constant rate. Or they may be constant throughout life. Or they may be high at birth, increase through early adulthood, and decrease dramatically in old age. Biologists are able to compute a survivorship curve from each of a series of survival probabilities through life (which may be age dependent), thus deriving a life table. A life table is simply an actuary table; indeed the concept was derived from the need of insurance companies to know the probability of survivorship for human clients of various ages so that they could compute premiums.

Generally for turtles, young animals are presumed to have high mortality and thus low rates of survivorship; survivorship likely increases at some unknown rate as they grow older. At some point, the probability of dying decreases substantially or even becomes negligible, and the probability of surviving from one year to the next becomes quite high. However, no life tables have yet been derived for box turtles, so annual rates of survivorship have not been computed. It is likely that box turtles have a rather constant survivorship once they reach adulthood, much as other turtles do (Gibbons, 1987). That is, an adult box turtle has the same probability of surviving from one year to next in a stable population, regardless of its initial age. Although there are no estimates of annual survivorship for any box turtle population, weekly survivorship between April 1991 and June 1993 on Egmont Key ranged between 93.7 and 100 percent (Langtimm et al., 1996).

POPULATION CHANGES THROUGH TIME

There is every reason to believe that the numbers of box turtles within a population should fluctuate somewhat from one period to the next. Many factors influence population size, so it is not surprising to observe changes in populations. On the other hand, the longevity and high adult survivorship, coupled with a rather sedentary lifestyle, certainly suggest the potential for a high degree of population stability. Until more long-term data are assembled on a greater number of populations, observed population trends may be difficult to put into context. At the same time, it would be unwise to dismiss inferences of population declines based on historical but anecdotal observations.

There have been a number of long-term studies conducted on box turtle populations. Three of these have been on *T. c. carolina*—on Long Island in New York (1915–present), in Allee Memorial Woods in Indiana (1958–83), and at the Patuxent Wildlife Research Center in Maryland (1944–present)—and the fourth was on *T. c. triunguis* in central Missouri (1965–83). Partial results from the Long Island study were published in 1939 (Nichols, 1939a, 1939b), but these did not include population trends. Unfortunately, no other results are available from this study, although data on the population are continuing to be gathered (Lipske, 1989). All of the remaining populations showed declines during the period of observation (Schwartz et al., 1984; Williams and Parker, 1987; Stickel, 1978; Hall et al., 1999) despite their occurrence on protected lands.

In Missouri and Indiana, long-term changes appeared associated with changing vegetation structure and/or changes in adjacent land use. In Maryland, the population decline was thought to be the result of human-exacerbated floods that occurred in 1972. As of 1995, this population still had not recovered to preflood levels despite its location on a large protected reserve (Hall et al., 1999). Follow-up studies planned for the Missouri population should lend insight into the long-term trends shown by this population. On Egmont Key, Florida, studies conducted between 1991 and 1998 show no discernible trends. Turtles disappearing from the western side of the island may be casualties of the tremendous amount of beach erosion occurring on that side of the island; this does not indicate an overall population decline.

Future Directions

There are two main considerations when collecting data and interpreting the results on the population and demographic topics reported in the second part of this chapter.

SAMPLING CONSIDERATIONS. All population data must be taken in as unbiased a manner as possible. If biases are present (e.g., seasonal, temporal, or sexual differences in capture probabilities), they should be acknowledged and considered during interpretation. If biases are not known, research should be directed at determining what they might be. Limitations on data collection will always be present, and data collected under less than optimal conditions will be the norm rather than the exception. Yet such data are not worthless; indeed, they may be quite valuable in lending insight into biological populations. Biologists need to plan field research carefully in order to avoid problems resulting from sampling biases that might arise during the interpretation of their results.

LONG-TERM STUDIES. There is a critical need for long-term studies on these long-lived chelonians. As I have pointed out, "long-term studies of long-lived chelonians are vital to ensure that slow processes, rare events or episodic phenomena, processes with a high degree of variability, and subtle and complex processes are fully appreciated and understood" (Dodd, 1997b:1505). Studies carried out over a short period are like snapshots. While giving a glimpse of the present, they do not provide an understanding of the processes that shaped the present. It is hard to imagine a more suitable animal than *Terrapene* for long-term biological studies.

In the world of box turtles, the long-term studies at Patuxent Wildlife Research Center, Egmont Key, the Nichols estate on Long Island, Allee Memorial Woods in Indiana, and on the Schwartz farm in Missouri all hold great potential. Some of these studies are ongoing, and follow-up studies are planned, at least in Missouri. Results of such studies need to be disseminated. In addition, follow-up surveys and research would be desirable on some populations studied long ago, such as at Dolbeer's study site in Tennessee, Legler's site in Kansas, and at Cuatro Ciénegas. More recent studies, such as Terry Farrell and Peter May's work at Lake Woodruff in Florida, need to be continued. Public lands offer the ideal location for long-term studies. Federal and state parks and wildlife refuges should be encouraged to support long-term studies on box turtles.

BODY SIZE AND SIZE-CLASS STRUCTURE. Biologists know little about such basic information as body size and size-class structure in the Mexican species and subspecies of *Terrapene* or, for that matter, *T. ornata*. Fruitful research could be directed at understanding the interrelated roles of growth, genetics, geographic variation, and resource availability in the evolution of sexual size dimorphism. Are larger males really at a mechanical advantage during mating, or can a more parsimonious explanation for SSD be advanced?

GROWTH. A particular problem with growth data in the literature is that results may be biased by the way turtles were sampled (e.g., road-cruising, St. Clair, 1995; museum specimens collected from a large geographic area, Ernst et al., 1998b). Biased sampling diminishes the value of the data. In addition, a few authors have used unquestioningly the assumptions that one growth ring equals one year of life or that box turtles mature at a uniform or equivalent size. Again, these assumptions, if incorrect, diminish the value of the conclusions derived. More good data are needed on known-age animals from long-term studies, such as those of Stickel and Bunck (1989), before generalizations can be drawn about the universality of growth curves.

AGE-CLASS STRUCTURE. In effect, nothing is known concerning the age structure of box turtle populations. Aging techniques, such as scute counts, need to be verified on known-age animals, and skeletochronology should be tried. Are juveniles naturally rare in populations, or is juvenile rarity an artifact of collecting technique? Might the scarcity of juveniles in some populations result from the overabundance of certain predators, such as raccoons?

SEX RATIOS. Although a good deal of information is available on box turtle sex ratios, much of it was gathered over short periods and on populations in which age at maturity was assumed or approximated. Long-term data are needed on marked populations. In addition, it might be interesting to know the sex ratios of hatchlings and juveniles to determine whether differential survivorship exists between the sexes and, if so, at what age. Advanced sex determination techniques using various hormone titres are now available. In addition, the underlying mechanisms for imbalanced sex ratios in well-studied populations need investigation.

NUMBER AND BIOMASS OF TURTLES. Better estimation of population size, density, and biomass should now be possible using advanced computer programs. Again, long-term data collected using a sampling regime as unbiased as possible should lend insight into what the range of "normal" population density might be. It should be possible to assess whether populations are unusually large (as some biologists claim for island populations) or small (e.g., from human disturbance). I have always been intrigued by the huge population densities (and biomass) we see for terrestrial turtles in some parts of the world (e.g., giant land tortoises or even gopher tortoises). Might not huge population sizes be the norm for terrestrial box turtles if they were left undisturbed by humans and our development?

As an additional consideration, biologists must ensure that the assumptions of the statistical tests and population models we use are met. It behooves us to avoid scenarios in which the assumptions of statistical tests, especially those used to estimate population size, are either assumed to be met or are ignored. With the new computer techniques available, all capture assumptions need to be tested.

SURVIVORSHIP. A life table now seems possible for several well-studied populations.

GENETIC POPULATION STRUCTURE. The genetic structure has not been determined for any box turtle population. It might prove interesting to examine the relatedness among local residents of this very sedentary creature. Perhaps many aspects of box turtle behavior and activity would be better understood once the genetic relatedness of local populations was known. Knowledge of population genetics could aid in understanding population expansion and the colonization of islands by box turtles; did they colonize islands naturally or were they transported by humans? Further, it would aid in conservation programs, such as in relocation and repatriation of individuals out of harm's way or to augment depleted populations. The lack of information on the genetics of local populations seems an obvious and inexplicable oversight.

MEXICAN TAXA. With the exception of *T. coahuila*, data on the population biology of all Mexican taxa are lacking. Gathering such data would seem to be a most interesting area of future research.

9 | Predators, Parasites, and Disease

> Box turtles deserve a place in the turtle hall of fame as having perfected the ability to protect their vulnerable parts by sealing these within the shell.
>
> CLIFFORD POPE, 1939

As with all living creatures, box turtles are subject to predation, parasites, and diseases. The literature, however, offers few clues as to how these variables affect populations or whether they have significant impact. This chapter examines the ways in which predation, parasitism, and disease may influence box turtles, and I also include a few other topics that come under the general category of health.

Predation

The most prominent feature of box turtles, and indeed the morphological characteristic that gives them their common name, is their shell. Unlike most species of turtles, the carapace of adult box turtles consists of fused or nearly fused neural, costal, and peripheral bones; overlapping scutes provide additional strength and protection, much as shingles do on a roof. Therefore, the places where these bones contact one another, the sutures, are not weak points as they are in some of the water turtles, such as sliders (*Trachemys*) and cooters (*Pseudemys*). A predator may pick up a box turtle and try to break the shell, but it would take a massive amount of force to crush the arched dome of an adult's shell.

The hinged plastron affords protection from an underside attack. The forepart of the plastron consists of the epiplastral and hyoplastral bones (chapter 1). These bones are fused and joined to the posterior part of the plastron by a flexible hinge. The posterior part of the plastron consists of the fused hypoplastron and xiphiplastron (fig. 1-3b). Together, the fore and posterior plastron elements form a nearly impenetrable shield that fits tightly against the carapace. In many box turtles, it is impossible to fit even a fingernail between the plastron and carapace; in others, however, a small gap may be evident due to prolonged wear, abrasion, or simply a difference in shape. Excessive body mass also prevents a few overweight turtles from completely closing the shell.

Unlike in adults, the shells of juvenile box turtles are not nearly as strongly ossified, which makes them vulnerable to predators. The shells of hatchlings are soft and quite flexible. Because hatchlings are so small (less than 30 mm CL), they are in danger from even the smallest predators, such as shrews (Harding, 1997). A hatchling is simply a quick bite for a larger predator, and some predators, such as snakes (e.g., the copperhead, *Agkistrodon contortrix*; Legler, 1960), may swallow hatchlings whole. Calcification occurs rapidly as the turtle grows, but even then juveniles remain vulnerable because of their small size and incomplete calcification of the shell. Juvenile shells have many openings in the developing carapace as bone growth occurs, giving their skeletal structure a spidery appearance. Although overlapping scutes cover these openings (or fenestrae), the shell is not solid enough to deter predators until the turtle is several years old. Based on morphology (rather than on empirical data), the hatchling and juvenile stages are thought to be the most vulnerable life stages after hatching.

Perhaps the most vulnerable life history stage of all for a box turtle is its time in the egg. Box turtles do not have any form of nest defense, and the nest is concealed only as well as the nearby materials and the experience of the female allow. The hazards for developing eggs are greatest shortly after deposition, when a disturbed area or strong egg or female scent can lead predators to the nest. Many, if not most, turtle nests are destroyed within twenty-four hours of laying, but little is known concerning predation rates on box turtle nests. However, the nest is vulnerable throughout the two months or longer that the eggs are in the ground. Even within a nest or during nesting, eggs may be eaten by burrowing snakes (e.g., scarlet snakes, *Cemophora coccinea*; hognose snakes, *Heterodon*, and kingsnakes, *Lampropeltis*, Ernst et al., 1994; bullsnakes, *Pituophis melanoleucus*, in Legler, 1960; black rat snakes, *Elaphe obsoleta*, Palmer and Braswell, 1995) or by ants or other invertebrates. Whether invertebrates actually break through the eggshell or take advantage of breaks caused by other predators or because of mechanical factors, such as invading tree roots, is unknown.

After hatching, baby turtles are vulnerable to all forms of predators. Even if they escape detection by larger animals, the fluids associated with the egg likely attract ants, especially fire ants (*Solenopsis invicta*). These voracious nonindigenous predators of the southeastern United States have undoubtedly caused severe declines in ground-nesting reptiles and many other species (Allen et al., 1994). Both adult and juvenile box turtles have been killed by fire ants (e.g., in Mount, 1981; Montgomery, 1996), but there are no data on long-term impacts.

Very small box turtles are quite adept at concealment, as all field biologists who have tried to find them know. Larger box turtles also rely on cryptic coloration to blend into their environment as a defense against predators. In particular, the striped shells of *T. c. bauri* and *T. ornata* make them extremely difficult to see in grassy habitats common to the savannas of peninsular Florida and the arid North American Midwest and Southwest, respectively. *Terrapene coahuila* also blend into the background of their aquatic habitat (Brown, 1974). Hatchling box turtles are reported to have a malodorous scent much like that of the musk turtles (*Sternotherus* sp.) (Neill, 1948b). Although many biologists have assumed that the scent has a predator-deterring function (e.g., Norris and Zweifel, 1950), this has not been demonstrated. For example, Kool (1981) could not demonstrate a defensive basis for the musky scent of the Australian turtle *Chelodina longicollis*. Musky scents may serve social functions as well as or in place of deterring predators.

In addition to the shell and concealment, box turtles sometimes defend themselves by biting (based on personal experience, an unpleasant event!) and by exuding a foul-smelling urine (Norris and Zweifel, 1950) and fecal matter. These behaviors, while unpleasant to humans, are unlikely to thwart a determined predator and certainly are of little help to juveniles. Box turtles also may attempt to "run" or to dive into concealment (*T. coahuila*; Brown, 1974). Ornate box turtles are more likely to run and bite than eastern box turtles (Smith, 1961), but there is a great deal of variation in individual temperament.

The most common predators of box turtles are likely small to medium-sized carnivorous mammals and predatory birds. Mammals often mentioned in the literature include raccoons (*Procyon lotor*), skunks (*Mephitis mephitis, Spilogale*), minks (*Mustela vison*), dogs and coyotes (*Canis* spp.), and rodents (*Rattus* spp.; Allard, 1949), although badgers (*Taxidea*), opossums (*Didelphis*), foxes (*Vulpes, Urocyon*), armadillos (*Dasypus*), coatis (*Nasuta*), weasels (*Mustela*), and other species are likely to eat box turtles if they can (Ernst et al., 1994). Avian predators include crows (*Corvus brachyrhynchos*; Legler, 1960), ravens (*C. cryptoleucus*; Legler, 1960), vultures (*Cathartes*), Mississippi kites (*Ictinia*), barn owls (*Tyto*), herring gulls (*Larus*), turkey vultures (*Cathartes aura*; Germano, 1999), and possibly bald eagles (Clark, 1982; Klemens, 1993; Ernst et al., 1994). Snake predators include racers (*Coluber*), cottonmouths (*Agkistrodon piscivorus*), and copperheads (*A. contortrix*) (Klimstra, 1959; Legler, 1960; Murphy, 1964; Ernst et al., 1994). Small box turtles, especially, may be eaten by just about any predator. Small and medium-sized mammals may not be able to breach the defenses of a healthy adult box turtle, but they may be able to kill weakened animals. In addition, many box turtles, for whatever reason, react to danger not by closure within the impregnable shell but by trying to walk or run away. This leaves the limbs and head vulnerable to attack, and box turtles with missing limbs are not uncommon (see later discussion).

During our study of Egmont Key's box turtles, Dick Franz and I had the opportunity to track the effect of a single raccoon on a box turtle population. Tracks of the raccoon were first observed in January 1992 concurrent with finding a rash of carcasses of juvenile box turtles. Juveniles were consumed in their entirety except for their shells, which showed bite marks and penetration of the shells by raccoon-sized teeth. Initially only small turtles were attacked, but as the season went on, the raccoon learned to attack larger turtles. Adults were usually decapitated and had the limbs chewed off. In three months, the raccoon was known to have killed at least twenty-six turtles. After he was removed from the island in April, predation ceased.

Raccoon populations, in particular, are at an abnormally high abundance because of the lack of natural predators (Garrott et al., 1993). Considering that raccoons are also voracious predators of turtle eggs, they likely exert considerable pressure on box turtle populations, especially at the stage of juvenile recruitment into the adult breeding population. Studies of other turtles have suggested that both the eggs (Grand and Beissinger, 1997) and the larger juveniles about to enter the breeding population (Crouse et al., 1987), in addition to breeding females (Congdon et al., 1994), are critical to the stability and survival of populations of long-lived turtles, especially if other threats are present. If this is true for box turtles, the unnatural overabundance of raccoons in certain habitats could have serious consequences for *Terrapene*. Because of the long life and secretive behavior of box turtles, negative effects might not be observed until population recovery is unlikely.

The only instance of mass predation on box turtles is the report by Culbertson (1907) on hog predation on *T. carolina*. He counted more than seventy-two juvenile and adult turtles in a large muddy pool during a heat wave. As he watched, hogs approached the pool and began mouthing and crushing even large adults. Because of their voracious appetites and keen sense of smell, feral hogs certainly could exert predation pressure on local populations of box turtles.

Box turtles often show scars or injuries attributed to predation attempts. Missing limbs undoubtedly result from bites by large predators, but many of the shell abrasions found on box turtles may have multiple causes. For example, box turtles are sometimes quite belligerent to conspecifics and have been known to take chunks off the peripherals of the shell. Brown (1974) found six *T. coahuila* with missing limbs and another six with bite marks; in Cuatro Ciénegas, the most likely predator responsible was the coyote (*Canis latrans*). On Egmont Key, 17.7 percent of the Florida box turtles had trauma to their marginals, although only a portion of this likely resulted from predators rather than from conspecifics (Dodd et al., 1997). The most likely predators on the island include the occasional escaped raccoon or dog or perhaps predatory birds such as herons or crows.

Finally, mosquitoes are certainly predators of box turtles. At least five species of *Aedes* (*atlanticus, canadensis, cantator, sollicitans, triseriatus*) feed on box turtles, and another genus (*Culex* sp.) alights on box turtles but does not appear to engorge on them (Crans and Rockel, 1968). Mosquitoes carry viruses, which are passed on to the turtles, including both eastern and western encephalitis, although there is no evidence that these in turn are passed on to people. Interestingly, box turtles seem to attract mosquitoes, which hover around them or feed on the soft tissues and at the sutures between scutes. In Florida and elsewhere, turtles bury themselves in the litter to escape hordes of mosquitoes. After a turtle leaves a form, mosquitoes often remain at the site, perhaps attracted through chemoreception to the turtle's former presence.

Parasites

ECTOPARASITES

Box turtles are parasitized by at least four types of ectoparasites: leeches, mites, ticks, and flies. Of these, the least information available is on leeches (Hirudinea). Brown (1974) recorded unidentified leeches on 4 percent (7 of 169) of *T. coahuila* in Cuatro Ciénegas. Most were rather small and attached to the skin at the rear of the turtle. Inasmuch as other species of *Terrapene* do not spend a great deal of time in water, leech parasitism is probably inconsequential.

At least four species of mites (chiggers, red bugs) occur on wild box turtles, *Trombicula alfreddugesi*, *T. irritans*, *T. lipovskyana*, and *T. montanensis*. The latter two have been found only in ornate box turtles, and *T. alfreddugesi* has been found in both *T. carolina* and

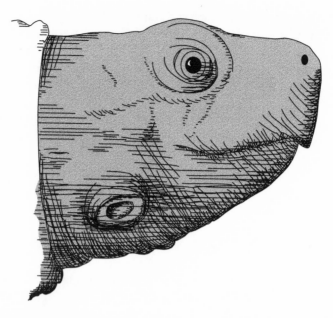

Figure 9-1. Infestation site of a sarcophagid fly, a common ectoparasite of box turtles. Infestations appear as mounds on the turtle's head, neck, or even in the body cavity. From McMullen (1940)

T. ornata (Loomis, 1956; Legler, 1960). In adults, mites usually occur on the soft parts of the skin in both the axial and inguinal areas and around the eyes, head, and neck. They also may be found at the junctures of the scutes on the carapace, especially in heavy infestations. Chiggers appear as bright red dots and are easily seen with the unaided eye. In Kansas, chigger infestations increase steadily from mid-June throughout July, then disappear usually by mid-September (Legler, 1960). Juveniles are more prone to infestation early in the season but, as the season progresses, all life stages may be covered by them. Mites do not appear to cause permanent harm to the turtles, although Legler (1960) noted a juvenile with an eye infection caused by chiggers. Ewing (1926:20) went so far as to suggest that "the finding of chiggers upon the common box-turtle may help explain the great abundance of chiggers in the swampy woods of the Atlantic Coast Region," but there is no basis for this statement.

Allen and Neill (1952) mentioned unidentified ticks on Florida box turtles, but I have never observed a tick on *T. c. bauri*, nor has Lehr Brisbin in South Carolina (pers. comm.). The tick *Ornithodoros turicata* is said to occur occasionally "in heavy infections" on wild box turtles (Flynn, 1973), but the basis for this statement is unknown to me.

The most commonly observed ectoparasites reported from box turtles are the sarcophagid (fleshfly) flies *Sarcophaga cistudinis*, found on both *T. carolina* and *T. ornata*, and *Phaenicia*, found in *T. c. triunguis* from Arkansas (McAllister, 1987). There are a host of short notes mentioning fly infestations (Packard, 1882; True, 1884; Leidy, 1888; Wheeler, 1890; Emerton, 1904; Cahn, 1937; McMullen 1940; Peters, 1948; Rokosky, 1948; Rodeck, 1949; Rainey, 1953; King and Griffo, 1958; Legler, 1960; Jackson et al., 1969). Infestations appear as small mounds (fig. 9-1) on the skin, usually around the head and neck; infestations of the body cavity also occur and may lead to the death of the animal (Peters, 1948; Rokosky, 1948; Rainey, 1953; King and Griffo, 1958). Death in Peters's animal resulted from larval infestation of the lymph glands and cloaca in addition to muscular and neural impairment. Larvae develop singly in a "clean" pocket embedded by means of a barb at the head, or may be found in clumps forming lesions. The lesions have been reported to contain up to eighteen larvae. When larvae pupate and exit the cavity, wounds may heal without bacterial infection or any sign of harm to the turtle.

ENDOPARASITES

Internal parasites are a natural component of animals, and box turtles are no exception. The presence of such parasites is not necessarily an indication of ill health, and there is no need to deparasitize captive animals unless there is a clear reason to do so. A host of parasites has been found in box turtles, and these have been summarized by Mays (1960), Ernst and Ernst (1977), and Baker (1987). Parasitic worms include the following:

Trematodes: *Brachycoelium salamandrae, Neopolystoma terrapensis, Polystomoidella oblongata, P. whartoni, Polystomoides coronatum, Telorchis corti, T. robustum, Telorchis* sp.

Cestodes: *Oochoristica whitentoni, Proteocephalus* sp., immature cyclophyllidian.

Nematodes: *Aplectana* sp., *Atractis carolinae, Angusticaecum holopterum, Camallanus microcephalus, C. trispinosus, Cardianema cistudinis, Cosmocercoides variabilis, C. dukae* (?), *Cruzia testudinis, Falcaustra affinis, F. chelydrae, F. longispiculata, Gnathostoma procyonis, Oswaldocruzia pipiens, Oxysomatium variabilis, Physaloptera terrapenis, Proleptus tortus, Serpinema trispinosus, Spiroxys constrictus, S. contorta, Urodelnema cryptobranchi*

Some of these worms may be host specific. Indeed, within any particular turtle, the worms are not evenly distributed throughout the alimentary tract, suggesting to Mays (1960) that there is a wide range of organ specificity among turtle helminth parasites. In Mays's (1960) study, 74 percent of *T. ornata* (66 of 89) and all *T. c. triunguis* (n = 77) were parasitized in the alimentary tract. A single unidentified filarial worm was found in the connective tissue adjacent to the heart of a three-toed box turtle.

In addition to worms, the non-hemoparasitic protozoans *Hexamita parva* and *Entamoeba knowlesi* have been reported from box turtles (Frank, 1984). In the case of *H. parva*, the protozoan was found in turtles held in captivity for a long time. Their presence is associated with a pathological condition affecting the intestinal tract, liver, kidneys, and especially the urinary bladder; the condition results in kidney failure and death. Like *Hexamita*, the presence of amoebas in box turtles is indicative of poor conditions in captivity, and there is no indication that these parasites seriously affect turtles in natural habitats.

Disease

Most of the information on box turtle diseases comes from animals held in captivity. In turn, most pathological conditions in captive animals reflect improper or inadequate care and feeding. Discussions on the proper care of box turtles can be found both in the herpetocultural literature (de Vosjoli, 1991; Patterson, 1994) and on the Internet. Many diseases or pathological conditions are found in captive turtles, but whether they are prevalent in wild populations, or what effect they may have, is unknown.

Certainly disease has the potential to affect wild box turtles adversely, just as it does in other turtle populations (e.g., Dodd, 1988). Recently, much attention has been focused on respiratory diseases in wild tortoises (Jacobson et al., 1991a) and fibropapillomas in sea turtles (Herbst, 1994). Fortunately, the herpes virus–induced fibropapillomas (Jacobson et al., 1991b) have not been observed in terrestrial turtles. Respiratory diseases, however, have been seen in free-ranging *Terrapene*.

Chronic upper respiratory tract disease in desert tortoises results from the pathogenic bacteria *Mycoplasma agassizii* and an unnamed *Mycoplasma*. A third *Mycoplasma*, in addition to *M. agassizii*, is known from gopher tortoises, but whether it is responsible for a similar respiratory disease is unknown (Epperson, 1997). Several tests for *M. agassizii* in box turtles have been negative (e.g., Belzer, 1996). However, Calle and colleagues (1996) documented serologic evidence of *Mycoplasma* sp. exposure in New York box turtles exhibiting signs of respiratory infection, and an infected Florida box turtle has been reported from the St. Johns River floodplain near Deland (Siefkas et al., 1998). Turtles with respiratory infections may exhibit signs of rhinitis, nasal discharge (sometimes appearing as bubbles), conjunctivitis, discharge from the eye, and swelling of the eyelids (palpebral edema). However, tortoises at least can test positively for the bacterium without exhibiting all or any of these signs. The infection is spread by direct contact, and may be introduced into wild populations through the release of infected captives, although this is by no means certain.

Chronic bacterial pneumonia also has been seen in free-ranging *T. carolina* (Evans, 1983). As with *Mycoplasma*-induced infections, box turtles with pneumonia also exhibit mucous discharge and general respiratory distress, with inflammation of the sinuses and lungs. Because tests for fungi, viruses, and protozoans proved negative, the pneumonia was attributed to gram-negative bacteria, including *Morganella morganii, Acineobacter calcoaceticus, Serratia marcescens*, and *Pseudomonas* sp. (Evans, 1983). Conjunctivitis associated with a bacterial infection (*Pseudomonas testoalcaligenes*) has been reported in a captive *T. c. triunguis* (Tully et al., 1996).

On Long Island, New York, nineteen box turtles were found between 1987 and 1994 that exhibited signs of listlessness, nasal discharge, rhinitis, conjunctivitis, and other symptoms indicating chronic bacterial infection. Numerous species of bacteria and yeasts were isolated from tissues (Tangredi and Evans, 1997). Analyses of the livers of three of these turtles revealed high levels of metabolites from the toxic chemicals chlordane (as much as 1,368 µ/kg of oxychlordane) or endosulfan. Despite the small sample size, the authors speculated that chronic immunosuppression resulting from long-term low-level exposure to these chemicals might be responsible for the infections. The extent to which chronic exposure to toxic chemicals may lead to disease problems in wild populations of box turtles certainly needs additional study.

In addition to the swellings on the neck associated with botfly infestations, many box turtles are found with sebaceous-like swellings on the neck (Allard, 1935; pers. obs.). For example, ten of 177 turtles (5.6 percent) examined in April 1998 on Egmont Key had cysts on one side of the cranium or both. Often, these cysts can be broken and cleaned out; my wife and I have treated them on *T. c. bauri* at Egmont Key, seemingly with no long-term detrimental effects. On other turtles, such cysts can result in massive infection and remodeling of the cranium, presumably with detrimental effects (Jackson et al., 1972). The cysts contain a caseous (cottage cheese–like) substance (see photo in Frye, 1973), are sterile, and may harden to a near hard plastic, acrylic-like consistency. Bacteria associated with massive infections include *Citrobacter, Enterobacter, Proteus morganii, P. rettgeri*, and *Pseudomonas*. Although the cause is unknown, such infections may result from insect or arachnid (ticks, mites) bites, from an infectious protozoan, or from injuries.

Pathological conditions can also result from abnormal functioning of the reproductive system. Jackson et al. (1971) reported a box turtle in Mississippi that had three extra-uterine eggs; that is, eggs outside the oviduct. Two of the eggs were attached to the liver by an overgrowth of connective tissue. Bacteria (*Micrococcus tetragenus*), associated with broken yolk, also were present. The turtle apparently did not exhibit any external sign of the condition, and whether the growth and bacterial infection would have led to more serious problems cannot be determined.

Reports of mass mortality in box turtles are rare, and most of them are associated with winter kill (chapter 3). However, there is at least one record of mass mortality in winter that may be associated with disease. In 1992, Whit Gibbons (Savannah River Ecology Laboratory) received a report of a massive die-off of *T. carolina* in Murray County, Georgia. The thirty to fifty turtles were found in a shallow water in February. Dead and dying turtles appeared sick, and at least one turtle had a subcutaneous abscess near the eye. Although the bacterium *Pasteurella* was isolated from the turtles, the cause of the sickness was undetermined (E. Jacobson, pers. comm.). On Egmont Key, we have occasionally observed sick, lethargic, and emaciated large old adults, but we have not determined the cause of these symptoms. Box turtles dying from unexplained causes, but exhibiting pneumonia-like symptoms, have recently been seen in Texas. Although local declines in *Terrapene* and perhaps other turtles had been attributed to the effects of fire ants, disease may have been responsible (M. Robinson, letter to E. Jacobson, 1998).

In response to infection, box turtles and other reptiles elevate their body temperatures, much as mammals do. However, because they are ectothermic, temperature elevation is accomplished by behavioral rather than by physiological methods, hence the term *behavioral fever*. Box turtles bask in direct sunlight and are able to elevate their body temperatures 4–5°C in response to infection by the bacterium *Aeromonas hydrophila* (Monagas and Gatten, 1983). Survivorship in infected reptiles is generally greater at higher temperatures than at low to moderate temperatures. Sick reptiles should always be kept rather warm.

Anomalies, Pits/Exposed Bone, and Radiation

DEVELOPMENTAL ANOMALIES

The most common developmental anomalies in box turtles involve the carapace (Knoll, 1935; Lynn, 1937; Zangerl and Johnson, 1957; Dodd et al., 1997). It is not uncommon for shells to have supernumerary scutes, particularly among the marginals and vertebrals. In Florida, most abnormalities among the vertebrals involve vertebrals 3 and 4, and most supernumerary marginals are found at the rear of the carapace. We have seen box turtles with extra costals and, on the plastron, an extra small round scute between the femoral and anal scutes. Of the Florida box turtles examined on Egmont Key, 1.4 percent had supernumerary scutes (15 of 1,042) (Dodd et al., 1997). In these turtles, at least, there was no evidence of deleterious effects from the presence of supernumerary scutes. Brown (1971) reported either supernumerary or a reduced number of scutes in 5 percent (11 of 218) of *T. coahuila* he examined from Cuatro Ciénegas.

In addition to supernumerary scutes, we have observed two small holes in the plastrons of some box turtles on Egmont Key. The holes appear to be in the position of the extra plastron scutes already mentioned (fig. 9-2) and are covered by tough membranous tissue internally. Such holes are unlikely to be the result of predation attempts, but I am unsure as to whether they are developmental anomalies or the result of abrasion from the bones of the pelvis. There do not appear to be reports of similar holes in other populations.

Other types of developmental abnormalities appear to be much rarer. Mitchell (1994) reports a two-headed hatchling found in 1979 in Virginia. A photograph of a hatchling *T. carolina* lacking a mouth and jaw is in Ewert (1979).

CARAPACE PITS AND EXPOSED BONE

Carapace pits have been found in *T. c. triunguis* from Oklahoma and Missouri (Carpenter, 1956; Schwartz and Schwartz, 1974). These pits are generally associated with the suture between the second and third costal scutes on the carapace in the central half of the suture line between the marginals and the vertebrals. Many are only slight indentations, whereas others penetrate into the underlying bone of the carapace. Of the 375 shells examined, Carpenter (1956) noted pits on 46 percent of the turtles, 33 percent of the males and 62 percent of the females; only turtles greater than 100 mm had pits. The cause of the pits could not be determined.

On Egmont Key, I have observed many turtles (n = 68 of 1,042; 6.5 percent) with patches of exposed bone on the carapace. Most of the patches are small (4–5 mm) and singular, but multiple patches occur on some turtles and patches can be as large as several cm (Dodd et al., 1997). The patches of exposed bone do not appear to be associated with bone regrowth or carapace replacement due to fire damage (chapter 10), and no evidence of fungal infection (Hunt, 1957) is present. In other box turtle populations, occasional individuals have patches of exposed bone (C. Ernst and I. Brisbin, pers. comm.), but the prevalence of these patches in other populations does not appear as great as on Egmont Key.

Figure 9-2. Adult female Florida box turtle (135 mm CL, photographed 18 October 1992) showing plastral holes. Egmont Key, Florida.

EFFECTS OF RADIATION

In the early 1950s, the development of nuclear weapons generated intense interest in the effects of irradiation on animals and plants. Included in the list of test animals were box turtles collected from Montgomery County, Maryland. Box turtles (n = 109) were subjected to doses of from 500 to 10,000 rads (r) of X-radiation in the laboratory; all turtles died from exposure to doses greater than 1,500 r. White blood cell counts decreased at all doses, and all marrow cells were destroyed at doses of 10,000 r. All turtles receiving doses of 500 r survived 270 days after irradiation. Box turtles were thus considered more tolerant of radiation than were endotherms (Altland et al., 1951). Cosgrove (1965) extended these studies, again exposing *T. carolina* from Tennessee to X-rays of from 500 to 7,000 r. He reported an LD$_{50}$ (see glossary) near 850 r (internal dose) after 120 days at 23°C, but many of his control and irradiated turtles had a purulent conjunctivitis, suggesting poor laboratory conditions. Ill health undoubtedly would affect the results from this study. Both studies noted that the shell served as a partial protective shield against irradiation.

The effects of irradiation on turtles have more relevance now than they did when the experiments described were carried out on the hapless turtles. Radiographs are now widely used to determine clutch size in turtles because shelled eggs are clearly visible (Gibbons and Greene, 1979; Dodd, 1997a). The use of radiographs to determine clutch size is certainly more humane and informative than killing highly valuable reproductive females to observe a snapshot of their reproductive biology, but biologists have been concerned about the possible effects of X-radiation on both the female and her developing eggs. If the technique has deleterious side effects, it should be discontinued.

Although the question cannot be answered definitively for box turtles, extensive work on the reproductive biology of turtles at the Savannah River Ecology Laboratory suggests that the 1.17 mGy (100 r = 1 Gray, abbrev. Gy) that turtle embryos are estimated to receive during one-time X-irradiation is well below the chronic exposure limit (10 mGy/day) that might harm plant or animal populations (reviewed by Hinton et al., 1997). In addition, there is no evidence to suggest that turtles are especially sensitive to radiation, nor is there evidence for increased incidences of deformities or decreased hatching success from irradiated turtle eggs. It is not surprising that eggs within the female are not affected by irradiation since rapid cell division does not occur at that time (chapter 6). For these reasons, the use of X-rays is probably the safest, most humane, and most cost-effective method to determine important reproductive parameters, especially as they pertain to conservation and management.

Future Directions

There is little quantitative information on predators, parasites, and diseases or their effects on wild populations of *T. carolina* and *T. ornata*, and I can find nothing at all on the Mexican species and subspecies. Endoparasites appear to be present in small numbers in nearly all turtles (e.g., Mays, 1960), ectoparasites are common on many populations of *T. carolina*, diseases—notably respiratory disease—are seen occasionally, and turtles are eaten by a great variety of predators.

Certainly, predators have the potential to impact box turtle populations seriously, especially in the egg and hatchling stages, and a few mammalian species like raccoons thrive in close contact with humans where the larger natural predators have been eliminated. It might appear as if urban and suburban populations of box turtles would be most vulnerable to predation effects, but is this so? Rural populations of medium-sized mammals may also attain high densities. In any case, quantitative data are needed to assess the impacts of all these factors on *Terrapene*.

One of the most important unknowns in the study of box turtles is the extent of disease in natural populations. Diseases have had serious effects on populations of flattened musk turtles (*Sternotherus depressus*), green turtles (*Chelonia mydas*), and tortoises (*Gopherus* spp.). Certainly the potential is there for disease to impact long-lived, sedentary, box turtles, and perhaps the symptoms observed in some animals reflect a more serious problem than is currently recognized. We know virtually nothing concerning the demographic impacts of pathologic conditions commonly seen in wild turtles, such as the neck cysts. Yet we can become complacent, along the lines that the common occurrence of a condition somehow means such conditions are not very serious. The sick turtles (i.e., those with neck cysts) that we have examined on Egmont Key are usually lethargic, emaciated, and/or dehydrated, and they usually have swollen eyelids. Clearly, they are impaired as regards feeding and drinking and, in the presence of predators, would not be able to fend off an attack. If left alone, as they are on Egmont, some may recover. However, the effects of chronic infection are not known.

Sick turtles need to be examined by veterinarians familiar with turtle diseases, and the etiology and treatment of diseases need to be refined. In addition, we need to know the fate of sick or debilitated turtles within natural populations and their effects on healthy turtles. This is especially urgent because of the many attempts to rehabilitate, relocate, or otherwise conserve individual turtles (chapter 10). We certainly do not want to devastate native box turtle populations through the introduction of respiratory tract diseases or other illnesses from captive or sick animals, as seems to have been the case in some tortoise populations.

It is important to recognize that proximate symptoms of pathology, whether shown by obvious signs of disease, increased levels of parasitism, or adverse effects on reproduction, may be reflective of a problem that might be difficult to identify. Proximate symptoms do not always lead to the ultimate cause, and examination procedures need to be developed accordingly. In flattened musk turtles, the symptoms I observed were indicative of a more serious problem affecting the turtles. Although the turtles had different symptoms (Dodd, 1988) and may have died from more than one immediate cause, they all apparently had compromised immune systems. The reason for the collapse of the immune system remains unknown.

As more and more concern is expressed over the potential impacts of endocrine disrupters and other xenobiotic compounds (see glossary), biologists need to know much more about how these chemicals function in reptiles, their effects, and about their impacts on reptile immune systems. If endocrine-mimicking compounds have affected freshwater turtles and alligators (Guillette, 1994; Guillette et al., 1994), could they also affect terrestrial box turtles? Reports of sick, diseased, or otherwise abnormal box turtles need to be maintained in a common forum to ensure that disease outbreaks, population declines, and turtles that appear strange or behave unusually receive appropriate attention.

10 | Conservation Biology

> The wheels of civilization move all too swiftly now-a-days, and it is a pity that so many harmless and interesting of Nature's creatures are sacrificed to speed and greed!
>
> DORIS COCHRAN, 1927

> The end result of our conservation efforts must be to establish self-sustaining turtle populations in healthy habitats.
>
> NAT FRAZER, 1997

 Box turtles are termed "common," and in many areas they are not protected. But are box turtles truly common? They certainly were common in northern Virginia where I grew up, but they are gone now from the areas I roamed as a child. Their habitat has been replaced by housing developments, strip malls, frighteningly busy roads, and the general mayhem of an urban and suburban lifestyle. We tend to remember things as they were, rather than seeing them as they are; if box turtles were once common, they must be still. It is often easier to focus on the needs of exotic wildlife in far-off places than to promote active conservation at home—which might bear some immediate and local costs.

I have sometimes been asked why we should be concerned with the conservation of box turtles. Surprisingly (to me, anyway), such questions occasionally are posed by natural resource managers, who seem only concerned about the legal, rather than ethical, ramifications of conservation. The problem is perception.

Box turtles may or may not be common, but it is well documented that in recent years massive changes have occurred in their habitat, that even well protected populations have declined, that a huge trade has occurred despite knowledge that it could not (and cannot) be sustained, and that turtle populations worldwide are in deep and serious trouble (Dodd and Franz, 1993).

The world will not end if any one species or genus disappears, let alone *Terrapene*. But box turtles are the product of millions of years of evolution; or, depending on your point of view, they are the direct creation of an all-knowing God. It is senseless for us to destroy a marvelous creature for short-sighted gains or through ignorance. There are critical self-centered reasons for being concerned about the continuance of human life on earth, and hence for an interest in conservation, but for me, the protection of box turtles is more of an ethical concern. We have responsibilities as the dominant species in our environment; we have responsibilities to the creatures with which we share our world. We should be concerned about box turtles because they are here, have been here a long time, and deserve to continue to be here a long time into the future. It is the moral thing to do.

In this chapter, I discuss threats to box turtles and the constraints and possible solutions to the dilemma of their conservation. I do not restate problems from predation and disease covered elsewhere (chapter 9). We need to refocus our attention to ensure that the threats outlined are not compounded by complacency born of old memories of how common box turtles once were or by lack of information on their present status.

Threats to Box Turtles

LANDSCAPE CHANGES

Although it has never been adequately quantified, the loss or alteration of habitat is probably the greatest threat to the continued existence of box turtles. Ever since humans arrived in North America, we have been changing the environment. Native Americans burned the prairies and forest to drive game, to improve pasture, and to clear land for agriculture. Native American populations were dense in some regions, and people farmed the land intensively to support their sedentary populace. Land clearing was systematic around population centers and open corridors may have connected these (Adler, 1970; Hammett, 1992). Undoubtedly, box turtles were collected for food, as pets, and for making ceremonial items, and many were lost as the habitat was modified. As Native American populations crashed because of disease and warfare with early Europeans, box turtles may have been able to reclaim parts of their former territory.

When Europeans began to flood North America, however, the pace of land alteration accelerated as colonists pushed ever farther west. Lands were cleared, the great forests were felled, and the prairies were plowed; and gradually even the agricultural society faded into the modern industrial and service society with its intensive, seemingly permanent landscape changes. Given the extent of habitat loss, it is surprising that box turtles have survived in some of the enclaves where they have, but it is unlikely that they will continue to do so much longer as human populations explode and mindless consumption drives the society.

Literally millions of hectares of land that once supported box turtles no longer do so. Millions more hectares have been degraded. Much of the suitable turtle habitat left is not in conservation status and not contiguous with other appropriate tracts of land. In Florida, for example, forests declined 22 percent, herbaceous wetlands declined 51 percent, agricultural lands increased 60 percent, and urban lands increased 632 percent between 1936 and 1995 (Kautz, 1998). The trends point to a continued loss in overall biological diversity within the state, and some communities, such as the pine rocklands in south Florida known to have been inhabited by sizable box turtle populations, have nearly disappeared (Kautz et al., 1993). Similar trends, especially the increase in urban lands, are evident throughout the range of box turtles.

HABITAT FRAGMENTATION

As forests are cleared and prairies plowed, remaining tracts of land become increasingly isolated. Natural or seminatural habitats are separated from similar habitats, and the plants and animals within each area become isolated from conspecifics on other fragments. Habitat fragmentation can be appreciated best from the air. What look like large tracts of land from the ground can be seen from above to be patches of somewhat natural habitat in a sea of housing developments, agricultural fields, quarries, clearcuts, roads, and other transportation corridors. Ecologist Peter Feinsinger remarked that habitat *shredding* was a better term than fragmentation, for it appears from the air as if eastern forests have been shredded linearly by modern civilization. I get the same feeling flying over what was once prairie and seeing hundreds of irrigation wheels spotted across the landscape.

Habitat fragmentation threatens box turtles in several ways. For one thing, box turtles tend to wander away from the habitat patch in order to forage, find mates, explore, or move as transients. The greater a turtle's propensity to wander becomes, the greater will be the threat of movement away from a habitat patch. This exposes individuals to an increased chance of predation, mortality (in crossing roads and other barriers, such as railroad tracks), and threats from collection. For example, box turtles are unlikely to cross busy highways safely, and even if they do, it is unlikely that they will return safely. If adjacent areas include human occupation, box turtles may be picked up by children, killed by dogs or garbage-eating raccoons, run over by lawnmowers, or burned in leaf piles. Even if an area is protected, box turtle populations may decline because of a continual loss of individuals, though the loss appears rather small annually. The decline of box turtles at several well-studied protected sites (Schwartz et al., 1984; Williams and Parker, 1987) is thought to result from land use changes that have occurred on surrounding property, rather than from some sort of detrimental impact directly on site.

Another potential detrimental result of habitat fragmentation is the edge effect. The amount of edge bordering a habitat patch is inverse to the size of the patch; that is, small habitat patches have a relatively large amount of edge. Turtles residing in habitat fragments with a great deal of edge may be more likely to leave the patch than those residing in areas with little edge. Edges may increase the likelihood of predation (many predators such as raccoons are edge specialists) and may make the turtles subject to environmental extremes emanating from outside the patch. Predators are more likely to destroy turtle nests at or near a habitat edge than in its center (Temple, 1987). Extremes of heat and cold and fluctuations in humidity are more noticeable at habitat edges than in the center of the site. Changes in temperature and humidity could affect activity, habitat use, and survival, especially during overwintering (chapters 3, 4). On the other hand, habitat edges increase the choice of microhabitats, and box turtles often seem to prefer edge habitats.

There is another subtle way that habitat fragmentation may adversely affect box turtle populations. If the entire habitat patch were to be altered in some way, perhaps as a result of a lack of management, the box turtles in that habitat might be subject to environmental conditions that would threaten their persistence. For example, a habitat patch could undergo succession from a natural (in terms of the historic landscape) to a modified habitat type, such as from prairie to woodland. Small fragments are much less likely to be managed than larger patches, and they often are neglected. As habitats change, so do their biophysical conditions and habitat structure, and an area once suitable for box turtles may become unsuitable and may affect life history traits.

In a series of comparisons between ornate box turtle populations in contiguous versus severely fragmented prairie and savanna habitats, Curtin (1995, 1997) demonstrated that box turtles in the fragmented habitats had shorter activity seasons (155 vs. 177 days), larger home ranges (8.7 vs. 2.5 ha), and longer egg incubation periods (80 vs. 60 days) than turtles in contiguous habitats. This means that they were at greater risk from environmental extremes because they might not be active long enough to gather energy reserves for overwintering (making them more prone to winterkill); that they were more prone to mortality because they moved over a greater home range; and that their eggs might not have sufficient time to develop and hatch successfully (resulting in low recruitment). The differences Curtin documented in life history traits resulted from the biophysical differences in the habitats. Specifically, the grassland-inhabiting ornate box turtles were forced to spend greater amounts of time in the cooler woodlands. These woodlands took longer to warm up in the spring, thus reducing the time for box turtle activity. Ultimately, the shorter activity season adversely affected their ability to survive.

In this example, box turtle populations were adversely affected even though the habitat patches were of sufficient size to sustain a population. Curtin (1997) suggested that the decline observed in a population previously studied by Doroff and Keith (1990) might have been the result of subtle changes in the biophysical environment, rather than deriving from predation, overcollection, or movement outside the study area. Habitat deterioration, especially in isolated habitat patches, could be a more serious threat than has previously been recognized. This is because individuals might persist for a long period despite the habitat change and the virtual lack of recruitment. The turtle population would appear to be declining without direct human impact, and the decline might even be termed "mysterious." Subtle changes to box turtles' biophysical environment could be especially important at the periphery of their range where they are already experiencing natural limits to their survival.

COMMERCIAL TRADE

People have always been attracted to box turtles, and countless animals must have been picked up through the centuries and taken home as pets. Some escaped, some were released (usually at inappropriate locations), but a great many died in captivity because so little was known concerning proper care. In the past, commercial trade in the United States was not great, and few animals appear to have been exported (e.g., twenty-two into Britain in 1981; Warwick, 1993). In 1984, however, that changed.

Europeans have always had a fondness for tortoises, and literally hundreds of thousands of *Testudo graeca, T. hermanii,* and *T. marginata* were imported from southern Europe and north Africa to satisfy the pet markets; 150,000 tortoises were imported into the United Kingdom alone between 1980 and 1984 (Warwick, 1993). With the creation of the European Economic Community in 1984, that trade was banned because tortoise populations were being decimated, and importers turned to a different source. They discovered the North American box turtle.

Unfortunately, the U.S. government did not keep trade statistics on the export of domestic species not federally protected, and data on exports are therefore incomplete. However, between 1986 and 1990, approximately 10,000 *T. carolina* and 2,000 *T. ornata* entered Britain from the United States (Zug, 1994). From 1990 to 1993, information compiled by TRAFFIC USA, based on U.S. Fish and Wildlife Service figures but known to be incomplete data, showed that at least 81,233 box turtles worth $494,845 were exported to Europe (especially Britain and Germany), Japan, and Hong Kong. These figures underestimate the actual total exported, and they do not include any domestic commercial trade. Certainly well over 100,000 wild *Terrapene* were removed from their homes to be someone's pet in a foreign land. Since turtles were collected from the wild, nearly all were mature adults. An outcry from concerned biologists and others led to CITES listing in 1994 (Lieberman, 1994; see later discussion), and regulations have halted this unconscionable exploitation, at least internationally.

In a revealing series of articles, Warwick (1993) and Highfield (1993) documented the way in which box turtles were captured to be brought into Britain and recorded their fate once in the Old World. Professional turtle hunters often caught the turtles, arranged for their confinement and transport, and took them to wholesalers for shipment overseas. A circuit rider would then travel to pick up turtles from a series of local collectors on a route that might extend for hundreds of miles, during which time the turtles were neither fed nor watered but were confined to crowded, unhealthy conditions. Box turtles then were stored en masse until they could be sent to the wholesaler. Once at the wholesaler, the turtles often were treated inhumanely; they could be kept in crowded unsanitary conditions, with or without food and water, and without regard for thermal stress. Even before leaving the country, many of the turtles observed by Warwick (1993) were thin and dehydrated.

Once in Britain, the turtles sold for about fifty dollars (in 1992). Most purchasers did not receive information on how to care for the turtle, or the information was incorrect. Sometimes the turtles were misidentified as Chinese wood turtles or as an "ordinary" tortoise. In a British survey, 65 percent of the respondents reported veterinary problems, especially ear abscesses and eye infections. Box turtles were commonly in poor condition in the British pet shops visited by Highfield (1993). As with the vast majority of tortoises and turtles imported into Britain, most box turtles met a similar fate; they died within a year as a result of the stress of capture, shipment, confinement, and improper care in a climate alien and thermally inadequate. Is this any way to treat a sixty-year-old homebody? Additional information on the disturbing international trade in turtles can be found in Luiijf (1997).

Although there is ample evidence to suggest that wild-caught box turtles do not make good pets, commercial trade continues within the United States. Indeed, a note in *Pet Business* recently advised dealers that "both the common box turtle and ornate box turtle are popular land tortoises [*sic*] that you'll want to stock" (Ramus, 1997:48). Prices for box turtles range from ten to eighty dollars in the U.S. domestic market to well into the hundreds of dollars in the now black markets of Japan and Europe. I have never seen information on box turtle care distributed in a pet store, and I have seen sick box turtles (swollen-eyed, lethargic) for sale without explanation. Most box turtles in U.S. pet shops probably meet the same fate as their exported kin. In any case, they are certainly dead in relation to the viability of the population from which they originated.

The extent of black market trade in box turtles is difficult to assess. Undercover operations have confiscated box turtles thought to have been illegally collected, but most of the trade is quiet and hard to track. As recently as October 1997, two men were arrested in Topeka, Kansas, and later convicted on charges of illegally buying and selling more than a thousand box turtles (Beltz, 1998). This was probably not an isolated instance.

Human-Caused Mortality

Human-caused box turtle mortality for the most part is indirect and inadvertent; few people go out of their way to kill or injure box turtles. This has not always been the case. Farmers and others sometimes deliberately killed these harmless turtles in the mistaken belief that they caused serious damage to vegetable crops, particularly tomatoes (Allard, 1935). Undoubtedly box turtles will take advantage of a readily available food supply, but they are not a pest to gardeners. Indeed, they consume deleterious insects and other invertebrates. Methods of keeping "marauding" turtles out of gardens, such as by using screen or mesh fencing, are readily available.

Although many people do not recognize it as mortality, simply removing an animal from its natural habitat has the same effect as death; the turtle ceases to be a member of a breeding population. Since its genes are removed from the population, evolutionary potential is terminated. Of course, the continuous removal of animals from a population leads to the population's decline and extirpation. Belzer (1997) recorded the demise of a box turtle population in Pennsylvania during the height of human recreational activity in the area from 1936 to 1962. Although common in the 1930s, box turtles had disappeared by the early 1960s. People just love to take box turtles home.

Another serious threat to box turtles is mortality and injury from mowing and land clearing. Many box turtles are killed each year on lawns and pastures as people mow high grass and brush. This is a particular problem in grasslands, where ornate box turtles reside. We have observed adult Florida box turtles killed as a result of lawn mowing on Egmont Key. In most cases, the drivers of lawn mowers and tractors are unaware of the turtles, but there are always those who are too lazy or uninterested to avoid a fleeing turtle. On Egmont Key, mowing lawns during the heat of the day would reduce the chance of mortality, since box turtles congregate on the lawns mostly in early morning to take advantage of cool temperatures and moisture (Dodd et al., 1997). John Sealy (pers. comm.) found that mowing pastures in the heat of mid- to late summer in North Carolina reduced box turtle mortality. Unfortunately, most mowing occurs in spring and early summer and, as Sealy noted in a letter to me, it undoubtedly takes "a terrible toll on turtle populations." If at all possible, pastures should be mowed when box turtles are not present. If box turtles are expected to be in an area to be mowed or cleared, the area should be searched prior to mowing.

The most serious direct threat to box turtles comes from the automobile. Literally thousands are killed each year on highways, and this slaughter has been ongoing for a long time. In 1985, I drove 19,000 km during the course of fieldwork in northern Alabama, and recorded 136 box turtles on roads (Dodd et al., 1989), 100 of which were dead. This number may not seem like much, but multiplied throughout eastern North America year after year, the toll of road-killed *Terrapene* quickly becomes enormous. Even in the 1930s biologists expressed concern about box turtle mortality on roads (e.g., Burt and Hoyle, 1934). High rates of mortality on highways should not be unexpected considering the turtle's propensity to move and the presence of transients in populations, particularly in light of the vast numbers of roads of every type that crisscross our landscape. Highway mortality is a continuous drain on box turtle populations.

Although many people have decried the loss of box turtles on highways, few people ever do anything about it except to stop and move a turtle out of harm's way. These people deserve our thanks. Those who deliberately run over box turtles for sport deserve another fate. As Roger Barbour (1968:33) put it, "Many [box turtles] are killed on the highways by witless or curiously sadistic drivers who deliberately run over them to hear them pop. There probably isn't much that can be done about such people except to hope they burst a tire and skid." But there *is* something that can be done. Barrier fencing can be constructed to prevent access to roads; such fences have been effective in reducing desert tortoise mortality in areas of the Mojave Desert. In other areas, highway wildlife underpasses, in concert with fencing, could allow passage yet prevent mortality. These construction options need consideration in areas of particularly high population densities. Deliberately running over turtles should warrant a traffic citation, and anyone performing such callous actions should be subject to animal cruelty statutes.

We have also created a direct predation threat to box turtles, in addition to allowing an overabundance of some native predators that decimate turtles and their eggs (chapter 9). This predation threat is the domestic dog. Many dogs roam free and readily attack and kill box turtles and other turtles found away from the safety of pond or burrow. As with the tremendous destruction of wildlife caused by cats, dog owners often are in denial or think that the problem is not serious. It can be, however, and every effort should be made to control depredation by free-ranging dogs.

Finally, there are persons who simply cannot resist the urge to pick up a turtle and put it in a race. For decades, tortoise racing was popular in Florida. Gopher tortoises were carted to a fair ground, put in pens with or without food, water, or shelter, and placed in trackways to have children chase them to the finish line. After the race, the tortoise was carted home to be eaten, kept as a pet, or dumped back into the nearest patch of sandhills, far from home, to fend for itself. Fortunately, this practice has ceased, and without any economic loss to sponsors. Mechanical turtles work just as well. The towns of Leoti and Onaga, Kansas, still have races each year using ornate box turtles as racers. Concerns about housing, treatment, and release have been raised, as they were in Florida. Sponsors promise that the turtles will be humanely treated, and they often recommend that the turtles be released where they were captured. Chances are, however, that the trauma associated with such events takes its toll, and it is certainly unnecessary. Perhaps Kansas officials should consult officials in San Antonio, Florida, to learn of alternatives.

FIRE

Box turtles are particularly susceptible to fire. Native Americans and European settlers both set fires to open habitats for game and agriculture. Today, fires are deliberately set in acts of vandalism, or they are used as a management tool to maintain healthy ecosystems. On the southeastern coastal plain and in the prairies of the Midwest, fire is a natural phenomenon necessary in structuring plant and animal communities; whole communities of species are specially fire adapted, and such communities are reservoirs of great biotic diversity.

Still, fire takes a toll on box turtles residing in these communities (Babbitt and Babbitt, 1951; Carr, 1952). On Egmont Key and elsewhere, I have seen numbers of box turtles with shells virtually melted and fused, leading to wholesale bone restructuring and carapace replacement (Smith, 1958; Rose, 1986; Dodd et al., 1997). The effects of fire on box turtle populations have not been systematically assessed using unbiased sampling procedures, though there is a study based on museum specimens (Ernst et al., 1995). Undoubtedly, juvenile and subadult individuals are greatly at risk from fire, especially during the warm season activity period (year-round in Florida).

CONTAMINANTS

Our society is awash in chemicals. Many of these are benign to the health of wild species, but many others are not. With the addition of thousands of chemicals each year, it is nearly impossible to determine in advance which chemicals affect wildlife and how. Adverse effects from chemicals need not lead to direct mortality. Sublethal effects may be just as deleterious in the long run. For example, sublethal effects, such as chronic exposure to chemical contaminants, may depress immune systems, making the species vulnerable to other stress factors, such as disease or cold. Keepers of box turtles are well aware that an obviously sick turtle should never be cool and dormant during the winter as a healthy animal might be. Unfortunately, turtles often look healthy when they are not. If an animal's immune system is stressed, external symptoms may not be present and subsequent mortality may be reported as mysterious or unexplained.

A second consideration is that most chemicals in the environment have multiple personalities. By this I mean that they often act differently in concert with one another. One chemical may be rather inert until it comes in contact with another. The resulting combination might have more potent effects than either component singly. And the reverse may occur: one detrimental chemical may be neutralized by the presence of another. Thus, the environment in which the chemical is found in nature is important in predicting its potential effects. With the thousands of chemical contaminants pervasive in modern society, the potential for synergistic interactions is always present.

A third consideration is that chemical compounds in the environment break down into other compounds. Again, the by-products of chemical breakdown may be benign, or the by-products may be as lethal as the parent compounds or more so. These by-products are then free to interact, with the same potential consequences.

In order to assess the impact of chemical contaminants, it is necessary to understand their mode of action. Traditional methods of assessment have relied on a measure of lethality: dose the animal under captive conditions and determine if it dies or whether there is behavioral or reproductive impairment. Whereas this method is still used by some researchers, new concern about sublethal and chronic effects, in addition to the shear volume of new and old potential toxics, make an understanding of modes of action critical. Moreover, a great deal of concern has been expressed about the effects of chemicals that mimic chemicals naturally occurring in the body, especially those involving the endocrine system. If a synthetic chemical in the environment mimics a chemical in the body, such as a hormone, it could cause a disruption in development or in the maintenance of homeostasis. For example, there has been widespread concern about the potential effects of various pesticides in the environment, since at least some of them are known to mimic the activity of estrogen. An estrogen-mimicking slush (dicofol and DDT and its metabolites DDD and DDE) was dumped into Lake Apopka, Florida, in 1980 and completely disrupted the reproductive system of resident alligators and turtles, leading to severe population declines (Guillette et al., 1994). Because hormones naturally work in very small concentrations, the presence of even minute quantities of estrogen-mimicking compounds in the environment is of great concern to both wildlife and humans.

Unfortunately, little is known concerning the effects that toxic chemicals have had, or are capable of having, on box turtles. Given the rather sedentary lifestyle of most individuals and their close-to-the-ground stance, it would seem reasonable that they and their prey might be exposed to adverse interaction with many of today's chemical compounds. Most reports are anecdotal, however. In Maryland, Stickel (1951) found no differences in sex ratios, growth, or abundance of eastern box turtles in DDT-treated and untreated sites over a period of four years. In Mississippi, Ferguson (1963) reported a single *T. carolina* possibly killed by the pesticide heptachlor, although others were found unharmed; no tissue analyses were performed. Box turtles living in areas treated with mirex had high concentrations of the pesticide in both liver and eggs (Holcomb and Parker, 1979). In all these observations, sample sizes were small and detrimental effects could not be proven.

Exposure to chemicals in the environment need not result from direct application. Some chemicals are transported aerially or more likely through the food chain, usually with unknown effects. In West Virginia, box turtles living in close proximity to lead smelters had much higher concentrations of lead in their tissues than turtles living at distant sites (Beresford et al., 1981). The authors speculated that some of this exposure resulted from inhalation, whereas the remainder probably was picked up in the diet. The turtles appeared to concentrate lead to some extent. Unfortunately, the authors offered no insight into the effects that the reported levels might have had on the turtles' biology, except to state that the levels were above those of some species and below those of others, depending on location and source of exposure. Box turtles are known to pick up radioactive strontium-90 in the skeleton, although levels are low compared to those for other terrestrial and many freshwater turtles (Jackson et al., 1974). Strontium-90 probably enters the box turtle through its invertebrate prey, and its effects, if any, are unknown.

Biological Constraints to Conservation

In the past, Richard Seigel and I have argued that there are two sets of constraints to the successful conservation and management of a species (Dodd and Seigel, 1991; Seigel and Dodd, 2000). The most important are the biological constraints imposed by the species, which are products of its long evolutionary history in a particular ecosystem. Examples of such constraints for box turtles include the attributes needed for successful development (e.g., sunny locations, friable soils, adequate temperature and moisture), thermal requirements, home range and habitat requirements, food preferences, and social behavior. If a box turtle needs a certain amount of habitat, no manner of human compromise will change that habitat requirement. Biological constraints form the limits within which conservation programs must function. If these limits are breached, regardless of human intention, the program will fail.

The second set of constraints to conservation are human imposed; that is, the limits within which human activities are able to perform. Examples of such constraints include finances, manpower, initiative, public support and understanding, politics, habitat availability, logistics, and the many other factors associated with carrying out a conservation program. These factors are important, but they are often more flexible than the biological constraints limiting the options. If the human-imposed constraints are inadequate or are used to override the reality of the biological constraints, then again a conservation program will fail, no matter how noble are the motives of those who implement it. This concept is simple, but it is often lost on those forced to make decisions in the real world. In effect, the conservation of box turtles is a people problem, not a turtle problem.

Those attributes of box turtles which most constrain conservation options are the same life history traits that affect other long-lived chelonians, namely a long, somewhat sedentary life, a low rate of recruitment, high adult survivorship, high egg and hatchling mortality, relatively late maturity, and low fecundity. Congdon et al. (1994) discuss the implications of these traits for the conservation and management of long-lived species. Basically, the high adult survivorship and low rates of recruitment make it difficult for populations to recover from stress, such as the loss of a proportion of the adult population through emigration or collecting. Removing adults is not compensated for by an increase in juvenile survivorship or an increase in the already high adult survivorship, either of which could otherwise allow population recovery. Instead, populations can take decades to recover (e.g., Hall et al., 1999), if they do at all.

Conservation Options

HABITAT PROTECTION

The only real long-term solution to box turtle conservation is to protect natural habitats. Of course, habitat protection helps many species. Protection can include a whole range of options, from complete prevention of access and exploitation to carefully controlled management. If habitat is to be protected for box turtles, conservation must have both a spatial and a temporal component. Simply stated, there must be enough space to allow a population to persist in perpetuity and there must be provisions to protect the habitat through time. In both, the biological and human-related constraints to conservation must be considered.

In terms of space, box turtles need room for their daily activities, nesting, basking, and overwintering. Habitats must include both a sufficient quantity and quality of food and water. Turtles need to be protected from people, overabundant human-associated predators—raccoons and dogs—traffic, and all kinds of physical disturbance. Habitats need to be large enough to support a *population* through time, not just *individuals*. This is an important consideration on which little work has been done. Cook (1996) suggested that repatriation sites should contain a minimum of from 300 to 500 ha of good to high quality habitat, but a resident population probably can be maintained on a smaller scale. Still, box turtle populations have declined on protected reserves because of adverse adjacent land use, edge effects, human trespass, biophysical changes, and the turtles' natural propensity to wander. Needless to say, the largest preserve which contains the least amount of edges, in high quality habitat, is the most desirable.

Once a reserve or other protected area is established, it cannot be neglected. As Curtin (1995, 1997) has so ably demonstrated, neglect of habitat can lead to structural and biophysical changes that adversely affect the species to be protected. In addition, it may be necessary to restrict access to the area. This is not a popular option since many public agencies operate under the notion that all persons have rightful access to lands acquired with public funds. In a troubling study, Garber and Burger (1995) documented the disappearance of wood turtles (*Clemmys insculpta*) from two areas under long-term protection after people were allowed access for recreation (fishing, hiking, etc.). Although the habitat quality remained unchanged, the turtle population declined because of lack of recruitment and the outright loss of adult females. They concluded that recreational access to protected areas adversely affected the survival of wood turtles, a conclusion that can reasonably be extended to the similarly sized and terrestrial box turtle.

Sometimes, events outside a completely protected reserve have drastic consequences on resident box turtles. At the Patuxent Wildlife Research Center in Maryland, the box turtle population studied by Stickel (1950) underwent a severe decline by the late 1970s (Stickel, 1978). Careful review of land use in the watershed determined that the likely cause was the severe floods in the area in the early to mid-1970s, floods which had been exacerbated by the far-upstream flood control activities of the U.S. Army Corps of Engineers. By the late 1990s, the population still had not recovered to preflood population levels, offering a dramatic example of the influence of life history traits on the potential for a box turtle population to recover from stress (Hall et al., 1999).

All reserves need a carefully planned and adequately funded management plan, with clearly stated goals and objectives, to guide land stewardship on a long-term basis. On Egmont Key, we are trying to balance the expected increase in public visitation as the island becomes more popular with the obligation to protect its resident box turtle and tortoise populations. Because of the difficulties in reaching the island and restrictions on entry to many parts of it, it may be possible to juggle the needs of wildlife and human visitors; and in that the area is a national wildlife refuge, the requirements of wildlife should be paramount. A management plan overseen and administered cooperatively by a variety of public agencies, and reviewed by scientists, is helping to guide the long-term survival of Egmont Key's irreplaceable box turtle population.

Reserve oversight involves more than just visitor management, especially if active land management is undertaken. For example, if exotic vegetation is removed in an area inhabited by box turtles (an admittedly desirable goal), vegetation restoration must occur simultaneously in order to maintain habitat structure and the biophysical environment. One would not want a huge roller-chopper to remove exotic vegetation if the result were the decimation of the resident turtle population by crushing and killing. Management needs to be guided by the best scientific data available, as specified in a management plan, rather than by whim, opportunity, or local fiat.

Habitat protection is not the sole responsibility of public agencies; we all have a stake in the protection of natural areas. Private landowners can help protect and conserve box turtles on additional land by following the same guidelines that govern conservation elsewhere. If you want to help box turtles, know their biological constraints and plan accordingly. An excellent set of guidelines to assist private landowners in the protection of box turtles has been developed by Habitat From Humanity, a Michigan-based organization concerned with land use issues. Their Internet site (http://www.wtgrain.org/turtle/w2needs.htm) contains eight informative leaflets on all aspects of the needs of box turtles within their environment and ways to accommodate them. Landowners may consider formalizing protection through conservation easements or agreements.

Some private organizations, notably the Nature Conservancy, have already helped substantially in protecting box turtle habitat, and members should be vigilant to ensure that the needs of these species are considered along with the needs of the more charismatic large mammals and birds. Most conservation organizations, however, have been woefully negligent in considering habitat protection for reptile conservation; it is time these attitudes changed. Governments can help both individuals and organizations that promote habitat protection by offering tax breaks and incentives to landowners who manage land for box turtles and other wildlife. Incentives exist to destroy natural habitat; they should also be available to protect it.

LAWS AND REGULATIONS

STATE/PROVINCIAL. The simplest conservation measure to protect box turtles is to afford them some blanket measure of statutory protection. Protection may involve complete prohibitions on collection ("take"), as is usually the case with species listed as Endangered, Threatened, or in similar categories denoting that the species is in trouble from a survival or persistence standpoint. In North America, a number of U.S. states and Ontario, Canada, have listed box turtles in such categories, especially at the periphery of the species' range (table 10-1). Endangered species regulations may or may not afford some measure of habitat protection or oversight, such as a review of projects to be located in critical habitats.

TABLE 10-1. A brief review of U.S. state regulations as they pertain to box turtles. Permits are required for otherwise prohibited activities. Always check with a state's wildlife management agency prior to collecting any specimen or conducting scientific research. Information from Levell (1997). **Tc** = *Terrapene carolina*; **To** = *T. ornata*.

Alabama (Tc)	Cannot be collected, offered for sale, sold, or traded for anything of value
Arkansas (To)	Cannot be taken or possessed from the wild
Colorado	Sale of wild-caught native species prohibited
Connecticut (Tc)	Season and possession limit
Florida (Tc)	Possession limit; may not be sold commercially
Illinois	Sale of wild-caught native species prohibited
Indiana (Tc)	Endangered; fully protected
Iowa (To)	Threatened; fully protected
Kansas	Sale of wild-caught native species prohibited
Kentucky	Collecting box turtles prohibited
Louisiana	Possession limit; no commercial collecting
Maine (Tc)	Endangered; fully protected
Maryland (Tc)	Possession limit
Massachusetts (Tc)	Special Concern; fully protected
Michigan (Tc)	Special Concern; fully protected
Mississippi	Sale of wild-caught native species prohibited
Missouri	Sale of wild-caught native species prohibited
Nebraska	Commercial permit required
New Hampshire (Tc)	Controlled; fully protected
New Jersey (Tc)	Protected
New York (Tc)	Protected
Oklahoma	Sale of wild-caught native species prohibited
Pennsylvania	Sale of wild-caught native species prohibited
Rhode Island (Tc)	Protected
Tennessee	Sale of wild-caught native species prohibited
Virginia	Sale of wild-caught native species prohibited
West Virginia	Sale of wild-caught native species prohibited
Wisconsin (To)	Endangered; fully protected

Even if box turtles are not endangered or threatened, prohibitions sometimes prevent commercial collecting while allowing take by individuals (table 10-1). Although it seems well ingrained in wildlife management agencies that wild mammals and birds should not be collected as pets, this philosophy has rarely been extended to reptiles, and there is considerable debate within the herpetological public as to whether and to what extent it should be. Other statutes may regulate seasons of take, possession limits, or life-stage prohibitions (for example, the protection of eggs or young, but not adults). Partial prohibitions are infrequently based on the biology of long-lived species, and few states have programs directed at assessing the effectiveness of their regulations.

All states allow for some take, even of protected species, for research or conservation purposes. Before working with box turtles, individuals should inquire of the state natural resource agency as to the status of box turtles and whether permits are required for possession. Addresses for the various agencies are in Levell (1997), and most states have home pages on the Internet where more information can be found.

The effectiveness of state regulations varies considerably from one state to another. As with all regulatory and conservation programs, effectiveness is only as good as the commitment and resources supporting the regulations. If administrators care about box turtles and adequately fund enforcement and monitoring efforts, then regulations may be quite effective at identifying and conserving local populations, and especially at protecting them from the scourge of commercial collecting. If enforcement is lax or arbitrarily directed at one segment of the public, then respect diminishes and regulations become ineffective or, worse, divisive. Ultimately, however, regulation of possession without attention to habitat protection will not conserve box turtles.

NATIONAL. There are no national statutes in the United States specifically protecting box turtles, although the Coahuilan box turtle (*T. coahuila*) is listed as Endangered under provisions of the Endangered Species Act of 1973, as amended. As such, the importation and sale of this species is prohibited except by permit. As reptiles, box turtles are included under provisions of the federal Lacey Act, however. This law makes it a federal crime to take a specimen across state or international borders if the specimen was illegally obtained. For example, it would be a violation of the Lacey Act to collect an ornate box turtle in Wisconsin and transport it to Florida without a Wisconsin state permit; the person responsible would be subject to federal prosecution. Unfortunately, the hodgepodge of state regulations makes enforcement of the Lacey Act difficult since it is often difficult to prove where a box turtle originated. Unscrupulous individuals try to avoid the law by claiming confiscated turtles come from unregulated states, even states from which the species is unknown.

In addition, the commercial sale of box turtles less than four inches in carapace length is prohibited by the U.S. Food and Drug Administration in order to prevent the spread of salmonella (see Levell, 1997). Likewise, importation of turtles smaller than this size is prohibited by the U.S. Public Health Service for the same reason.

Mexican law is somewhat vague about the protection of box turtles (they are considered "species subject to special protection"), although it would appear that *T. coahuila* and *T. nelsoni* do have some form of statutory protection. Commercial exploitation of

T. c. yucatana and *T. c. mexicana* is prohibited. Mexico has rather stringent requirements for scientific research, and permits are necessary.

INTERNATIONAL. The genus *Terrapene* is listed on Appendix II of the Convention on International Trade in Endangered Species of Wild Fauna and Flora (CITES), and *T. coahuila* is listed on Appendix I. This international treaty regulates and monitors trade in species that either are or might become endangered by trade. Commercial trade in Appendix I species is prohibited, and importation and exportation require permits. Commercial trade in Appendix II species is allowed if accompanied by a permit from the country of origin. Trade in Appendix II species is strictly monitored. In addition, an important provision of CITES affecting Appendix II species is that permits cannot be issued unless the country of origin has proof that trade will not be detrimental to the species. Canada, Mexico, and the United States are all parties to CITES.

CITES has proven an important weapon in the regulation of the immense and unsustainable international trade that occurred in box turtles prior to listing. Box turtles were exported until 1995, but in 1996 the U.S. Fish and Wildlife Service provided a zero export quota since it could not be demonstrated that export would not be detrimental to box turtles in Louisiana, at that time the only state lobbying to continue the trade. Indeed, as numerous biologists and organizations pointed out, there is every reason to believe that massive and virtually unregulated trade would have severe effects on population viability and the ability of populations to recover. Fortunately, the Fish and Wildlife Service has continued to maintain a zero quota despite intense pressure to sanction export, and thanks to the tireless efforts of Martha Messinger and George Patton, Louisiana has since adopted legislation ending commercial exploitation.

As discussed previously, the biological constraints imposed by the evolutionary history of a species define the limits to management and the response to exploitation or other forms of population-related stress. There is no compromising these constraints without predictable adverse consequences. Clearly, the life history traits of box turtles do not permit large-scale exploitation, certainly not to satisfy the whims of a fickle and consumptive international market. In this regard, CITES has played a most valuable and effective role, one based on science rather than politics.

MANIPULATING POPULATIONS

Conservation biologists have often faced the dilemma of what to do with animals that are displaced from their native habitat. Some animals are unwanted pets, whereas others have been moved to safety away from traffic or bulldozers. In certain places, development threatens populations, and statutory assistance is unavailable to prevent the destruction of their habitat. What should be done with these animals? There are no easy answers. Sometimes the goals of protecting individuals and of conserving the species are compatible, and sometimes they are not. I would never recommend ignoring the plight of animals about to be killed by advancing "development." However, measures adopted to prevent unwanted deaths should not be used as a screen for ignoring the problem of habitat loss and fragmentation, or to give positive publicity when it is not warranted.

Several labor-intensive and expensive methods have been promoted as management options when turtle populations are threatened by declines or habitat loss. Because these methods often treat the symptoms of a problem rather than the underlying cause—moving turtles rather than protecting habitat—and depend on technological solutions, they can fall under the term "halfway technology" (Frazer, 1992, 1997). Unfortunately, relocation may be the only option available in emergency situations. Protection of individuals usually is handled on a case by case basis.

HEADSTARTING, CAPTIVE PROPAGATION. If predation is perceived as a problem, or if the egg to juvenile life stages have high mortality, turtles can be reared in a protected environment until such time as they can better fend for themselves. In theory, such "headstarted" turtles should have greater survivorship than eggs and hatchlings left in the wild because of their larger size. Headstarting has not been attempted for box turtles. Captive propagation on a large scale, whether for commercial or conservation purposes, also has not been undertaken for any *Terrapene*. The Durrell Wildlife Conservation Trust and some zoos in the United States have small captive colonies of *T. coahuila*, however. It is debatable whether captive propagation to supply the pet trade is either ethical or beneficial to the conservation of wild populations.

REPATRIATION, TRANSLOCATION, RELOCATION (RRT). The release of an individual into an area formerly or currently occupied by that species is termed repatriation, and the release of an individual into an area not known to contain the species is a translocation. Translocation includes the movement of animals into newly created habitats (see later discussion). The movement of animals out of harm's way, preferably to an area of suitable habitat, is a relocation. Collectively, these three activities are called RRT projects, and they all involve moving numbers of animals. The goals are laudable—to move animals out of harm's way—but do they work as a conservation strategy? Again the answer is not straightforward.

As the preceding pages have demonstrated, box turtles have specific biophysical and environmental requirements that must be met (biological constraints). At the same time, adults are rather sedentary, not completely social, and have well-defined home ranges (except, of course, for the transients). Displaced animals tend to try to return home, and they expend considerable time and energy doing so, often from far distances. Long-term oriented movement exposes them to hazards (predators, roads) in unfamiliar territory, perhaps across seasons with severe weather extremes. A homeward-moving turtle may be sidetracked, but rarely are they entirely discouraged. Few turtles remain stationary and immediately establish home ranges in unfamiliar territory. Therefore, if box turtles are moved in RRT projects, what are the chances of success?

Few studies have examined these factors in connection with a box turtle RRT project. In general, however, RRT programs have rarely been successful for reptiles, and most biologists consider them experiments at best, rather than proven management techniques (Dodd and Seigel, 1991; Reinert, 1991; Seigel and Dodd, 2000). In Wisconsin, Curtin (1995, pers. comm.) moved twenty ornate box turtles from degraded sites to a field enclosure. Results suggested that only one third to half of the turtles remained on site after one year. Belzer (1997) also attempted to repatriate eastern box turtles in Pennsylvania. Although precautions were taken prior to release, few of his twenty turtles established home ranges at the release site. The problem is simple: box turtles tend to leave the site. This makes the establishment of new populations very difficult and does little to conserve threatened populations.

The only scientific study to examine the translocation of box turtles in depth is that of Cook (1996). From 1987 to 1990, he moved 335 *T. carolina* from various areas within a mean distance of 70 km from New York to a newly created 580 ha protected site in Brooklyn. The turtles were then monitored for a period of up to seven years. As with other displaced *Terrapene*, the translocated turtles oriented generally in a homeward direction, and many started moving immediately upon release. Although many turtles established home ranges within three to five years, survivorship was lower in the translocated turtles (71 percent) than in populations not translocated, especially during the first two years after release. The greatest mortality was due to winterkill. The density of translocated *Terrapene* at Floyd Bennett Field was between 0.87 and 1.19 per ha (Cook, 1996), slightly above the value of 0.62 per ha calculated by Mosimann (1958) as the minimum population density at which box turtles could find one another. Based on telemetry, Cook (1996) estimated that a translocation site must have a minimum of 527 ha of good quality habitat if it is to retain 100 percent of the translocated individuals at a minimum density for survival. Habitats to which box turtles are moved need 200 to 300 ha to retain approximately 80 percent of the released animals.

Much remains to be learned about the effectiveness of RRT programs as conservation tools. Still, it is clear that they are not panaceas if long-term population establishment is the goal of the effort. Cook (1996) intensively monitored his population, protected on National Park Service land, using the best available technology. He did not have to secure the land and arrange for long-term protection, an important consideration when moving animals around. He also moved a large number of animals. Still, he could not conclude that the project was entirely successful; it may yet be, but it will take many more years to be sure. Individuals and organizations interested in pursuing RRT programs for conservation reasons should read Cook's (1996) study carefully for insight and guidance. It is hard to circumvent those biological constraints.

Leave Box Turtles Alone

Ultimately, the best advice I can offer on box turtle conservation is to protect their habitats and leave them alone. Refrain from collecting them. Don't buy wild-caught animals. Support and assist organizations that promote their study and conservation, and oppose land use changes that lead to loss of habitat. Disseminate accurate information on their needs and requirements, encourage conservation organizations to take more interest in their welfare, and support and promote research. In some instances, it may be desirable to move them out of harm's way; it is certainly appropriate to do so from a humane standpoint. If this becomes necessary, work carefully and courteously with landowners and local biologists, and minimize reliance on halfway technologies, if at all possible, regardless of how attractive they may be. Box turtles are best enjoyed in their native environment. If you have them on your land or in your neighborhood, be glad. You are lucky.

Future Directions

The results of a great many empirical studies have conservation applications. One important thing biologists who study box turtles can do is to look beyond the immediate results of their research and try to examine its broader implications. For example, examine the implications of home range size on the amount of habitat needed to protect a box turtle population rather than merely studying home range size in box turtles. Determine how or if human activity can be meshed with box turtle temporal and seasonal activity patterns instead of merely studying activity patterns. Examples of this type of research are found in the recommendations of Dodd et al. (1994), Dodd et al. (1997), and Curtin (1997). Good conservation and management begin with a solid foundation of life history information.

Much new insight into box turtle biology can be gained by examining population demography in fragmented populations, especially in those populations that have been protected over a long period. How does patch size influence population structure and survivorship? We need to know much more about box turtles living in human-occupied habitats. How do they survive, and how can they be conserved? If recreational activity leads to a gradual decline of box turtles as it did for wood turtles (Garber and Burger, 1995), should recreation be promoted on public conservation lands? If edges are particularly detrimental to turtles at the northern extremes of their ranges, might not edges be beneficial in other regions by allowing more choice for thermoregulation, providing a greater variety of food sources, and extending activity periods? In this regard, more information is needed on the biophysical environment of box turtles.

Mortality from automobiles is known to exact a high toll on box turtles. It might be interesting to compare data on the population structure and life history of box turtles adjacent to and far away from a highway system. Is mortality continuous through time, or are there seasonal peaks? Are the animals killed local residents, or are they mostly transients? Are certain size classes affected more heavily? Finally, what effects on population persistence does this mortality have? Population viability analysis could lead to some unsettling insights. Research needs to identify major geographic regions of highway mortality and possible ways to deter turtles from entering or crossing highway rights-of-way.

In tandem with these efforts, research needs to examine the effects of removing animals from a population, whether through highway mortality, emigration from small habitats, commercial collection, predation by domestic pets or overfed raccoons, or gathering turtles to race. Are certain life stages—juveniles, females—more vulnerable than others? If males are removed for commerce, as was once recommended by Louisiana, what is the effect on social structure, mating, and survivorship of those left behind? There is ample evidence from studies on other long-lived chelonians to suggest that removal of any segment of the population is detrimental to the persistence of the species, but can models be developed that demonstrate this?

In terms of contaminants, we know so little that virtually any of the topics popular right now (sublethal effects, threshold dosage effects, chemical synergy, endocrine disrupters) have applications to box turtle conservation. Techniques using small amounts of tissue or even the bones from deceased animals or specimens in museums could be valuable in tracing the history and effects of chemical contamination and assessing bioaccumulation. Meyers-Schöne and Walton (1994) have suggested that turtles have both advantages and limitations as environmental monitors. One of the limitations cited by these authors is the lack of information on specific biochemical indicators of contaminant exposure.

Finally, we need much better information on techniques involving the manipulation of box turtle populations. The work of Cook (1996) presents an excellent example of the integration of a life history study with a dispassionate examination of a possible management technique. If life history constraints suggest that RRT will not work, what are we to do with box turtles moved for humane reasons? Just as ethics play a role in medical research, the ethics of conservation options need exploration. We also need much better information on the effects of disease on box turtles and to determine if humans play a part in facilitating or spreading disease. Can box turtles truly be left alone if they are to survive as functioning members of their ecosystems?

Identification Key to *Terrapene* Species and Subspecies

1a. Plastron without a well-developed hinge between abdominal and pectoral scutes .... Not a box turtle!
1b. Plastron with a well-developed hinge between abdominal and pectoral scutes (fig. 1-2b) 2

2a. Upper jaw notched; chin and throat bright yellow .... Blanding's turtle (*Emydoidea blandingi*)
2b. Upper jaw without a notch; chin and throat may have yellow, especially in patches or streaks, but normally not a uniform bright yellow .... box turtle (*Terrapene*); 3

3a. Carapace keeled with keel normally present; first marginal scute usually rectangular; interfemoral seam short (see fig. 1-2b); carapace vaulted toward rear of bridge and somewhat elongate (normally); inner toe of male like other toes; pattern extremely variable .... Carolina group; 4
3b. Carapace usually without dorsal keel; first marginal scute irregularly oval or triangular in shape (see fig. 1-2a); interfemoral seam long; carapace vaulted before the bridge and generally round in appearance; inner toe of male capable of being turned inward at sharp angle; pattern of radiating lines or spots on carapace .... Ornata group; 5

4a. Carapace usually elongate and narrow, domed but less than 40 percent of carapace length; uniform coloration; head may be mottled but limbs, neck, and tail grayish brown to olive; 4 toes on hind foot; found only in Coahuila, Mexico .... Coahuilan box turtle, *T. coahuila*
4b. Carapace usually elongate and domed, but may be wide or nearly oval, greater than 42 percent of carapace length; coloration of carapace uniform to highly variable patterns of yellow and orange blotches to stripes; limb coloration highly variable; 3–4 toes on hind foot; found throughout the eastern and midwestern United States, and in scattered locations in east-central Mexico and on the Yucatán Peninsula, but not in Coahuila .... Eastern box turtle, *T. carolina*; 6

5a. Interabdominal seam greater than or equal to 38 percent of the plastral hind lobe length; interfemoral seam (fig. 1-2b) length 16 percent or less of plastral hind lobe length; dark brown to tan carapace, spotted, although spotting occasionally may be absent; found west of the Sierra Madre Occidental mountains in Mexico .... Spotted box turtle, *T. nelsoni;* 11

5b. Interabdominal seam less than or equal to 32 percent of plastron hind lobe length; interfemoral seam 18 percent or greater of plastral hind lobe length; carapace and plastron with radiating patterns of yellow or cream-colored lines; found mostly in the mid-continent of North America in sandy or arid habitats, especially grasslands and scrub . . . . Ornate box turtle, *T. ornata*; 12

6a. Carapace with a series of radiating yellow lines; plastron variable from either uniform yellow to black, with much variation between these extremes; head variable, but often with longitudinal lines; rear toes 3 or 4; carapace may or may not show flaring; extreme southeast Georgia and throughout Florida Peninsula . . . .
. . . . Florida box turtle, *T. carolina bauri*
6b. Carapace does not possess radiating lines; found outside the Florida Peninsula . . 7

7a. Carapace high domed with third vertebral elevated into small hump; carapace tan or straw colored with dark radiations or black scute borders; some marginal flaring; 4 toes on rear feet; found only on the Yucatán Peninsula . . . .
. . . . Yucatán box turtle, *T. carolina yucatana*
7b. Not as above; found outside the Yucatán Peninsula 8

8a. Carapace pattern indistinct, uniformly unmarked to patterned, dark chocolate to black in color; rear marginals flared; 4 toes on hind feet; head normally uniformly dark, often with large white patches laterally; large size, often greater than 200 mm carapace length; found along northern Gulf Coast from Florida Panhandle to Louisiana; next to the Coahuilan box turtle, the most aquatic of box turtles, often found in or near marshes . . . . Gulf Coast box turtle, *T. carolina major*
8b. Not as above; found outside the northern Gulf Coast region 9

9a. Carapace brown to black, highly patterned with various arrays of blotches, smudges, or other marks of yellow and orange; plastron unmarked to extremely pigmented; marginals vertical to only slightly flared; head extremely variable, often very colorful with yellow or orange markings; 4 toes on each hind foot; found throughout much of the eastern and central United States . . . .
. . . . Eastern box turtle, *T. carolina carolina*
9b. Carapace usually tan, olive, or straw colored, pattern either absent or only weakly discernible; 3 toes normally found on each hind foot 10

10a. Carapace elongated and high domed, with third vertebral elevated into a small hump; marginals may be slightly flared; some individuals pale yellow with dark markings on the marginal borders; found only in east-central Mexico . . . .
. . . . Mexican box turtle, *T. carolina mexicana*
10b. Carapace tan or olive, sometimes with obscure pattern; orange or yellow spots on forelimbs and head, but some males have red heads; concavity of male shallow; found in the central United States . . . . Three-toed box turtle, *T. carolina triunguis*

11a. Carapace straw colored, tan, or dark brown; light spots relatively large and uncommon; interhumeral seam and interpectoral seam (fig. 1-2b) average 16 percent and 35 percent, respectively, of anterior plastral lobe's length; first vertebral scute concave; found only in the vicinity of Pedro Pablo, Nayarit, Mexico . . . .
. . . . Southern spotted box turtle, *T. nelsoni nelsoni*

11b. Carapace tan to dark brown or even greenish brown; light spots relatively small and numerous; interhumeral seam and interpectoral seam average 18 percent and 33 percent, respectively, of anterior plastral lobe's length; first vertebral scute flattened; found in Sinaloa and southwestern Sonora, Mexico . . . .
. . . . Northern spotted box turtle, *T. nelsoni klauberi*

12a. Radiating lines on second pleural scute number 5–8; generally lines are yellow or cream on a rather dark background; found on the Plains grasslands in the central United States . . . . Ornate box turtle, *T. ornata ornata*

12b. Radiating lines of the second pleural scute number 11–14; carapace generally yellowish; some shells show no pattern at all; found on the grasslands of southwestern United States . . . . Desert box turtle, *T. ornata luteola*

Species Accounts

The following accounts provide additional information on the taxonomy and life history of box turtles not contained elsewhere in the book. Generally, I do not repeat information in the text. I follow standard common names in English (Collins, 1997) and Spanish (Liner, 1994). Synonymies follow Ward (1978), Smith and Smith (1979), Iverson (1982a, b), and Ernst and McBreen (1991a, b), although I do not include early spelling errors (termed *lapsus calami*). Museum abbreviations generally follow Leviton et al. (1980).

Identification is provided on the basis of many published papers and my personal experience. The brief life history sections are intended to cover regional details of interest (such as clutch size variation) and other tidbits of information not included in the main text. Readers are urged to use these data, but with caution. I have found that regional guides often pirate information from other guides or papers, leading to a certain degree of inaccuracy; know thy source! The best sources are those which state how the data were obtained rather than simply providing unsubstantiated numbers. Finally, I single out a few important or summary references that may further aid the reader in obtaining information on North American box turtles.

Box Turtle, Genus *Terrapene* Merrem, 1820

ETYMOLOGY: The generic name is derived from an Algonkian word for turtle.

SYNONYMY:
> *Didicla* Rafinesque, 1815. Nomen nudum.
> *Monoclida* Rafinesque, 1815. Nomen nudum.
> *Terrapene* Merrem, 1820
> *Cistuda* Fleming, 1822
> *Cistudo* Say, 1825
> *Emys* Wagler, 1830 (in part)
> *Pyxidemis* Fitzinger, 1835
> *Emyoides* Gray, 1844
> *Onychotria* Strauch, 1862
> *Pariemys* Cope, 1895
> *Toxaspis* Cope, 1895

KARYOTYPE: The karyotype of *Terrapene* consists of a diploid chromosome number of 50 (26 macrochromosomes and 24 microchromosomes) (Killebrew, 1977).

REFERENCES: Taylor (1895), Milstead (1969); summaries in Ditmars (1934), Carr (1952), Murphy (1976), Smith and Smith (1979), Ernst and Barbour (1989), Ernst et al. (1994).

Eastern Box Turtle, *Terrapene carolina* (Linnaeus, 1758)

Tortuga carolina (Spanish); *Tortue tabatière* (French Canada)

ETYMOLOGY: The specific epithet refers to the Carolina region of the southeast Atlantic Coast of the United States. The subspecies names were derived as follows: *bauri*—named for George C. L. Baur, a specialist in the study of turtles in the late nineteenth century; *major*—Latin for larger or greater, referring to the large size of this subspecies; *mexicana*—referring to Mexico; *putnami*—named for F. W. Putnam, American Museum of Natural History, who first collected the bones of this fossil species in the Alafia (misspelled Alifia in Hay, 1906) River, Florida; *triunguis*—Latin for three (*tri*) and nail or claw (*unguiculus*), referring to the three toes on each hind foot; *yucatana*—referring to the Yucatán region of Mexico.

SYNONYMY:

Testudo carolina Linnaeus, 1758

Testudo carinata Linnaeus, 1758

Testudo brevi-caudata Lacépède, 1788

Testudo incarcerata Bonnaterre, 1789

Testudo incarcerato-striata Bonnaterre, 1789

Testudo clausa Gmelin, 1789

Testudo virgulata Latreille, in Sonnini and Latreille, 1801

Emys clausa Schweigger, 1814

Emys virgulata Schweigger, 1814

Emys schneideri Schweigger, 1814

Terrapene clausa Merrem, 1820

Monoclida kentuckensis Rafinesque, 1822

Cistudo clausa Say, 1825

Terrapene carolina Bell, 1825

Terrapene maculata Bell, 1825

Terrapene nebulosa Bell, 1825

Emys tridentaculata Saint Hillaire, in Cuvier, 1829. Nomen nudum.

Cistudo carolina Gray, 1831

Emys kinosternoides Gray, 1831

Cistudo mexicana Gray, 1849

Cistudo major Agassiz, 1857

Cistudo triunguis Agassiz, 1857

Cistudo virginea Agassiz, 1857

Terrapene carinata Strauch, 1862

Terrapene eurypygia Cope, 1869

Cistudo marnochi Cope, 1878

Onychotria mexicana Dugés, 1888

Cistudo carolina mexicana Boulenger, 1889

Cistudo yucatana Boulenger, 1895

Terrapene bauri Taylor, 1895

Terrapene triunguis Taylor, 1895

Terrapene major Taylor, 1895

Terrapene putnami Hay, 1906

Terrapene yucatana Siebenrock, 1909

Terrapene carolina triunguis Strecker, 1910

Terrapene formosa Hay, 1916

Terrapene antipex Hay, 1916

Terrapene whitneyi Hay, 1916

Terrapene innoxia Hay, 1916

Terrapene carolina carolina Stejneger and Barbour, 1917

Terrapene bulverda Hay, 1920

Terrapene impressa Hay, 1924

Terrapene singletoni Gilmore, 1928

Terrapene goldmani Stejneger, 1933

Terrapene carolina major Carr, 1940

Terrapene carolina bauri Carr, 1940

Terrapene llanensis Oelrich, 1953

Terrapene canaliculata Milstead, 1956

Terrapene carolina putnami Auffenberg, 1958

Terrapene carolina mexicana Milstead, 1967

Terrapene carolina yucatana Milstead, 1967

CONTENT AND DISTRIBUTION: Six extant and one fossil subspecies are currently recognized.

TERRAPENE CAROLINA CAROLINA (LINNAEUS, 1758): Eastern box turtle. Holotype: Undesignated. The range of the eastern box turtle extends from southern Maine along the eastern seaboard to the Piedmont and coastal plain of southern Georgia, and thence westward to the Mississippi River, at least in the north (map 1). There are relatively few records for New York; elsewhere in the north, there are a few records for extreme southern Ontario (but see chapter 2), and the species occurs northward in the state of Michigan along Lake Michigan to Grand Traverse County. It is absent from the Prairie Peninsula of Illinois. To the south and southwest, there is an extensive zone of intergradation with *T. c. bauri, T. c. major* (west of the Okefenokee Basin) and *T. c. triunguis*. In the zones of intergradation, especially in the western part of south Georgia, it may be impossible to determine subspecific status (M. Frick, pers. comm.). In addition, the eastern box turtle has been picked up, transported, and released since paleo-Indian times. It is not uncommon to find a specimen of this species (or of the other subspecies, for that matter) far outside its normal range. For example, eastern box turtles have been reported in Penobscot County, Maine, 150 km east of their "normal" range (Hunter et al., 1992). Important references on the distribution of the eastern box turtle include books on the herpetology of Connecticut (Klemens, 1993), Virginia (Mitchell, 1994), North Carolina (Palmer and Braswell, 1995), Illinois (Smith, 1961), Indiana (Minton, 1972), Ohio (Conant, 1938) and the Great Lakes region (Harding, 1997).

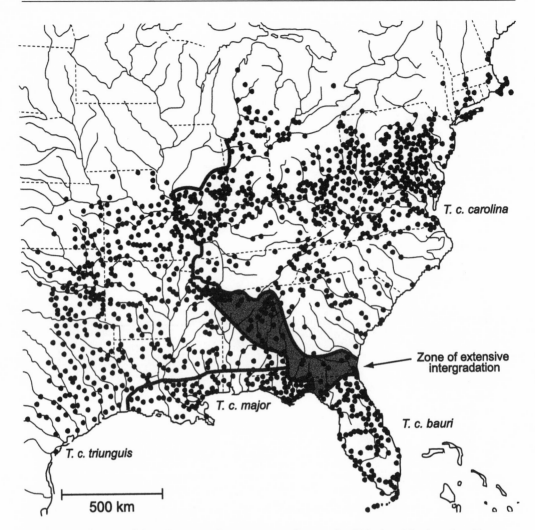

Map 1. Distribution of the subspecies of *Terrapene carolina* north of Mexico. Map based on Ernst and McBreen (1991b), Iverson (1992b) and Minx (1996). The shaded area marks a zone of extensive intergradation.

TERRAPENE CAROLINA BAURI TAYLOR, 1894: Florida box turtle. Holotype: USNM #8352, collected in 1875 by F.B. Meek. The Florida box turtle is found from the extreme southeast corner of Georgia (McIntosh to Camden counties; M. Frick, pers. comm.) south throughout the Florida Peninsula and into the Florida Keys (map 1). In the north, it intergrades with *T. c. carolina*, and in the northwest it intergrades with both *T. c. major* and *T. c. triunguis*. Iverson and Etchberger (1989) provide specific locality records in Florida, and Dodd and Franz (1993) review museum holdings.

TERRAPENE CAROLINA MAJOR (AGASSIZ, 1857): Gulf Coast box turtle. Syntypes: (6), MCZ 1505-1510. The Gulf Coast box turtle has at least three somewhat different and differently distributed morphological patterns (chapter 2). It occurs along the northern Gulf Coast from the Florida Panhandle westward to about the Beckwith River in Louisiana (map 1). This subspecies intergrades with *T. c. carolina, T. c. bauri,* and *T. c. triunguis.* Important geographic references include herpetology guides for Alabama (Mount, 1975), Florida (Iverson and Etchberger, 1989), and Louisiana (Dundee and Rossman, 1989).

TERRAPENE CAROLINA MEXICANA (GRAY, 1849): Mexican box turtle. *Tortuga méxicana* (Spanish). Type specimens: (2) in BMNH #48.7.28.29-30, collector unknown. Known from the eastern portions of the Mexican states of San Luis Potosí, Tamaulipas, and Veracruz (map 2). The best review of records for and distribution of this subspecies is Smith and Smith (1979).

TERRAPENE CAROLINA PUTNAMI HAY, 1906: Giant box turtle. Known only as fossils. See chapter 2.

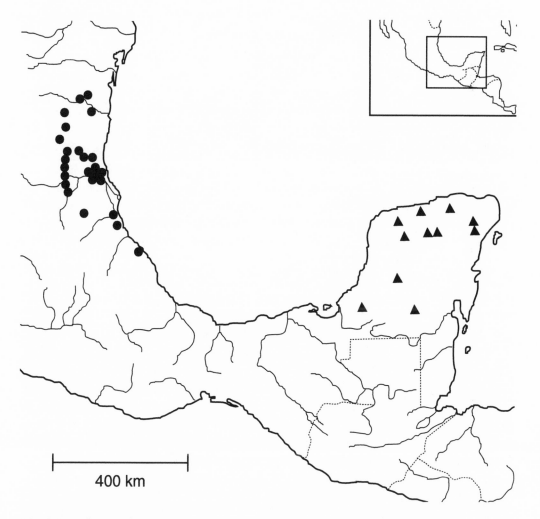

Map 2. Distribution of *T. c. mexicana* (circles) and *T. c. yucatana* (triangles) in Mexico. Map based on Iverson (1992b) and Smith et al. (1996).

TERRAPENE CAROLINA TRIUNGUIS (AGASSIZ, 1857): Three-toed box turtle. Syntypes: (9), MCZ #1519, 1522, collected by N. P. Benedict. The three-toed box turtle is found throughout central North America. In the northern part of its range, it is generally found west of the Mississippi River, although there are a few records of it in Illinois (Smith, 1961; Paukstis and Janzen, 1988, 1993; Tucker and Hatcher, 1994). To the south, it occurs in northern and central Mississippi into the Black Belt of Alabama (map 1). It does not enter the immediate Gulf Coastal Plain in Alabama and Mississippi, but does so in Texas. The western limit of the subspecies' range extends as far as the mesic deciduous woodlands. As the climate becomes more arid and the habitat changes to grasslands, *T. c. triunguis* drops out and is replaced by the ornate box turtle. In much of northern Alabama, extensive intergradation occurs with *T. c. carolina*; in the south, with *T. c. major*; and in the panhandle of Florida, with *T. c. bauri*. Information on its distribution is found as follows: Alabama (Mount, 1975), Louisiana (Dundee and Rossman, 1989), Texas (Dixon, 1987), Oklahoma (Webb, 1970), Kansas (Collins, 1993), and Missouri (Johnson, 1987).

TERRAPENE CAROLINA YUCATANA (BOULENGER, 1895): Yucatán box turtle. *Tortuga yucateca* (Spanish); *Ac* or *coc ac* (Mayan). Syntypes: (3), BMNH #94.3.23.2-4, collected by Mr. Gaumer, but presented to the museum by O. Salvin. The Yucatán box turtle occurs only in the states of Campeche, Yucatán, and Quintana Roo, Mexico (map 2). The best references on this turtle are Smith and Smith (1979) and Lee (1996). Smith et al. (1996) provide a range extension.

IDENTIFICATION AND DESCRIPTION: Eastern box turtles are characterized by a great deal of variation in shell color and shape, in the color and markings on the limbs, head, and neck, in maximum size, in the number of toes (claws) on the hind foot, and even in variation in eye color. In general, the carapace of an eastern box turtle is somewhat elongate, possesses a marked dorsal keel on vertebrals 2–4, and is greatest in depth at the midpoint or posterior to the hinge on the plastron. The first vertebral is steeply angled, and the first marginal is usually rectangular. The carapace is usually dark brown, although in some subspecies it ranges from light brown to yellowish brown (*triunguis*, *mexicana*, *yucatana*). The plastron has a single hinge, the hinge is usually present at the fifth marginal, and there is no bridge between the carapace and plastron. The plastron and carapace may be nearly equal in straight-line length. Plastrons range from completely yellow and unmarked to uniformly black, with every variation in between. Indeed, a great deal of phenotypic variation may exist within a single population. The skin of the head and limbs ranges from black to light tan, with much variation in color pattern (stripes, blotches, spots) and intensity (brilliant reds, yellows, and oranges are not uncommon; some *triunguis* even have blue heads).

SEXUAL DIMORPHISM: Sexual dimorphism is prevalent. Mature males of most subspecies have a red iris, although this does not hold true for *bauri* and *yucatana* and can even vary within a population of *carolina* (Drotos, 1974). Females usually have a brown or yellowish brown iris. In males, the plastron is concave to fit onto the female's carapace during mating. The depth of the concavity may vary considerably among individuals and subspecies. The plastron of the female is usually straight without any indentations. However, there are a few individuals with a very slight concavity that leads one to wonder about the sex. Males usually have shorter hind foot claws than females. Although it is often claimed that males have longer, thicker tails than females, this may not be a reliable method for distinguishing sex (Mitchell, 1994). Males are usually larger than females (in straight-line carapace length) but females may weigh more at a particular carapace length.

HATCHLINGS: A hatchling box turtle is much rounder than an adult, and about the size of a Ritz cracker. The carapace is grayish to black, and much lower and more flattened than in an adult, but the median keel is more pronounced (as knobs or lines) and very light (yellow) in color. Light markings on the carapace may be present although they are not pronounced; the carapace may be bordered by a light yellow line around its edge; the plastron is dark with yellow margins; the umbilicus and egg caruncle are obvious in recently hatched individuals; the hinge is nonfunctional. Hatchling box turtles have a noticeable odor when they are harassed (Neill, 1948b).

SKULL: See figure SA-1, UF/FMNH 22160, female, 18 km south of Waynesboro on Highway 56, Burke County, Georgia. Also see fig. 1-4 for variation in the zygomatic arch among the subspecies.

SUBSPECIES CHARACTERISTICS
Some individual characteristics among the subspecies are as follows.

T. C. CAROLINA. Carapace—usually dark brown with a great degree of pattern variation; often with yellow, orange, or red splotches, streaks, blotches, or dabs; pattern may be random or bilaterally symmetrical. Plastron—yellow to black, with or without patterns; every possible combination in between may be seen. Head, neck, legs—usually dark brown with some pattern involving yellow or orange streaks or blotches. Phalangeal formula of forefeet—mostly 2-3-3-3-2 (Minx, 1992). Phalangeal formula of hind feet—mostly either 2-3-3-3-2 or 2-3-3-3-1 (Minx, 1992). Toes—usually 4 on hind foot.

T. C. BAURI. Carapace—usually dark with streaks of radiating light yellow lines, most of which are continuous; shell relatively narrow and elongate, although some females may be nearly oval; most rear marginals not flared, although occasional individuals have extensive rear marginal flaring. Plastron—may be immaculately yellow or with extensive brown streaks or patterns resulting in a nearly uniform plastron coloration. Head, neck, legs—dark brown to nearly black, usually with moderate to dull yellow markings; often two parallel lateral stripes on side of head; the eye of the male is brown, not red as in other subspecies. Hatchlings—initially very similar in appearance to *carolina*, but often quickly assuming a somewhat broader appearance; the median keel of very small juveniles is broad and relatively bright yellow, and lateral markings on the carapace also appear more marked and conspicuous; they may appear as little gems of bright yellow on a black background. Phalangeal formula of forefeet—mostly 2-3-3-3-2 (Minx, 1992). Phalangeal formula of hind feet—mostly either 2-3-3-3-2 or 2-3-3-3-1 (Minx, 1992). Toes—usually 3 on rear hind foot, but some populations may have many individuals with 4 toes per hind foot, and a few turtles may have 3 toes on one foot and 4 on the other.

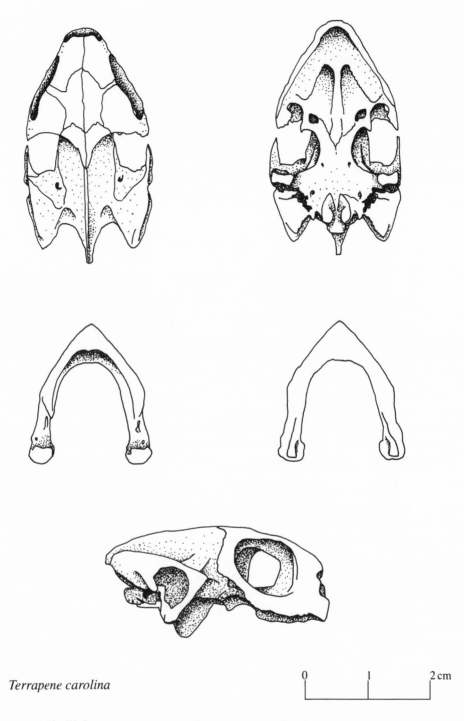

Terrapene carolina

0   1   2 cm

Figure SA-1. Skull of *Terrapene carolina.* UF/FMNH 22160, female, 18 km south of Waynesboro on Highway 56, Burke County, Georgia.

T. C. MAJOR. Carapace—relatively elongate and high, with the highest point in the middle of the carapace; keeled, with rear marginals flared; dark brown to nearly black, often with a pattern of dull scattered spots or radiating lines. Plastron—deeply black to dark brown; plastron of males deeply concave. Head, neck, legs—deeply jet black to dark brown, uniform to patterned; adult males may have a blotch or extensive white patches on the lateral and dorsal reaches of the head. Phalangeal formula of forefeet—mostly 2-3-3-3-2 (Minx, 1992). Phalangeal formula of hind feet—mostly 2-3-3-3-2 (Minx, 1992). Toes—usually 4 on the hind foot. According to Carr (1952), males have larger hind legs and a more distally placed vent than females. This is the largest extant box turtle, with adults commonly reaching more than 200 mm in carapace length.

T. C. MEXICANA. Carapace—elongated and domed, with a small hump on the third vertebral; moderate flaring of the posterior marginals; sometimes patterned. Head, neck, legs—generally uniform dark gray to brown; some light spotting may occur laterally on the head. Phalangeal formula of forefeet—mostly 2-3-3-2-2 (Minx, 1992). Phalangeal formula of hind feet—mostly 2-3-3-3-1 (Minx, 1992). Toes—usually 3 per hind foot (6 of 32 specimens examined by Smith (1939) had 4 toes on the hind foot).

T. C. TRIUNGUIS. Carapace—narrow and keeled, with some flaring at the posterior margin; highest point on the carapace well toward the rear, the most posterior of any of the subspecies; coloration tan, light yellowish, to olive; may have slight pattern or be rather uniform in color. Plastron—frequently solid yellow and unmarked; dark borders along the seams may be present; male plastron not as concave as in some of the other subspecies. Head, neck, legs—spotting (bright oranges, reds, yellows) usually present on head and forelimbs; males often have very colorful heads, including brilliant reds and even blue; the skin may be dark brown to black; white pigment may be present on upper jaw. Phalangeal formula of forefeet—mostly 2-3-3-2-2 (Minx, 1992). Phalangeal formula of hind feet—mostly 2-3-3-3-1 (Minx, 1992). Toes—usually 3, occasionally 4, on each hind foot.

T. C. YUCATANA. Carapace—domed, with a hump on the third vertebral; median keel distinct; some flaring on the posterior marginals; coloration tan to yellowish, often with black along the scute borders; carapace may have some dark radiations. Plastron—nearly solid black to dirty yellow. Head, neck, legs—may be rather light, pale yellow to dull yellowish; jaw notched. Phalangeal formula of forefeet—mostly 2-3-3-3-2 (Minx, 1992). Phalangeal formula of hind feet—mostly 2-3-3-3-2 (Minx, 1992). Toes—generally 4 per hind foot. There is a striking sexual dichromatism between male and female Yucatan box turtles (Buskirk, 1993). Females usually have pale brown limbs and heads, which may grade to yellow and brown in color. Males, however, have primarily white heads that may contain blue or pink flecking on the eyelids and throats. The iris of the male ranges from off-white to the color of the female's iris, yellow. Males generally have darker carapaces than females, and the carapace may even take on a reddish cast. Distinct reddish brown smudges are present on the underside of the posterior marginals of adult males, and the plastron has only a shallow concavity (Buskirk, 1993).

TAXONOMIC COMMENTS: As noted, there is great variation in the phenotypic appearance of this species. In areas where the subspecies come into contact, extensive intergradation occurs, blurring subspecific differences even further. In such areas, it may be impossible to determine which subspecies predominate.

LIFE HISTORY

ACTIVITY (NOCTURNAL): (North Carolina) Two instances of nocturnal activity (one animal crossing a road at 10:00 P.M. in Randolph County, June 29; a second animal crossing a road at 11:00 P.M. in Montgomery County, July 13) were reported in Palmer and Braswell (1995). Both observations occurred on rainy nights.

ACTIVITY SEASON: (New England) Late April to mid-October for *carolina*, but a hatchling found as early as March 8 (Klemens, 1993). (Kansas) April to October for *triunguis* (Collins, 1993). (Kentucky) Although *carolina* normally overwinters beginning in October, active individuals have been found as late as December 10 (Barbour, 1971). (North Carolina) Box turtles have been observed in every month (Palmer and Braswell, 1995). (Ohio) April to October, but occasionally through the winter on warm days, for *carolina* (Conant, 1938).

AGE: (New York) Of the many box turtles marked by J. T. Nichols at the Floyd Estate on Long Island, New York, from 1924 to 1956, eighteen were recaptured by Richard Stavdal of the National Park Service between 1980 and 1989 (see chapter 1). The minimum ages of these turtles ranged between forty-eight and eighty-six years (complete records in Klemens, 1993); twelve of the eighteen turtles were more than seventy years of age.

EGGS/CLUTCH SIZE: (New England) 3–9 for *carolina* (Klemens, 1993). (Illinois) 4–6 for *carolina* (Pope, 1938). Cahn (1937) records 3–8 eggs for Illinois *carolina*, with average dimensions of 33×19.5 mm (range 35×19 mm to 30.5×18.5 mm). (Kansas) 2–8 for *triunguis* (Collins, 1993). (Kentucky) 2–7 eggs, but usually 4–5, deposited by *carolina* (Barbour, 1971). (North Carolina) 2–7 ($\bar{x}$ = 3.67, mode = 3) for *carolina* (Stuart and Miller, 1987; Palmer and Braswell, 1995). (Virginia) A single clutch of 2–7 eggs for *carolina* (Mitchell, 1994).

ELEVATION: In New England, *carolina* seem most common up to 150 m in elevation but are found sporadically up to about 215 m (Klemens, 1993). In the South, box turtles may be found well over 1,300 m in elevation (Palmer and Braswell, 1995).

FEEDING: In captivity, feeding hierarchies may be established that persist between seasons. One turtle may be able to dominate accessibility to food to the detriment, even resulting in death, of more subordinate turtles (Boice et al., 1974). Ernst et al. (1994) misinterpret an abstract based on these experiments, which were not referenced, to suggest that box turtles and American toads (*Bufo americanus*) exhibit an interspecific social facilitation in feeding behavior.

HINGE: (Indiana) According to Minton (1972), the hinge on the plastron does not become functional until the turtle is 50–60 mm PL in *carolina*; this length presumably refers to PL, although this is not specified.

MALFORMATION: (North Carolina) Two-headed hatchling *carolina*. Carapace scute counts can show considerable variation (Palmer and Braswell, 1995).

MATING: (Indiana) Mating usually takes place in late April and May, but copulation has been observed in September in *carolina* in southern Indiana (Minton, 1972). Most authors report a spring mating peak, but mating routinely occurs into the autumn as well.

MORTALITY: (Kansas) Collins (1993) cites a paper in the *Kansas Herpetological Society Newsletter* reporting that approximately one third of the seventy-eight *triunguis* observed along a 122-mile stretch of highway on a single day in May were killed by auto traffic.

NESTING SEASON: (New England) Generally mid-May to late June for *carolina* (Klemens, 1993). (Indiana/Illinois) In southern Indiana and northern Illinois, nesting of *carolina* begins in June, with hatching in August or September (Pope, 1938; Smith, 1961; Minton, 1972). (Kansas) May to July for *triunguis* (Collins, 1993). (Virginia) Late May to late July for *carolina* (Mitchell, 1994).

SEXUAL DIMORPHISM: (Virginia) Although some authors claim that male box turtles have longer and thicker tails than females (e.g., Ernst and Barbour, 1989), Mitchell (1994) notes that great variation in this character makes it unreliable as a means to determine sex. Mitchell (1994) could not demonstrate strong sexual size dimorphism in Virginia *carolina*.

SIZE: (New England) According to Klemens (1993), New England mature male *carolina* exceed the CL of adult females by 8–9 mm. Klemens (1993) also provides data on size of adults from various New England states. (Indiana) *carolina* in northern Indiana are larger than in southern Indiana (Minton, 1972). (Illinois) The largest known *carolina* is 151 mm CL (Smith, 1961). (Kansas) The largest known *triunguis* in Kansas was 179 mm, although adults are normally 113–150 mm in CL (Collins, 1993). (Missouri) The largest *triunguis* in Missouri was recorded at 142 mm CL (in Johnson, 1987). (North Carolina) The largest *carolina* in North Carolina measured 151 mm CL (male) and 149 mm CL (female) (Palmer and Braswell, 1995). (Virginia) The maximum known CL for *carolina* is 156 mm and 603 g (Mitchell, 1994).

STATUS: (Indiana) "They are decidedly less common today than when I began my herpetological field observations in the 1930's" (Minton, 1972:166).

REMARKS: In North Carolina the eastern box turtle has the vernacular name "highland terrapin" (Palmer and Braswell, 1995). The specific density of this species has been measured for two juveniles at 0.73 and 0.8 g/cm^3 (Williams and Han, 1964). As such, the specific density is less than in the aquatic *T. coahuila*. Box turtles are rather adept climbers. For example, Willbern (1982) records that individual *T. c. triunguis* were able to climb a 77 cm high vertical wire mesh fence and escape from a holding pen. The eastern box turtle is the state reptile of both North Carolina (since 1979) and Tennessee.

REFERENCES: Stickel (1950), Smith and Smith (1979).

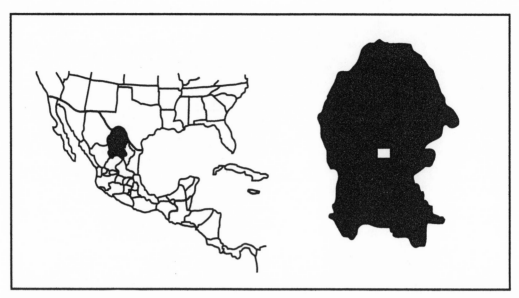

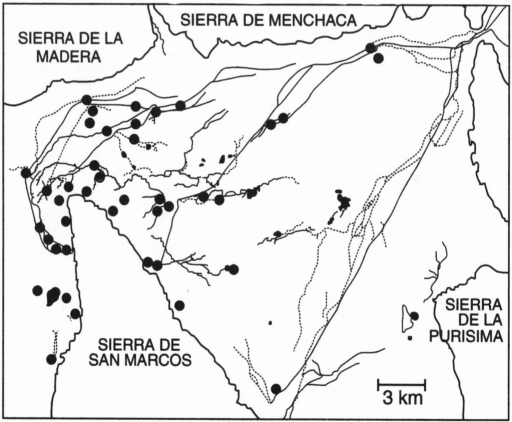

Map 3. Distribution of *Terrapene coahuila* in Coahuila, Mexico. Map based on Brown (1974) and M. A. Nickerson (pers. comm.).

Coahuilan Box Turtle, *Terrapene coahuila* Schmidt and Owens, 1944

Tortuga de Cuatro Ciénegas (Spanish)

ETYMOLOGY: The specific epithet refers to the Mexican state of Coahuila where the species occurs.

SYNONYMY:

> *Terrapene coahuila* Schmidt and Owens, 1944
> *Terrapene ornata coahuila* Mertens and Wermuth, 1955

CONTENT AND DISTRIBUTION: No subspecies are recognized. Holotype: FMNH, #41234, collected in 1939 by E.G. Marsh, Jr. The Coahuilan box turtle is found only at Cuatro Ciénegas in the Mexican state of Coahuila, north-central Mexico (map 3).

IDENTIFICATION AND DESCRIPTION: The carapace of the Coahuilan box turtle is elongate and narrow, much more so than in other *Terrapene* species. It is domed, but somewhat flattened dorsally, and a median keel may be present, but it is not very noticeable. Vertebral 1 is wedge shaped. The posterior marginals of the carapace are not serrated. The carapace has a dark brown to somewhat olive coloration, and about 70 percent of the turtles have small, irregular yellow lines, likened to worm tracks by Brown (1971). The plastron is large and well formed. An axillary scute is usually present at the bridge. Plastron color is dull yellow to dark, sometimes with dark seams and occasionally with traces of flecking. The head, neck, and legs can be gray, brown, or olive, but they do not have a pattern. The phalangeal formula of the forefeet is mostly 2-3-3-3-2 (Minx, 1992). Phalangeal formula of hind feet–2-3-3-3-2 (Minx, 1992). Generally, 4 toes are present on each hind foot.

SEXUAL DIMORPHISM: Males are generally larger than females, and they have a shell depth about 43 percent of the carapace length. In females, this ratio is about 46 percent (Brown, 1971). Males have a concave plastron, larger and heavier tails than in females, and older males are flatter than females. The iris in males is brownish, but in the female it is more yellow in color.

HATCHLINGS: The carapace of hatchlings is mottled brown with a slight trace of a pattern. The marginals are dull yellow, and there is a prominent dorsal keel on vertebrals 2 to 4. The plastron is light grayish yellow, with thin dark lines at the scute seams. The head has a light postocular stripe, which may form a blotch. Scales on the forelegs are light yellow-gray and may form a solid stripe; there may be a stripe on the dorsal surface of the tail (Brown, 1971).

SKULL: See figure SA-2, PCHP 4979, (male?), Cuatro Ciénegas, Coahuila, Mexico.

TAXONOMIC COMMENTS: Mertens and Wermuth (1955) placed *Terrapene coahuila* in synonymy with *Terrapene ornata* without explanation. There is no justification for this taxonomic arrangement.

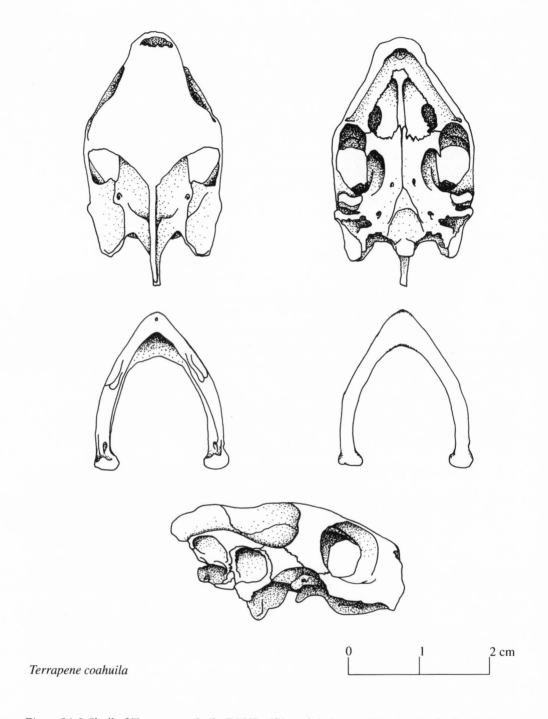

Terrapene coahuila

0   1   2 cm

Figure SA-2. Skull of *Terrapene coahuila*. PCHP 4979, male?, Cuatro Ciénegas, Coahuila, Mexico.

REMARKS: The specific density of this species has been measured at ca. 0.95 g/cm^3 (Williams and Han, 1964). As such, it is higher than in the terrestrial *T. carolina*. The present conservation status of the Coahuilan box turtle needs to be reevaluated.

REFERENCES: Schmidt and Owens (1944), Brown (1974).

Spotted Box Turtle, *Terrapene nelsoni* Stejneger, 1925
Tortuga manchas (Spanish)

ETYMOLOGY: The name *nelsoni* refers to E. W. Nelson, former chief biologist of the U.S. Biological Survey and collector of the holotype. The subspecific name *klauberi* refers to Lawrence M. Klauber, a distinguished herpetologist best known for his studies on rattlesnakes and the herpetofauna of North American deserts.

SYNONYMY:

Terrapene nelsoni Stejneger, 1925
Terrapene goldmani Ditmars, 1934 (in part)
Terrapene mexicana Mueller, 1936 (in part)
Terrapene klauberi Bogert, 1943
Terrapene nelsoni klauberi Mertens and Wermuth, 1955

CONTENT AND DISTRIBUTION: Two subspecies of the spotted box turtle are recognized.

TERRAPENE NELSONI NELSONI STEJNEGER, 1925: Southern spotted box turtle. *Tortuga manchada meridional*. Holotype: USNM #46252, collected in 1897 by E. W. Nelson and A. E. Goldman. Known only from the vicinity of the type locality in the state of Nayarit, Mexico (near Pedro Pablo, Sierra de Teponahuastla; see map 4, triangle).

TERRAPENE NELSONI KLAUBERI BOGERT, 1943: Northern spotted box turtle. *Tortuga manchada septentrional*. Holotype: AMNH #63751, collected by J. W. Hilton in 1941. The northern spotted box turtle is found in the Mexican states of Sonora and Sinaloa (see map 4, circles).

IDENTIFICATION AND DESCRIPTION: The spotted box turtle has an elongate and domed carapace but, like the Coahuilan box turtle, the carapace is somewhat flattened dorsally. The median keel is very faint or it may be absent altogether. The vertebral scutes are more broad than long, and the posterior marginals may flare over the hind limbs. The color of the carapace ranges from brown to tan or beige, or it may be dark brown to olive. There is usually a pattern of light spots. The plastron is large and well formed, dark brown, and bordered with yellow; small spots or streaks may be present. Axillary scutes are generally absent, although they occasionally may be present and located at the fifth marginals. The jaw is hooked and the head is large; as with the limbs and neck, head color is yellowish brown to dark brown. Small spots may be present. The phalangeal formula of the forefeet of both subspecies is 2-2-2-2-2 (Minx, 1992). There are 4 toes on each hind foot.

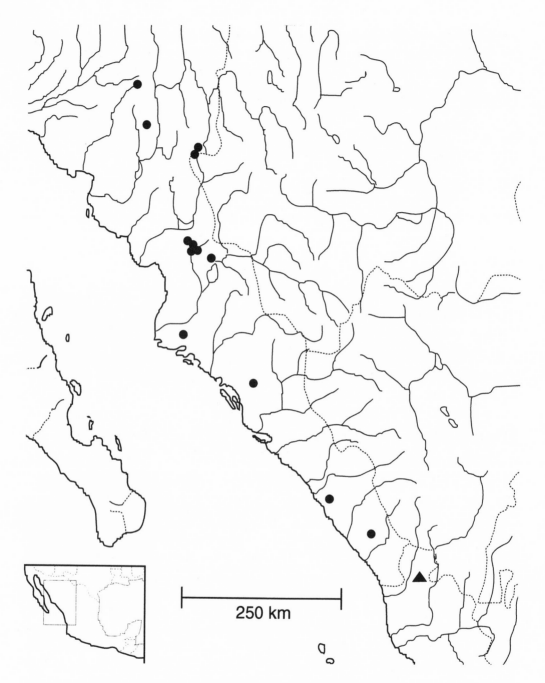

Map 4. Distribution of *Terrapene nelsoni nelsoni* (triangle) in Nayarit and *T. n. klauberi* (circles) in Sonora and Sinaloa, western Mexico. Map based on Iverson (1982b, 1992b).

SEXUAL DIMORPHISM: The male has a shallow concave plastron, whereas the female's plastron in straight or slightly convex. Like *T. ornata*, male *T. nelsoni* are capable of rotating the first toe of the hind foot and using it as a clasper to hook into the female's carapace during copulation. Males have thicker and longer tails than females. According to Shaw (1952), males have unspotted heads and forelimbs whereas in females, these structures are spotted.

SKULL: See figure SA-3, PCHP 1842, female, 80 km north of Mazatlan, Sinaloa, Mexico.

SUBSPECIES CHARACTERISTICS
Some individual characteristics between the subspecies are as follows:

T. N. NELSONI. Carapace—straw-colored, tan, or dark brown; light spots relatively large and uncommon. Upper jaw not notched. In addition, there are slight differences in the ratios of plastron scutes and in the shape of the first vertebral (see Identification Key). Phalangeal formula of hind feet—2-3-3-3-1 (Minx, 1992).

T. N. KLAUBERI. Carapace—tan to dark brown or even greenish brown; light spots relatively small and numerous. Upper jaw notched. In addition, there are slight differences in the ratios of plastron scutes and in the shape of the first vertebral (see Identification Key). Phalangeal formula of hind feet—either 2-3-3-3-2 or 2-3-3-3-1 (Minx, 1992).

TAXONOMIC COMMENTS: The taxonomic relationship and geographic partitioning between the subspecies needs a great deal of clarification. Taxonomic recognition of two subspecies may not be warranted.

REMARKS: Next to nothing is known about the life history of the spotted box turtle.

REFERENCES: Bogert (1943), Smith and Smith (1979).

Ornate Box Turtle, *Terrapene ornata* (Agassiz, 1857)
Tortuga de adornos (Spanish)

ETYMOLOGY: The specific epithet is derived from the Latin *ornatus*, meaning ornamented (or "handsome, bedecked, splendid"; in Smith and Smith, 1979), and refers to the yellow radiating lines on the scutes of the carapace. The subspecific name *luteola* comes from the Latin *luteolus* (yellowish) and refers to the drab yellowish color of the carapace.

SYNONYMY:
   Cistudo ornata Agassiz, 1857
   Terrapene ornata Baur, 1891
   Terrapene ornata var. *cimarronensis* Cragin, 1894
   Terrapene longinsulae Hay, 1908
   Terrapene ornata luteola Smith and Ramsey, 1952
   Terrapene ornata longinsulae Milstead, 1967

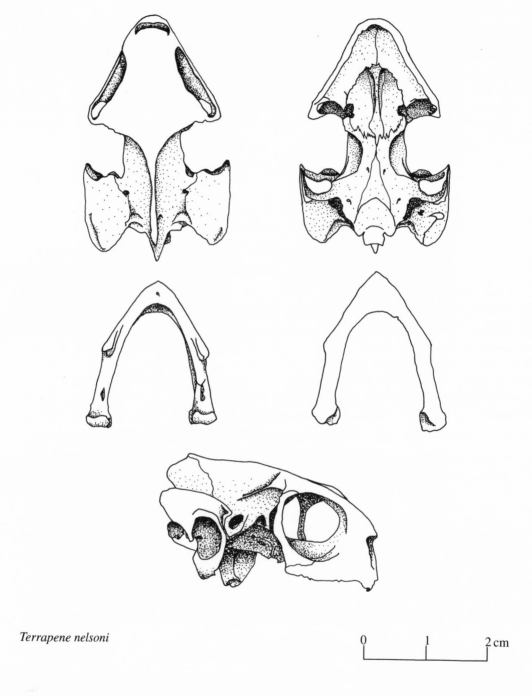

Terrapene nelsoni

0   1   2 cm

Figure SA-3. Skull of *Terrapene nelsoni*. PCHP 1842, female, 80 km north of Mazatlan, Sinaloa, Mexico.

CONTENT AND DISTRIBUTION: Two subspecies of the ornate box turtle are recognized.

TERRAPENE ORNATA ORNATA (AGASSIZ, 1857). Ornate box turtle. Syntypes: (6) USNM #7541, 7547, 7692, 7862, 131837, MCZ #1536, collected by J. Rauch. The ornate box turtle is found in both the northwest and southwest corners of Indiana and southern Wisconsin, south to Louisiana west of the Mississippi River. The subspecies' range extends westward north of the Rio Grande, thence northwest of the Pecos River in Texas and New Mexico (see map 5, circles). A zone of intergradation with *T. o. luteola* is found between the Rio Grande in New Mexico and the New Mexico–Texas border northward to the Canadian River. In the northern part of its range, *T. o. ornata* is found on the flat prairies of Colorado to south-central South Dakota. There are few locations in Iowa. In addition to the references noted on the map legend, see List (1951) and Minton (1972) for Indiana, Smith (1961) for Illinois, Vogt (1981) for Wisconsin, Johnson (1987) for Missouri, Rossman (1965) and Dundee and Rossman (1989) for Louisiana, Dixon (1987) for Texas, Webb (1970) for Oklahoma, Collins (1993) for Kansas, Hammerson (1982) for Colorado, and Degenhardt et al. (1996) for New Mexico.

TERRAPENE ORNATA LUTEOLA SMITH AND RAMSEY, 1952. Desert box turtle. *Tortuga ornada del desierto*. Holotype: Texas Christian University #1280, collected in 1950 by W. E. Smith. The desert box turtle occurs west of the Pecos River in Texas and New Mexico, west to southeastern Arizona (Santa Cruz County) and the Mexican states of Sonora and Chihuahua, and north to Sandoval and perhaps Santa Fe counties in the Rio Grande Valley of New Mexico (see map 5, triangles). A zone of intergradation with *T. o. ornata* is found between the Rio Grande in New Mexico and the New Mexico–Texas border northward to the Canadian River, but the exact relationships in this area need further study (Degenhardt et al., 1996). Distribution records for this subspecies for New Mexico are found in Degenhardt et al. (1996) and for Texas in Dixon (1987).

IDENTIFICATION AND DESCRIPTION: The carapace of ornate box turtles is rather broad and oval, much more so than in the other species, all of which are elongate. Although domed, it is flattened on the top and usually lacks a dorsal keel. The highest point (greatest shell depth) occurs just anterior to the level of the hinge, thus making it more anterior than in the other species. The first marginal scute is oval or triangular, not square as in *T. carolina*. The rear of the carapace is neither serrated nor flared. Coloration is dark, ranging from near black through dark gray to reddish brown. Light lines radiate out from the center of the carapacial scutes, much as they do in *T. c. bauri*, another grassland/savanna inhabitant. The central bright line is usually broken. According to Carr (1952), the plastron may be as long as or even longer than the carapace. As with the carapace, it has a series of light radiating lines on a dark brown to chocolate background. The head and legs are yellow spotted, especially dorsally. Each hind foot has 4 toes, although a few individuals may only have 3 toes per hind foot.

SEXUAL DIMORPHISM: Sexual dimorphism is not as obvious in this species as it is in the other species. Eye color is often similar between the sexes, and the male's plastron does not have the obvious concave indentation that the eastern box turtle has; it is, instead,

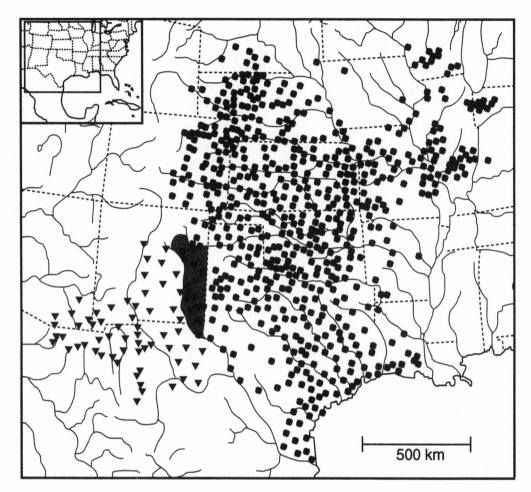

Map 5. The distribution of *Terrapene ornata ornata* (circles) and *T. o. luteola* (triangles). The shaded area marks a zone of extensive intergradation. Map based on Ward (1978) and Iverson (1992b).

shallow. However, most males have a red iris, and females usually have a yellow-brown iris. Males have a more distally located vent and, like male *T. nelsoni*, are capable of rotating the first toe of the hind foot and using it as a clasper to hook into the female's carapace during copulation. According to Cahn (1937), males have long tails and females have short tails.

HATCHLINGS: The hatchlings are nearly round, flat, and show no elongation. A small dorsal crest may be present (Cahn, 1937). The hatchlings are dark, but the dorsal ridge is yellow and there may be faint lines on the carapace. The plastron has light margins but lacks light spots; most of the plastron, especially the interior, is dark.

SKULL: See figure SA-4, composite based on USNM 030813, female, Chihuahua, Mexico, and USNM 092654, female, 23 km northwest of Vernon, Wilbarger County, Texas.

SUBSPECIES CHARACTERISTICS

Some individual characteristics between the subspecies are as follows:

T. O. ORNATA. Carapace—usually 5–9 radiating lines on the second pleural scute; generally dark in coloration. Old individuals retain their dark color and indications of their pattern. Phalangeal formula of forefeet—mostly 2-2-2-2-2 (Minx, 1992). Phalangeal formula of hind feet—2-3-3-3-1 (Minx, 1992).

T. O. LUTEOLA. Carapace—usually 10–16 radiating lines on the second pleural scute; generally much lighter than in *T. o. ornata*, more tan to straw colored. Older individuals become lighter and may lose their carapace pattern. Phalangeal formula of hind feet—2-3-3-3-1 (Minx, 1992).

TAXONOMIC COMMENTS: The uniqueness of the taxon *T. ornata* has never been questioned. It appears that there are no valid reasons for recognizing *Terrapene ornata longinsulae* as uniquely different from *Terrapene ornata*.

LIFE HISTORY

ACTIVITY: (Indiana) Mid-May to mid-September (Minton, 1972). (New Mexico) In New Mexico, *luteola* may be active well before sunrise, and around sunset, to avoid the heat of the day during the driest part of the summer. They are active from April to October (Degenhardt et al., 1996). (Wisconsin) Vogt (1980) reports that the earliest he saw *ornata* active was April 26.

EGGS/CLUTCH SIZE: (Indiana) 4–6 with an average incubation period of sixty-five days for *ornata* (Minton, 1972). (Kansas) 2–8 for *ornata* (Collins, 1993). (New Mexico) 1–4 ($\bar{x}$ = 2.68) for *luteola*, deposited from May to early August. Eggs measure 31–41 mm × 20–26 mm. Egg retention of up to fifty days has been reported (Nieuwolt, 1993). (Wisconsin) Only two eggs in each of two females (Vogt, 1980).

HATCHLING: (Indiana) Minton (1972) reports a single hatchling at 28.8 mm CL found on May 26.

MATURITY: (Kansas) Reached in 7–8 years for *ornata* (Collins, 1993).

MORTALITY: (Kansas) Collins (1993) cites a paper in the *Kansas Herpetological Society Newsletter* recording 178 *ornata* observed along a 220-mile stretch of highway on a single day in May. As in other box turtles, highway mortality may be quite high, although generally only anecdotal accounts are available.

NESTING: (Kansas) Common in June, but may extend from May to Autumn for *ornata* (Collins, 1993).

REFUGIA: (Nebraska/New Mexico). *Terrapene ornata* frequently use the burrows of kangaroo rats (*Dipodomys*) as refugia from adverse conditions (Degenhardt et al., 1996).

SEXUAL DIMORPHISM: (New Mexico) Females are generally larger than males (Degenhardt et al., 1996).

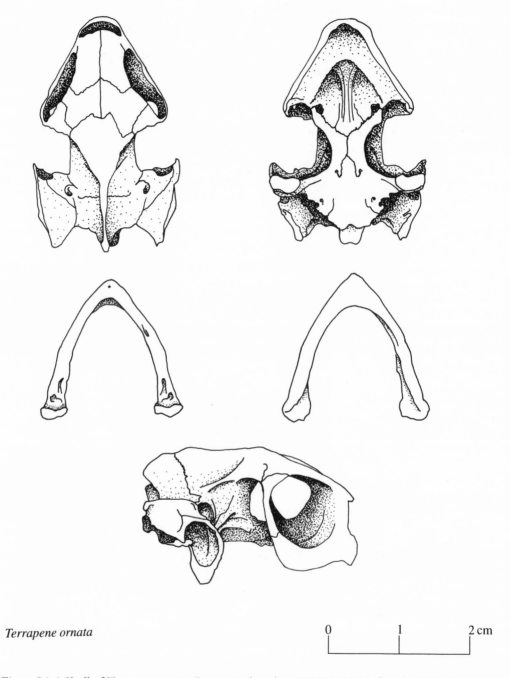

Terrapene ornata

0   1   2 cm

Figure SA-4. Skull of *Terrapene ornata*. Composite based on USNM 030813, female, Chihuahua, Mexico, and USNM 092654, female, 23 km northwest of Vernon, Wilbarger County, Texas.

SIZE: (Indiana/Illinois) In the eastern part of its range, *ornata* is considerably smaller than in the western part of its range (Minton, 1972). (Illinois) Largest known *ornata* is 128 mm CL (Smith, 1961). (Kansas) The largest known *ornata* is from Barber County and measured 154 mm CL (Collins, 1993).

STATUS: (Wisconsin) "A decade ago, many isolated pockets abounded in box turtles" (Vogt, 1980:101).

REMARKS: Ornate box turtles may be rather adept climbers. Willbern (1982) records that individual *T. o. ornata* were able to climb a 77 cm high vertical wire mesh fence and escape from a holding pen. Medium-sized individuals were most able to scale the fence, and they seemed more agile than the *T. c. triunguis* kept in the same pen. A photograph accompanying Willbern's article shows a determined individual as it climbed.

On November 4, 1930, someone let loose more than five hundred box turtles, mostly *T. o. ornata*, on Michigan Avenue in Chicago, Illinois. Most of these were collected by Karl Schmidt of the Field Museum and, after marking, were released near Waukegan. It is doubtful any of these turtles survived (see Cahn, 1937). Cahn (1937) suggested that the turtles were part of a turtle racing "stable," the owners of which went broke.

The ornate box turtle is the state reptile of Kansas (since 1986).

REFERENCES: Legler (1960), Smith and Smith (1979).

Glossary

actuary table: A life table. Life tables take life history information (e.g., age at maturity and first reproduction, mortality, birth rates, longevity) and use it to construct survivorship probabilities at different ages or stages of life.

anthropomorphic: Describing nonhuman objects in human form, e.g., rock art that depicts a god as having a human shape; regarding animals as possessing human qualities.

aliphatic: A class of organic (carbon-containing) compounds in which carbon and hydrogen molecules are arranged in straight or branched chains.

benthos: The biotic region or life zone at the bottom of a lake or other water body; the organisms living in such a region. Basically, the benthos are the organisms that live in the mud or at the water-substrate interface at the bottom of lakes, rivers, and other water bodies.

biomass (of a population): A quantitative estimate of the entire population of living organisms of a given habitat, considered collectively, and measured in terms of mass, volume, or energy in calories.

bridge: The part of a turtle's shell connecting the carapace and the plastron.

buccopharyngeal: Refers to the lining of the mouth and pharnyx. In some turtles, the buccopharyngeal region is highly vascularized, which allows gaseous exchange to occur in this area. Buccopharyngeal respiration supplements pulmonary gas exchange.

calcification: Deposition of calcium salts in various body tissues such as the muscles or bones.

carapace: The dorsal (upper) shell of a turtle (fig. 1-2a).

carpals: The series of bones in the wrist of the forelimb.

caruncle: The hard, pointed projection on the tip of a hatchling turtle's snout that helps it break through the tough eggshell and associated membranes at hatching.

caseous: Cheese-like mass.

celluolytic: Having the capacity to break down cellulose; used in reference to certain protozoans and bacteria that often occur in symbiosis with animals relying on a purely vegetarian diet.

chelonian: Any member of the Order Testudines; all turtles. The word is derived from the Greek for tortoise, *khelōnē*.

chemoreception: The action of the sense organs that respond to chemical stimulation, including the organs for taste (gustation) and smell (olfaction).

CITES: Convention on International Trade in Endangered Species of Wild Fauna and Flora, an international treaty set up to monitor and regulate trade in species either endangered or likely to become endangered through international trade.

CL: Carapace length, as measured in a straight line from the cervical scute (fig. 1-2a) to the posterior-most junction of marginal scutes 12, left and right.

clade: A taxon comprising an evolutionary tree made up of an ancestor and all of its descendants; an evolutionary lineage.

cloaca: The common body cavity into which genital, urinary, and digestive canals discharge in reptiles. The anus is actually the opening of the cloaca.

conjunctivitis: Inflammation of the mucous membrane that lines the eyelids and covers the exposed surface of the sclera.

conspecific: Of or relating to organisms belonging to the same species; an individual belonging to the same species as another.

contiguous: Occurring together; closely associated in time and space.

costal bones: The bones of a turtle's carapace lying between the neurals and the peripherals and which cover the ribs (fig. 1-3a).

Cryptodira: Turtle suborder; a cryptodire is able to pull its heads into its shell by bending the neck into an S shape.

cryoprotectants: Substances capable of protecting against injury due to freezing.

demographics: The characteristics of a specific population, such as its average age, reproductive status, and future life expectancy; systems or procedures that are based on such characteristics.

diapause: A "resting" stage accompanied by reduced metabolic activity and a delay in development and/or growth; usually employed during periods of unfavorable environmental conditions.

ecotone: A transition zone between two distinct habitats, such as between a forest and a grassland. An ecotone contains species from each area as well as organisms unique to it.

ectothermic: Refers to the maintenance of body temperature from sources outside the body. Ectotherms often are incorrectly termed "cold-blooded." In fact, ectotherms usually maintain a rather narrow and high preferred body temperature through behavioral means, such as basking. When ambient temperatures turn cold or extremely hot, however, ectotherms must seek protective shelter. The body temperature of ectothermic animals usually mirrors the immediate environmental temperature.

egestion: The process of eliminating fecal material at the inferior end of the digestive tract.

embryonic diapause: A period of delayed development or growth of an organism while in the embryo stage, associated with reduced metabolism and used as a mechanism for surviving adverse environmental conditions.

emydid: All turtles belonging to the mostly freshwater turtle family Emydidae.

Emydidae: A family of mostly freshwater cryptodiran (see *Cryptodira*) turtles that includes *Terrapene.* Other common members of this family include spotted, bog, and wood turtles (*Clemmys* spp.), Blanding's turtle (*Emydoidea blandingi*), map turtles (*Graptemys* spp.), painted turtles (*Chrysemys picta*), and pond turtles (*Pseudemys* spp., *Trachemys* spp.).

endotherm: An animal that generates a constant body heat through internal metabolic processes. Among living vertebrates, only birds and mammals are endotherms.

epididymis (plural epididymides): An elongated coiled structure along the posterior surface of the testis that merges with the ductus deferens and provides for the storage, transmission, and maturation of spermatozoa.

epiplastral bones: The pair of bones lying at the anterior end of the plastron (fig. 1-3b).

epithelium: An animal tissue composed of cells that are packed tightly together, with little intercellular matrix; it covers the external surface of the body and also internal surfaces such as the lining of tracts and vessels.

estivation: A dormant state of decreased metabolism in which animals pass the warm or dry parts of the year. A state of inactivity during the summer or dry season months.

etiology: The cause or origin of a disease or disorder; the study of the causes of diseases.

fecundity: The innate capacity of an organism to form reproductive elements, such as ova or sperm, and to produce offspring; the total number of eggs produced by an organism is a manifestation of its fecundity.

fibropapilloma: A noncancerous tumor of the epithelium in which the epithelial cells grow outward from a surface to form a lobed or branching structure constructed of fibrous tissue.

filarial: Pertaining to a group of nematode worms; adults parasitize the blood and tissue of vertebrates, while larvae are found in biting insects.

friable: Describing soils that when either wet or dry can be crumbled or reduced to powder. These are soils in which animals can readily dig.

gastropod: A member of the Mollusk class Gastropoda, which includes the snails, slugs, limpets, and conches.

gastrula: Pertaining to the stage of embryonic development of the germ layers.

genotypic sex determination: Sex determination controlled directly by genes located on specific sex chromosomes. For example, and embryo with a Y chromosome will develop into a male child in humans. Although a few turtles have genotypic sex determination (e.g., the softshells, *Apalone* spp.), most species, including box turtles, lack sex chromosomes.

geotaxis: The movement of an animal in response to gravitational forces.

harmonic radar tracking: A technique used to track small animals based on a tag that converts incoming radio signals to a specific harmonic frequency and reradiates this frequency in a wavelength that can be detected using specialized equipment. Although not yet used to track small turtles, the technique may hold promise for doing so (see Engelstoft et al., 1999, and references therein for further details).

hectare: A basic unit of area in the metric system, equal to 10,000 square meters or 2.471 acres.

holotype: A single specimen designated as representative of the species or subspecies by the author describing the species or subspecies at the time of publication of the description of a new taxon. Designation of a holotype ensures that future researchers always will know exactly what the animal being described looks like; it serves as a basic reference to that taxon.

hypoplastral bones: The pair of bones of the plastron lying between the hyoplastron and the xiphiplastron. The hinge of the box turtle lies on the anterior margin of the hypoplastron.

inguinal: Relating to or located in the inguinal region, or groin.

introgression: The incorporation of genes from one taxon with those of another taxon as a result of interbreeding.

karyotype: The number and structure of the chromosomes.

keel: See median keel.

keratinized: Containing a fibrous scleroprotein that is the principal constituent of hair, nails, and other epidermal structures.

LD$_{50}$: The number at which 50 percent of test animals either die or show an adverse reaction after exposure to toxic chemicals or conditions during controlled laboratory experiments.

lipid: Any of a group of fats and fatlike substance including fatty acids, neutral fats, waxes, and steroids; all contain aliphatic hydrocarbons, are water insoluble, and are easily stored in the body, serving as a source of fuel.

lumen: A general term referring to the space within a tubular or hollow organ such as an artery, a vein, or the intestine.

median carina: See median keel.

median keel: An elevated ridge extending and bisecting the length of the dome of the carapace of a turtle, dividing the animal into two mirror-image (but not necessarily in terms of coloration) halves in its midline path.

meristic: Refers to a characteristic that can be counted, such as the number of marginals, scales, phalanges in a toe, etc.

morphology: The study of the form and structure of organisms; the form and structure of a single organism considered as a whole.

myoglobins: Oxygen-transporting and -storing pigments in muscle cells, containing iron porphyrin, where oxygen binds.

Nearctic Region: One of the world's six zoogeographc realms. It includes Greenland and all of North America north of the Isthmus of Tehuantepec in Mexico.

neural bones: The medial bones running down the back of the carapace. The vertebrae of the turtle are fused internally with the neural bones that lie above them. Box turtles generally have seven neurals, although there is some variation among turtles as a group.

nominate species: The subordinate taxa (e.g., subspecies) that contain the type of the subdivided species and have the same name. For example, the nominate species *Terrapene ornata* contains the subspecies *T. o. ornata* and *T. o. luteola*.

olfactory receptors: Cells in the nasal epithelium that are stimulated by substances capable of producing impulses in the olfactory passage, thus giving rise to the sense of smell.

ontogenetic: Related to the developmental history of an individual organism.

oogenesis: The proliferation, growth, and maturation of the ova.

ossified: Having produced bone or turned into bone.

osteology: The study of bones and their relationships within skeletal structure.

peripheral bones: The small bones along the margins of the carapace. Most box turtles have eleven pairs of peripherals.

phalanges: General term referring to the bones in the fingers (carpals) and toes (tarsals).

PL: Plastron length. In box turtles, it may be measured as a straight line from the anterior-most point of the plastron where the gulars meet (fig. 1-2b) to the posterior junction of the anals. Alternatively, the front and rear sections of the plastron may be measured in a straight line independently and the sums added to obtain PL. (Front = anterior-most juncture of the gulars to the hinge at the interpectoral seam; rear = hinge at the anterior-most juncture of the interabdominal seam to the posterior-most part of the interanal seam.)

plastron: The ventral (bottom) portion of the shell of a turtle.

purulent: Containing pus or consisting of pus; forming pus.

rad: Radiation absorbed dose, a unit of measure for absorbed doses of ionizing radiation.

ramus (plural rami): Projecting parts or elongated processes of body parts, primarily of appendages.

rhinitis: Inflammation of the mucous membrane of the nasal passages, with profuse discharge of mucus.

sagittal: An imaginary plane though the body of bilaterally symmetrical animals, dividing the body into right and left; sometimes used to denote the midline. For example, a sagittal crest is a ridge that divides the skull into right and left sides.

sarcophagid: Pertaining to members of the Sarcophagidae, including the blowflies and scavenger flies, the eggs of which are laid in decaying or living animal matter, which is eaten by the larvae.

scutes: The scales covering the bones of the turtle's shell.

sebaceous: Relating to or secreting sebum, a fatty exudate of the sebaceous (hair or oil) gland, varying in consistency in different areas of the body.

seminiferous: Conveying or containing semen.

skeletochronology: The study of growth rings in bones (in turtles, usually the humerus or other long bones) as they relate to age. Presumably, one Line of Arrested Growth (LAG) is discernible for every nongrowing season (usually in the winter or dry season). LAGs thus delimit periods of growth. In theory, by counting the number of growth rings, it should be possible to determine the age of the organism, at least within certain limits of confidence. Although sometimes called annular rings, growth may occur at multiple times of the year, or, in some years, not at all. Hence, there may or may not be a direct correlation between the number of growth rings and the age of the animal.

spermatogenesis: The process by which undifferentiated male germ cells develop into mature spermatozoa.

subcutaneous: Located beneath the skin.

subfossil deposit: Geologic deposit containing remains of organisms that are clearly old but are not yet mineralized. A deposit containing remains in the process of becoming fossilized.

symbiosis: A relationship in which two dissimilar organisms live in close association.

synonymy: A chronological list of scientific names that have been applied to a particular taxon.

syntopic: Found or living in exactly the same spatial habitats at a specific location.

syntype: Every specimen in a type series in which no holotype was designated.

tarsals: The bones of the ankle of the hind limbs.

taxon (pl. taxa): A formally recognized group of organisms (i.e., one identified and named in accordance with the scientific rules of nomenclature and classification) sufficiently distinct to be named and to be ranked in a definite category. Examples: species, subspecies, family, class.

thermoregulation: The various physiological processes by which an animal regulates its internal temperature.

xenobiotic: Artificial (human-created) chemicals in the environment.

xeric: A location or habitat with very little moisture; a desert or other very dry place.

xiphiplastral bones: The paired posterior bones of a turtle's plastron (fig. 1-3b).

zygomatic arch: Bony bridge consisting of the jugal and squamosal bones in the skull (fig. 1-4). In box turtles, the zygomatic arch may be complete and robust or absent. There is much variation depending on individual, subspecies, and species.

Literature Cited

Adams, N. A., D. L. Claussen, and J. Skillings. 1989. Effects of temperature on voluntary loco-motion of the eastern box turtle, *Terrapene carolina carolina*. *Copeia* 1989:905–15.

Adler, K. 1968. Turtles from archeological sites in the Great Lakes region. *Michigan Archeologist* 14:147–63.

———. 1970. The influence of prehistoric man on the distribution of the box turtle. *Ann. Carnegie Mus.* 41(9):263–80.

Agassiz, L. 1857. *Contributions to the Natural History of the United States of America*. Vol. 2. Boston, Mass.: Little, Brown.

Allard, H. A. 1935. The natural history of the box turtle. *Sci. Monthly* 41:325–38.

———. 1939. Mating of the box turtle ending in death to the male. *Copeia* 1939:109.

———. 1948. The eastern box turtle and its behavior. *J. Tennessee Acad. Sci.* 23:307–21.

———. 1949. The eastern box turtle and its behavior. *J. Tennessee Acad. Sci.* 24:146–52.

Allen, C. R., S. Demarais, and R. S. Lutz. 1994. Red imported fire ant impact on wildlife: An overview. *Texas J. Sci.* 46:51–59.

Allen, R., and W. T. Neill. 1952. The box turtles. *Florida Wildl.* 5(9):16, 38.

Altland, P. D. 1951. Observations on the structure of the reproductive organs of the box turtle. *J. Morph.* 89:599–621.

Altland, P. D., B. Highman, and B. Wood. 1951. Some effects of X-irradiation on turtles. *J. Exp. Zool.* 118:1–19.

Anton, T. G. 1990. Predation on the house sparrow, *Passer domesticus*, by the Gulf Coast box turtle, *Terrapene carolina major*, under seminatural conditions. *Bull. Chicago Herp. Soc.* 25:143–44.

Arndt, R. G. 1980. An albino eastern box turtle, *Terrapene c. carolina*, from North Carolina. *Herp. Rev.* 11:30.

Auffenberg, W. 1958. Fossil turtles of the genus *Terrapene* in Florida. *Bull. Florida Mus. Nat. Hist., Biol. Sci.* 3:53–92.

———. 1959. A Pleistocene *Terrapene* hibernaculum, with remarks on a second complete box turtle skull from Florida. *Quart. J. Florida Acad. Sci.* 22:49–53.

———. 1967. Further notes on fossil box turtles of Florida. *Copeia* 1967:319–25

Auffenberg, W. W., and W. W. Milstead. 1965. Reptiles in the Quaternary of North America. Pp. 557–68 in H. E. Wright, Jr., and D. G. Frey (eds.), *The Quaternary in the United States*. Princeton, N.J.: Princeton Univ. Press.

Avent, J. M. 1988. Initialed terrapin turns up in garden 47 years later. *Knoxville News-Sentinel*, Sept. 21.

Avise, J. C. 1986. Mitochondrial DNA and the evolutionary genetics of higher animals. *Phil. Trans. R. Soc. Lond.* 312B:325–42.

Avise, J. C., B. W. Bowen, T. Lamb, A. B. Meylan, and E. Bermingham. 1992. Mitochondrial DNA evolution at a turtle's pace: Evidence for low genetic variability and reduced microevolutionary rate in the Testudines. *Mol. Biol. Evol.* 9:457–73.

Babbitt, L. H., and C. H. Babbitt. 1951. A herpetological study in burned-over areas in Dade County, Florida. *Copeia* 1951:79.

Babcock, H. L. 1919. The turtles of New England. *Mem. Boston Soc. Nat. Hist.* 8:325–431.

Baker, M. R. 1987. Synopsis of the nematoda parasitic in amphibians and reptiles. *Mem. Univ. Newfoundland Occas. Pap. Biol.* (11):1–325.

Barbour, R. 1968. The box terrapin. *Kentucky Happy Hunting Ground* 24(5):33.

———. 1971. *Amphibians and Reptiles of Kentucky*. Lexington: Univ. Press of Kentucky.

Barbour, T., and H. C. Stetson. 1931. A revision of the Pleistocene species of *Terrapene* of Florida. *Bull. Mus. Comp. Zool.* 72:295–99.

Barton, B. S. 1796. *A Memoir Concerning the Fascinating Faculty Which Has Been Ascribed to the Rattle-snake and Other American Serpents*. Philadelphia: Henry Sweitzer.

Bayless, J. W. 1984. Home range studies of the eastern box turtle (*Terrapene carolina carolina*) using radio telemetry. Unpubl. M.S. thesis, George Mason Univ., Fairfax, Virginia.

Beltz, E. 1998. HerPet-pourri. *Bull. Chicago Herp. Soc.* 33:15–17.

Belusz, L. C., and R. J. Reed. 1969. Some epizoophytes on six turtle species collected in Massachusetts and Michigan. *Amer. Midl. Nat.* 81:598–601.

Belzer, B. 1996 (1995). Box turtle repatriation in northwestern Pennsylvania. *Box Turtle Newsl.* (4):12–13.

Belzer, W. 1997. Box turtle conservation issues. *Reptile & Amphibian* (Jul.–Aug.): 32–35.

Bentley, C. C., and J. L. Knight. 1998. Turtles (Reptilia: Testudines) of the Ardis Local Fauna Late Pleistocene (Rancholabrean) of South Carolina. *Brimleyana* 25:3–33.

Beresford, W. A., M. P. Donovan, J. H. Henninger, and M. P. Waalkes. 1981. Lead in the bone and soft tissues of box turtles caught near smelters. *Bull. Environ. Contam. Toxicol.* 27:349–52.

Bethea, N. J. 1972. Effects of temperature on heart rate and rates of cooling and warming in *Terrapene ornata*. *Comp. Biochem. Physiol.* 41A:301–5.

Blair, W. F. 1976. Some aspects of the biology of the ornate box turtle, *Terrapene ornata*. *Southwest. Nat.* 21:89–104.

Blaney, R. M. 1968. Hybridization of the box turtles *Terrapene carolina* and *T. ornata* in western Louisiana. *Proc. Louisiana Acad. Sci.* 31:54–57.

Bleakney, S. 1958. The significance of turtle bones from archeological sites in southern Ontario and Quebec. *Can. Field-Nat.* 72:1–5.

Bogert, C. M. 1943. A new box turtle from southeastern Sonora, Mexico. *Amer. Mus. Novitates* no. 1226, 7 pp.

Bogert, C. M., and R. B. Cowles. 1947. Moisture loss in relation to habitat selection in some Floridian reptiles. *Amer. Mus. Novitates* no. 1358, 34 pp.

Boice, R. 1970. Competitive feeding behaviours in captive *Terrapene c. carolina*. *Anim. Behav.* 18:703–10.

Boice, R., C. B. Quanty, and R. C. Williams. 1974. Competition and possible dominance in turtles, toads, and frogs. *J. Comp. Physiol. Psychol.* 86:1116–31.

Bonnemains, J., and R. Bour. 1996. Les chéloniens de la collection Lesueur du Muséum d'Histoire Naturelle du Havre. *Bull. Trim. Soc. Géol. Normandie et Amis Muséum du Havre* 83:5–45.

Bramble, D. M. 1974. Emydid shell kinesis: Biomechanics and evolution. *Copeia* 1974:707–27.

Braun, J., and G. R. Brooks, Jr. 1987. Box turtles (*Terrapene carolina*) as potential agents for seed dispersal. *Amer. Midl. Nat.* 117:312–18.

Breder, R. B. 1927. Turtle trailing: A new technique for studying the life habits of certain testudinata. *Zoologica* 9(4):231–43.

Brimley, C. S. 1943. Reptiles and Amphibians of North Carolina. *Carolina Tips* 6:2–3, 6–7, 10–11, 14–15, 18–19.

Brisbin, I. L., Jr. 1972. Seasonal variations in the live weights and major body components of captive box turtles. *Herpetologica* 28:70–75.

Brown, E. E. 1992. Notes on amphibians and reptiles of the western Piedmont of North Carolina. *J. Elisha Mitchell Sci. Soc.* 108:38–54.

Brown, W. S. 1971. Morphometrics of *Terrapene coahuila* (Chelonia, Emydidae), with comments on its evolutionary status. *Southwest. Nat.* 16:171–84.

———. 1974. Ecology of the aquatic box turtle, *Terrapene coahuila* (Chelonia, Emydidae) in northern Mexico. *Bull. Florida St. Mus., Biol. Sci.* 19:1–67.

Brumwell, M. J. 1940. Notes on the courtship of the turtle, *Terrapene ornata*. *Trans. Kansas Acad. Sci.* 43:391–92.

Burt, C. E., and W. L. Hoyle. 1934. Additional records of the reptiles of the Central Prairie Region of the United States. *Trans. Kansas Acad. Sci.* 37:193–216.

Bush, F. M. 1959. Foods of some Kentucky herptiles. *Herpetologica* 15:73–77.

Buskirk, J. R. 1993. Yucatan box turtle *Terrapene carolina yucatana*. *Tortuga Gazette* 29(5):1–4.

Cagle, F. R. 1939. A system for marking turtles for future identification. *Copeia* 1939:170–73.

Cahn, A. R. 1937. The turtles of Illinois. *Illinois Biol. Monogr.* 16:1–218.

Cahn, A. R., and E. Conder. 1932. Mating of the box turtles. *Copeia* 1932:86–88.

Calle, P. P., J. McDougal, and J. Behler. 1996. Health assessment, with an emphasis on *Mycoplasma*: Survey of eastern box turtles in Long Island's Central Pine Barrens Reserve. *Box Turtle Newsl.* (5):9.

Carpenter, C. C. 1956. Carapace pits in the three-toed box turtle, *Terrapene carolina triunguis* (Chelonia-Emydidae). *Southwest. Nat.* 1:83–86.

———. 1957. Hibernation, hibernacula and associated behavior of the three-toed box turtle (*Terrapene carolina triunguis*). *Copeia* 1957:278–82.

Carr, A. F. 1952. *Handbook of Turtles: The Turtles of the United States, Canada, and Baja California.* Ithaca, N.Y.: Cornell Univ. Press.

———. 1994. *A Naturalist in Florida: A Celebration of Eden.* New Haven, Conn.: Yale Univ. Press.

Catawba Cultural Heritage Project. 1995. *Catawba Pottery, Legacy of Survival: 7 Master Potters.* Columbia, S.C.: Nations Bank and MetLife.

Cerda, A., and D. Waugh. 1992. Status and management of the Mexican box terrapin *Terrapene coahuila* at the Jersey Wildlife Preservation Trust. *Dodo, J. Jersey Wildl. Preserv. Trust* 28:126–42.

Christiansen, J. L., and J. W. Bickham. 1989. Possible historic effects of pond drying and winterkill on the behavior of *Kinosternon flavescens* and *Chrysemys picta*. *J. Herpetol.* 23:91–94.

Clark, H. W. 1935. On the occurrence of a probable hybrid between the eastern and western box turtles, *Terrapene carolina* and *T. ornata*, near Lake Maxinkuckee, Indiana. *Copeia* 1935:148–50.

Clark, W. S. 1982. Turtles as a food source of nesting bald eagles in the Chesapeake Bay region. *J. Field Ornithol.* 53:49–51.

Claussen, D. L., P. M. Daniel, S. Jiang, and N. A. Adams. 1991. Hibernation in the eastern box turtle, *Terrapene c. carolina*. *J. Herpetol.* 25:334–41.

Claussen, D. L., M. S. Finkler, and M. M. Smith. 1997. Thread trailing of turtles: Methods for evaluating spatial movements and pathway structure. *Can. J. Zool.* 75:2120–28.

———. 1998. Erratum, Thread trailing of turtles: Methods for evaluating spatial movements and pathway structure. *Can. J. Zool.* 76:387–89.

Cochran, D. M. 1927. The box turtle. *Nature* (Sept.):151–53.

Collins, J. T. 1993. *Amphibians and Reptiles in Kansas.* 3rd ed.(rev.). Lawrence: Univ. of Kansas, Museum of Natural History.

———. 1997. Standard common and current scientific names for North American amphibians and reptiles. 4th ed. *SSAR Herp. Circ.* 25.

Conant, R. 1938. The reptiles of Ohio. *Amer. Midl. Nat.* 20:1–200.

Conant, R., and J. T. Collins. 1991. *A Field Guide to Reptiles and Amphibians, Eastern and Central North America.* 3rd ed. Boston, Mass.: Houghton Mifflin.

Congdon, J. D., and J. W. Gibbons. 1989. Biomass productivity of turtles in freshwater wetlands: A geographic comparison. Pp. 583–92 in R. Sharitz and J. W. Gibbons (eds.), *Freshwater Wetlands and Wildlife.* U.S. Dept. Energy Symposium Series 61, Oak Ridge, Tenn.

Congdon, J. D., R. E. Gatten, Jr., and S. J. Morreale. 1989. Overwintering activity of box turtles (*Terrapene carolina*) in South Carolina. *J. Herpetol.* 23:179–81.

Congdon, J. D., A. E. Dunham, and R. C. van Loben Sels. 1993. Delayed sexual maturity and demographics of Blanding's turtles (*Emydoidea blandingii*): Implications for conservation and management of long-lived organisms. *Conserv. Biol.* 7:826–33.

———. 1994. Demographics of common snapping turtles (*Chelydra serpentina*): Implications for conservation and management of long-lived organisms. *Amer. Zool.* 34: 397–408.

Congello, K. 1978. Nesting and egg laying behavior in *Terrapene carolina. Proc. Pennsylvania Acad. Sci.* 52:51–56.

Conklin, H. C., and W. C. Sturtevant. 1953. Seneca Indian singing tools at Coldspring longhouse: Musical instruments of the modern Iroquois. *Proc. Amer. Philos. Soc.* 97:262–90.

Cook, R. P. 1996. Movement and ecology of eastern box and painted turtles repatriated to human-created habitat. Unpubl. Ph.D. diss., City Univ. New York.

Cook, S., D. Abb, and W. Frair. 1972. A new record size box turtle. *Intern. Turtle & Tortoise Soc. J.* 6(3):8–17.

Cope, E. D. 1869. Synopsis of extinct Batrachia, Reptilia and Aves of North America. *Trans. Amer. Philos. Soc.* 14:1–124.

———. 1878. Description of new reptiles from the Upper Tertiary formations of the West. *Proc. Amer. Philos. Soc.* 17:229.

Cosgrove, G. E. 1965. The radiosensitivity of snakes and boxturtles. *Rad. Res.* 25:706–12.

Costanzo, J. P., and D. L. Claussen. 1990. Natural freeze tolerance in the terrestrial turtle, *Terrapene carolina. J. Exp. Zool.*254:228–32.

Costanzo, J. P., R. E. Lee, Jr., and M. F. Wright. 1993. Physiological responses to freezing in the turtle *Terrapene carolina. J. Herpetol.* 27:117–20.

Costanzo, J. P., J. B. Iverson, M.F. Wright, and R. E. Lee, Jr. 1995. Cold hardiness and overwintering strategies of hatchlings in an assemblage of northern turtles. *Ecology* 76:1772–85.

Cragin, F. W. 1885. Second contribution to the herpetology of Kansas, with observations on the Kansas fauna. *Trans. Kansas Acad. Sci.* 9:136–40.

Crans, W. J., and E. G. Rockel. 1968. The mosquitoes attracted to turtles. *Mosquito News* 28:332–37.

Creaser, E. P. 1940. A note on the food of the box turtle. *Copeia* 1940:131.

Crooks, F. P., and P. W. Smith. 1958. An instance of twinning in the box turtle. *Herpetologica* 14:170–71.

Crouse, D. T., L. B. Crowder, and H. Caswell. 1987. A stage-based population model for logger-head sea turtles and implications for conservation. *Ecology* 68:1412–23.

Culbertson, G. 1907. Some notes on the habits of the common box turtle (*Cistudo carolina*). *Proc. Indiana Acad. Sci.* 1907:78–79.

Cunningham, B., and E. Huene. 1938. Further studies in water absorption by reptile eggs. *Amer. Nat.* 72:380–85.

Curtin, C. G. 1995. Latitudinal gradients in biophysical constraints: Implications for species response to shifting land-use and climate. Unpubl. Ph.D. diss., Univ. Wisconsin, Madison.

————. 1997. Biophysical analysis of the impact of shifting land use on ornate box turtles, Wisconsin, USA. Pp. 31–36 in J. Van Abbema (ed.), *Proceedings: Conservation, Restoration, and Management of Tortoises and Turtles—An International Conference*. New York: New York Turtle & Tortoise Society.

————. 1998. Plasticity in ornate box turtle thermal preference. *J. Herpetol.* 32:298–301.

Davis, M. 1981. Aspects of the social and spatial experience of eastern box turtles, *Terrapene carolina carolina*. Unpubl. Ph.D. diss., Univ. Tennessee, Knoxville.

Degenhardt, W. G., C. W. Painter, and A. H. Price. 1996. *Amphibians and Reptiles of New Mexico*. Albuquerque: Univ. of New Mexico Press.

DeKay, J. E. 1842. *Zoology of New York*. Pt. 3: *Reptiles and Amphibia*. Albany, N.Y.: W. and A. White and J. Visscher.

DeRosa, C. T., and D. H. Taylor. 1980. Homeward orientation mechanisms in three species of turtles (*Trionyx spinifer*, *Chrysemys picta*, and *Terrapene carolina*). *Behav. Ecol.Sociobiol.* 7:15–23.

DeRosa, C. T., and D. H. Taylor. 1982. A comparison of compass orientation mechanisms in three turtles (*Trionyx spinifer*, *Chrysemys picta*, and *Terrapene carolina*). *Copeia* 1982:394–99.

De Queiroz, K. 1995. Phylogenetic approaches to classification and nomenclature, and the history of taxonomy (an alternative interpretation). *Herp. Rev.* 26:79–81.

————. 1997. The Linnaean hierarchy and the evolutionization of taxonomy, with emphasis on the problem of nomenclature. *Aliso* 15:125–44.

de Vosjoli, P. 1991. *The General Care and Maintenance of Box Turtles*. Lakeside, Calif.: Advanced Vivarium Systems.

Ditmars, R. L. 1934. A review of the box turtles. *Zoologica* 17:1–44.

Dixon, J. R. 1987. *Amphibians and Reptiles of Texas*. College Station: Texas A&M Univ. Press.

Dodd, C. K., Jr. 1988. Disease and population declines in the flattened musk turtle *Sternotherus depressus*. *Amer. Midl. Nat.* 119:394–401.

————. 1997a. Clutch size and frequency in Florida box turtles (*Terrapene carolina bauri*): Implications for conservation. *Chel. Conserv. Biol.* 2(3):370–77.

————. 1997b. Population structure and the evolution of sexual size dimorphism and sex ratios in an insular population of Florida box turtles (*Terrapene carolina bauri*). *Can. J. Zool.* 75:1495–1507.

————. 1998. Biomass of an island population of Florida box turtles (*Terrapene carolina bauri*). *J. Herpetol.* 32:150–52.

Dodd, C. K., Jr., and R. Seigel. 1991. Relocation, repatriation, and translocation of amphibians and reptiles: Are they conservation strategies that work? *Herpetologica* 47:336–50.

Dodd, C. K., Jr., and R. Franz. 1993. The need for status information on common herpetofaunal species. *Herp. Rev.* 24:47–50.

Dodd, C. K., Jr., K. M. Enge, and J. N. Stuart. 1989. Reptiles on highways in northern Alabama, USA. *J. Herpetol.* 23:197–200.

Dodd, C. K., Jr., R. Franz, and L. L. Smith. 1994. Activity patterns and habitat use of box turtles (*Terrapene carolina bauri*) on a Florida island, with recommendations for management. *Chel. Conserv. Biol.* 1(2):97–106.

Dodd, C. K., Jr., R. Franz, and S. A. Johnson. 1997. Shell injuries and anomalies in an insular population of Florida box turtles (*Terrapene carolina bauri*). *Herp. Nat. Hist.* 5:66–72.

Dodge, C. H., M. T. Dimond, and C. C. Wunder. 1978. Effect of temperature on the incubation time of eggs of the eastern box turtle (*Terrapene carolina carolina* Linné). *Florida Mar. Res. Publ.* (33):8–11.

Dolbeer, R. A. 1969. A study of population density, seasonal movements and weight changes, and winter behavior of the eastern box turtle, *Terrapene c. carolina* L., in eastern Tennessee. Unpubl. M.S. thesis, Univ. Tennessee, Knoxville.

———. 1971. Winter behavior of the eastern box turtle, *Terrapene c. carolina* L., in eastern Tennessee. *Copeia* 1971:758–60.

Doroff, A. M., and L. B. Keith. 1990. Demography and ecology of an ornate box turtle (*Terrapene ornata*) population in south-central Wisconsin. *Copeia* 1990:387–99.

Drotos, E. J. 1974. Natural history notes. The box turtle. *Virginia Wildl.*(May):7–8.

Dundee, H. A., and D. A. Rossman.1989. *The Amphibians and Reptiles of Louisiana*. Baton Rouge: Louisiana State Univ. Press.

Duvernoy, G. L. 1836. *Le Règne animal distribué d'après son organisation pour servir de base à l'histoire naturelle des animaux et d'introduction à l'anatomie comparée, par Georges Cuvier*. Tome 3. *Les Reptiles . . .avec un Atlas*. Paris: Libr. Fortin, Masson & Cie.

Eaton, T. H., Jr. 1947. Box turtle eating a horned toad. *Copeia* 1947:270.

Edney, J. M., and W. R. Allen. 1951. Age of the boxturtle, *Terrapene carolina carolina* (Linnaeus). *Copeia* 1951:312.

Ellner, L. R., and W. H. Karasov. 1993. Latitudinal variation in the thermal biology of ornate box turtles. *Copeia* 1993:447–55.

Emerton, J. H. 1904. A dipterous parasite of the box turtle. *Psyche* 11:34.

Engelhardt, G. P. 1916. Burrowing habits of the box turtle. *Copeia* (31):42–43.

Engelstoft, C., K. Ovaska, and N. Honkanen. 1999. The harmonic direction finder: A new method for tracking movements of small snakes. *Herp. Rev.* 30:84–87.

Epperson, D. M. 1997. Gopher tortoise (*Gopherus polyphemus*) populations: Activity patterns, upper respiratory tract disease, and management on a military installation in northeast Florida. Unpubl. M.S. thesis, Univ. Florida, Gainesville.

Ernst, C. H. 1981. Courtship behavior of male *Terrapene carolina major* (Reptilia, Testudines, Emydidae). *Herp. Rev.* 12:7–8.

Ernst, C. H., and R. W. Barbour. 1972. *Turtles of the United States*. Lexington: Univ. Press of Kentucky.

———. 1989. *Turtles of the World*. Washington, D.C.: Smithsonian Institution Press.

Ernst, C. H., and J. McBreen. 1991a. *Terrapene* Merrem: Box turtles. *Cat. Amer. Amphib. Rept.* 511.1–511.6.

Ernst, C. H., and J. McBreen. 1991b. *Terrapene carolina* (Linnaeus): Eastern box turtle. *Cat. Amer. Amphib. Rept.* 512.1–512.13.

Ernst, C. H., J. E. Lovich, and R. W. Barbour. 1994. *Turtles of the United States and Canada*. Washington, D.C.: Smithsonian Institution Press.

Ernst, C. H., T. P. Boucher, S. W. Sekscienski, and J. C. Wilgenbusch. 1995. Fire ecology of the Florida box turtle, *Terrapene carolina bauri*. *Herp. Rev.* 26:185–87.

Ernst, C. H., J. E. Lovich, A. F. Laemmerzahl, and S. Sekscienski. 1997. A comparison of plastral scute lengths among members of the box turtle genera *Cuora* and *Terrapene*. *Chel. Conserv. Biol.* 2:603–7.

Ernst, C. H., J. C. Wilgenbusch, T. P. Boucher, and S. W. Sekscienski. 1998a. Morphometrics of the fossil box turtle, *Terrapene innoxia* Hay 1916, from Florida. *Chel. Conserv. Biol.* 3:99–102.

———. 1998b. Growth, allometry and sexual size dimorphism in the Florida box turtle, *Terrapene carolina bauri*. *Herpetol. J.* 8:72–78.

Ernst, E. M., and C. H. Ernst. 1977. Synopsis of helminths endoparasitic in native turtles of the United States. *Bull. Maryland Herp. Soc.* 13:1–75.

Erskine, D. J., and V. H. Hutchison. 1981. Melatonin and behavioral thermoregulation in the turtle, *Terrapene carolina triunguis*. *Physiol. & Behav.* 26:991–94.

Evans, L. T. 1953. The courtship pattern of the box turtle, *Terrapene c. carolina*. *Herpetologica* 9:189–92.

———. 1968. The evolution of courtship in the turtle species, *Terrapene carolina*. *Amer. Zool.* 8:695–96.

Evans, R. H. 1983. Chronic bacterial pneumonia in free-ranging eastern box turtles (*Terrapene carolina carolina*). *J. Wildl. Dis.* 19:349–52.

Ewert, M. A. 1979. The embryo and its egg: development and natural history. Pp. 333–413 In: M. Harless and H. Morlock (eds.), Turtles. Perspectives and Research. John Wiley & Sons, New York.

———. 1985. Embryology of turtles. Pp. 75–267 In: C. Gans, F. Billett, and P. F. A. Maderson (eds.), Biology of the Reptilia. Volume 14. Development A. John Wiley & Sons, New York.

Ewert, M. A., and C. E. Nelson. 1991. Sex determination in turtles: Diverse patterns and some possible adaptive values. *Copeia* 1991:50–69.

Ewing, H. E. 1926. The common box-turtle, a natural host for chiggers. *Proc. Biol. Soc. Wash.* 39:19–20.

———. 1933. Reproduction in the eastern box turtle, *Terrapene c. carolina*. *Copeia* 1933:95.

———. 1935. Further notes on the reproduction of the eastern box turtle, *Terrapene carolina* (Linné). *Copeia* 1935:102.

———. 1937. Notes on a Florida box-turtle, *Terrapene bauri* Taylor, kept under Maryland conditions. *Copeia* 1937:141.

———. 1943. Continued fertility in female box turtles following mating. *Copeia* 1943:112–14.

Ferguson, D. E. 1963. Notes concerning the effects of heptachlor on certain poikilotherms. *Copeia* 1963:441–43.

Fitch, A. V. 1965. Sensory cues in the feeding of the ornate box turtle. *Trans. Kansas Acad. Sci.* 68:522–32.

Fitch, H. S. 1958. Home ranges, territories, and seasonal movements of vertebrates of the Natural History Reservation. *Univ. Kansas Publ. Mus. Nat. Hist.* 11(3):63–326.

Flynn, R. J. 1973. *Parasites of Laboratory Animals*. Ames: Iowa State Univ. Press.

Frank, W. 1984. Non-hemoparasitic protozoans. Pp. 259–384 in G. L. Hoff, F. L. Frye, and E. R. Jacobson (eds.), *Diseases of Amphibians and Reptiles*. New York: Plenum Press.

Frazer, N. B. 1992. Sea turtle conservation and halfway technology. *Conserv. Biol.* 6:179–84.

———. 1997. Turtle conservation and halfway technology: What is the problem? Pp. 422–25 in J. Van Abbema (ed.), *Proceedings: Conservation, Restoration, and Management of Tortoises and Turtles—An International Conference*. New York: New York Turtle & Tortoise Society.

Frothingham, L. 1936. Observations on young box turtles. *Bull. Boston Soc. Nat. Hist.* (78):3–8.

Frye, F. L. 1973. *Husbandry, Medicine and Surgery in Captive Reptiles*. Bonner Springs, Kans.: VM Publishing.

Gaffney, E. S., and P. A. Meylan. 1988. A phylogeny of turtles. Pp. 157–219 in M. J. Benton (ed.), *The Phylogeny and Classification of the Tetrapods*. Vol. 1: *Amphibians, Reptiles and Birds*. Oxford, U.K.: Clarendon Press.

Garber, S. D., and J. Burger. 1995. A 20-year study documenting the relationship between turtle decline and human recreation. *Ecol. Applic.* 5:1151–62.

Garrott, R. A., P. J. White, and C. A. V. White. 1993. Overabundance: An issue for conservation biologists? *Conserv. Biol.* 7:946–49.

Gatten, R. E., Jr. 1974. Effect of nutritional status on the preferred body temperature of the turtles *Pseudemys scripta* and *Terrapene ornata*. *Copeia* 1974:912–20.

———. 1987. Cardiovascular and other physiological correlates of hibernation in aquatic and terrestrial turtles. *Amer. Zool.* 27:59–68.

Germano, D. J. 1999. Life history notes, *Terrapene ornata luteola* (Desert box turtle): Attempted predation. *Herp. Rev.* 30:40–41.

Germano, D. J., and R. B. Bury. 1998. Age determination in turtles: Evidence for annual deposition of scute rings. *Chel. Conserv. Biol.* 3(1):123–32.

Germano, D. J., and P. Nieuwolt-Decanay. 1999. Life history notes, *Terrapene ornata luteola* (Desert box turtle): Homing. *Herp. Rev.* 30:96.

Gibbons, J. W. 1987. Why do turtles live so long? *Bioscience* 37:262–69.

Gibbons, J. W., and J. L. Greene. 1979. X-ray photography: A technique to determine reproductive patterns of freshwater turtles. *Herpetologica* 35:86–89.

Gillette, D. D. 1974. A proposed revision of the evolutionary history of *Terrapene carolina triunguis*. *Copeia* 1974:537–39.

Gilmore, C. W. 1927. On fossil turtles from the Pleistocene of Florida. *Proc. U.S. Natl. Mus.* 71:1–10.

Gould, E. 1957. Orientation in box turtles, *Terrapene c. carolina* (Linnaeus). *Biol. Bull.* 112:336–48.

———. 1959. Studies on the orientation of turtles. *Copeia* 1959:174–76.

Gould, J. L. 1984. Magnetic field sensitivity in animals. *Ann.Rev. Physiol.* 46:585–98.

Graham, R. W., and E. L. Lundelius, Jr. 1984. Coevolutionary disequilibrium and Pleistocene extinctions. Pp. 223–49 in P. S. Martin and R. G. Klein (eds.), *Quaternary Extinctions: A Prehistoric Revolution*. Tucson: Univ. of Arizona Press.

Graham, T., and V. H. Hutchison. 1969. Centenarian box turtles. *Intern. Turtle & Tortoise Soc. J.* 3(3):25–29.

Graham, T., A. Georges, and N. McElhinney. 1996. Terrestrial orientation by the eastern long-necked turtle, *Chelodina longicollis*, from Australia. *J. Herpetol.* 30:467–77.

Grand, J., and S. R. Beissinger. 1997. When relocation of loggerhead sea turtle (*Caretta caretta*) nests becomes a useful strategy. *J. Herpetol.* 31: 428–34.

Grobman, A. B. 1990. The effect of soil temperatures on emergence from hibernation of *Terrapene carolina* and *T. ornata*. *Amer. Midl. Nat.* 124:366–71.

Guillette, L. J., Jr. 1994. Endocrine-disrupting environmental contaminants and reproduction: Lessons from the study of wildlife. Pp. 201–7 in D. R. Popkin and L. J. Peddle (eds.), *Women's Health Today: Perspectives on Current Research and Clinical Practice*. New York: Parthenon Publishing Group.

Guillette, L. J., Jr., T. S. Gross, G. R. Masson, J. M. Matter, H. F. Percival, and A. R. Woodward. 1994. Developmental abnormalities of the gonad and abnormal sex hormone concentrations in juvenile alligators from contaminated and control lakes in Florida. *Environ. Health Perspec.* 102:680–88.

Hall, R. J., P. F. P. Henry, and C. M. Bunck. 1999. Fifty-year trends in a box turtle population in Maryland. *Biol. Conserv.* 88:165–72.

Hallgren-Scaffidi, L. 1986. Habitat, home range and population study of the eastern box turtle (*Terrapene carolina*). Unpubl. M.S. thesis, Univ. Maryland, College Park.

Hamilton, A. M. 2000. Evidence for ontogenetic shifts in box turtles: Activity patterns, movements, and use of microenvironments and habitats by juvenile *Terrapene carolina bauri* on Egmont Key, Florida. Unpubl. M.S. thesis, Univ. Florida, Gainesville.

Hammerson, G. A.1982. *Amphibians and Reptiles in Colorado*. Denver: Colorado Division of Wildlife.

Hammett, J. E. 1992. The shapes of adaptation: Historical ecology of anthropogenic landscapes in the southeastern United States. *Landscape Ecol.* 7:121–35.

Harding, J. H. 1997. *Amphibians and Reptiles of the Great Lakes Region*. Ann Arbor: Univ. of Michigan Press.

Hardy, L. M., and R. W. McDiarmid. 1969. The amphibians and reptiles of Sinaloa. *Univ. Kansas Publ. Mus. Nat. Hist.* 18:39–252.

Harlan, R. 1827. Genera of North American Reptilia, and a synopsis of the species. Pt 2. *J. Acad. Nat. Sci. Philadelphia* 6:7–34.

Harless, M. D., and C. W. Lambiotte. 1971. Behavior of captive ornate box turtles. *J. Biol. Psychol.* 13:17–23.

Hattan, L. R., and D. H. Gist. 1975. Seminal receptacles in the eastern box turtle, *Terrapene carolina*. *Copeia* 1975:505–10.

Hay, O. P. 1906. Descriptions of two new genera (*Echmatemys* and *Xenochelys*) and two new species (*Xenochelys formosa* and *Terrapene putnami*) of fossil turtles. *Bull. Amer. Mus. Nat. Hist.* 22:27–31.

———. 1907. Descriptions of seven new species of turtles from the Tertiary of the United States. *Bull. Amer. Mus. Nat. Hist.* 23:847–63.

———. 1908a. Descriptions of five species of North American fossil turtles, four of which are new. *Proc. U.S. Natl. Mus.* 35:161–69.

———. 1908b. *Fossil Turtles of North America*. Carnegie Inst. of Washington Publ. 75. 568 pp.

———. 1916a. Descriptions of some Floridian fossil vertebrates, belonging mostly to the Pleistocene. *Florida St. Geol. Surv.* 8:39–76.

———. 1916b. Descriptions of some fossil vertebrates found in Texas. *Bull. Univ. Texas* (71):1–24.

———. 1920. Descriptions of some Pleistocene vertebrates found in the United States. *Proc. U.S. Natl. Mus.* 58:83–146.

———. 1923. *The Pleistocene of North America and Its Vertebrated Animals from the States East of the Mississippi River and from the Canadian Provinces East of Longitude 95°*. Carnegie Inst. of Washington Publ. 322. 499 pp.

———. 1924. *The Pleistocene of the Middle Region of North America and Its Vertebrated Animals*. Carnegie Inst. of Washington Publ. 322a. 385 pp.

Herbst, L. H. 1994. Fibropapillomatosis of marine turtles. *Ann. Rev. Fish Dis.* 4:389–425.

Heth, C. (ed.). 1997. *Native American Dance: Ceremonies and Social Traditions*. Golden, Colo.: Fulcrum.

Highfield, A. C. 1993. The fate of American *Terrapene* box turtles imported into Britain. *New York Turtle & Tortoise Soc. Newsnotes* 4(1):16–18.

Hinton, T. G., P. D. Fledderman, J. E. Lovich, J. D. Congdon, and J. W. Gibbons. 1997. Radiographic determination of fecundity: Is the technique safe for developing turtle embryos? *Chel. Conserv. Biol.* 2:409–14.

Hirschfeld, S. E. 1968. Vertebrate fauna of Nichol's Hammock, a natural trap. *Quart. J. Florida Acad. Sci.* 31:177–89.

Hnatiuk, S. H. 1978. Plant dispersal by the Aldabran giant tortoise, *Geochelone gigantea* (Schweigger). *Oecologia* 36:345–50.

Holbrook, J. E. 1842. *North American Herpetology; or, A Description of the Reptiles inhabiting the United States*. Vol. 1. Philadelphia: J. Dobson.

Holcomb, C. M., and W. S. Parker. 1979. Mirex residues in eggs and livers of two long-lived reptiles (*Chrysemys scripta* and *Terrapene carolina*) in Mississippi, 1970–1977. *Bull. Environ.
   Contam. Toxicol.* 23:369–71.

Holman, J. A. 1965. A huge Pleistocene box turtle from Texas. *Quart. J. Florida Acad. Sci.*
   28:345–48.

———. 1975. Herpetofauna of the Wakeeney Local Fauna (Lower Pliocene: Clarendonian) of
   Trego, County, Kansas. *Univ. Michigan Pap. on Paleontol.* 12:49–66.

———. 1987. Herpetofauna of the Egelhoff site (Miocene: Barstovian) of north-central Nebraska.
   J. Vert. Paleontol. 7:109–20.

———. 1995. *Pleistocene Amphibians and Reptiles in North America*. New York: Oxford Univ.
   Press.

Holman, J. A., and R. G. Corner. 1985. A Miocene *Terrapene* (Testudines: Emydidae) and other
   Barstovian turtles from south-central Nebraska. *Herpetologica* 41:88–93.

Holy, L. L. 1995. Home range, homing ability, orientation and navigational mechanisms of the
   western box turtle (*Terrapene ornata*) from western Nebraska. Unpubl. M.S. thesis, Univ.
   Nebraska, Lincoln.

Hudson, G. E. 1942. *The Amphibians and Reptiles of Nebraska*. Nebraska Conserv. Bull. 24.

Hunt, T. J. 1957. Notes on diseases and mortality in Testudines. *Herpetologica* 13:19–23.

Hunter, M. L., Jr., J. Albright, and J. Arbuckle (eds.). 1992. *The Amphibians and Reptiles of Maine*.
   Maine Agric. Exper. Sta., Univ. Maine, Orono.

Hutchison, V. H., A. Vinegar, and R. J. Kosh. 1966. Critical thermal maxima in turtles.
   Herpetologica 22:32–41.

Iverson, J. B. 1977. Reproduction in freshwater and terrestrial turtles of north Florida.
   Herpetologica 33:205–12.

———. 1982a. *Terrapene coahuila* Schmidt and Owens: Coahuila box turtle. *Cat. Amer. Amphib.
   Rept.* 288.1–288.2.

———. 1982b. *Terrapene nelsoni* Stejneger: Nelson's box turtle. *Cat. Amer. Amphib. Rept.*
   289.1–289.2.

———. 1982c. Biomass in turtle populations: A neglected subject. *Oecologia* 55:69–76.

———. 1987. Tortoises, not dodos, and the tambalacoque tree. *J. Herpetol.* 21:229–30.

———. 1992a. Correlates of reproductive output in turtles (Order Testudines). *Herp. Monogr.*
   6:25–42.

———. 1992b. Revised checklist with distribution maps of turtles of the World. Privately publ.,
   Richmond, Indiana.

Iverson, J. B., and C. R. Etchberger. 1989. The distributions of the turtles of Florida. *Florida Sci.*
   52:119–44.

Iverson, J. B., C. P. Balgooyen, K. K. Byrd, and K. K. Lyddan. 1993. Latitudinal variation in egg
   and clutch size in turtles. *Can. J. Zool.* 71:2448–61.

Jackson, C. G., Jr., M. M. Jackson, and J. D. Davis. 1969. Cutaneous myiasis in the three-toed box
   turtle, *Terrapene carolina triunguis*. *Bull. Wildl. Dis. Assoc.* 5:114.

Jackson, C. G., Jr., M. M. Landry, and M. M. Jackson. 1971. Reproductive tract anomaly in a box
   turtle. *J. Wildl. Dis.* 7:175–77.

Jackson, C. G., Jr., M. Fulton, and M. M. Jackson. 1972. Cranial asymmetry with massive infection in a box turtle. *J. Wildl. Dis.* 8:275–77.

Jackson, C. G., Jr., and J. M. Kaye. 1974. Occurrence of box turtles, *Terrapene* (Testudines:
   Testudinidae) in the Pleistocene of Mississippi. *Herpetologica* 30:11–13.

Jackson, C .G., Jr., C. M. Holcomb, S. Kleinbergs-Krisans, and M. M. Jackson. 1974. Variation in strontium-90 exoskeleton burdens of turtles (Reptilia: Testudines) in southeastern United States. *Herpetologica* 30: 406–9.

Jackson, D. R. 1991. Multiple clutches and nesting behavior in the Gulf Coast box turtle. *Florida Field Nat.* 19:14–16.

Jacobson, E. R., J. M. Gaskin, M. B. Brown, R. K. Harris, C. H. Gardiner, J. L. LaPointe, H. P. Adams, and C. Reggiardo. 1991a. Chronic upper respiratory tract disease of free-ranging desert tortoises (*Xerobates agassizii*). *J. Wildl. Dis.* 27:296–316.

Jacobson, E. R., C. Buergelt, B. Williams, and R. K. Harris. 1991b. Herpesvirus in cutaneous fibropapillomas of the green turtle *Chelonia mydas. Dis. Aquatic Org.* 12:1–6.

James, D. 1961. The measurements of an aged box turtle. *Proc. Arkansas Acad. Sci.* 15:26–28.

Janzen, F. J. 1993. An experimental analysis of natural selection on body size of hatchling turtles. *Ecology* 74:332–41.

Jensen, J. B. 1999. Life history notes, *Terrapene carolina carolina* (Eastern box turtle): Diet. *Herp. Rev.* 30:95.

Johnson, T. R. 1987. *The Amphibians and Reptiles of Missouri.* Jefferson City: Missouri Department of Conservation.

Jordan, J. A. 1979a. Box turtles and stomp dancing. Pt. 1. *Stovall Newsl.* 5(1):1–2.

———. 1979b. Box turtles and stomp dancing. Pt. 2. *Stovall Newsl.* 5(2):1–2.

Kautz, R. S. 1998. Land use and land cover trends in Florida, 1936–1995. *Florida Sci.* 61:171–87.

Kautz, R. S., D. T. Gilbert, and G. M. Mauldin. 1993. Vegetative cover in Florida based on 1985–1989 Landsat Thematic Mapper imagery. *Florida Sci.* 56: 135–54.

Kiester, A. R., C. W. Schwartz, and E .R. Schwartz. 1982. Promotion of gene flow by transient individuals in an otherwise sedentary population of box turtles (*Terrapene carolina triunguis*). *Evolution* 36:617–19.

Killebrew, F. C. 1977. Mitotic chromosomes of turtles. Pt. 4: The Emydidae. *Texas J. Sci.* 29:245–53.

King, F. W., and J. V. Griffo, Jr. 1958. A box turtle fatality apparently caused by *Sarcophaga cistudinis* larvae. *Florida Entomol.* 41:44.

Klemens, M. W. 1993. Amphibians and Reptiles of Connecticut and Adjacent Regions. *State Geol. and Nat. Hist. Surv. of Connecticut Bull.* 112:1–318.

Klimstra, W. D. 1959. Food habits of the cottonmouth in southern Illinois. *Nat. Hist. Misc.* (168):1–8.

Klimstra, W. D., and F. Newsome. 1960. Some observations on the food coactions of the common box turtle, *Terrapene c. carolina. Ecology* 41:639–47.

Knoll, C. M. 1935. Shield variation, reduction, and age in a box terrapin, *Terrapene carolina. Copeia* 1935:100.

Kolbe, J. J. 1998. *Terrapene ornata ornata* (Ornate box turtle): Diet. *Herp. Rev.* 29:235.

Kool, K. 1981. Is the musk of the long-necked turtle, *Chelodina longicollis*, a deterrent to predators? *Aust. J. Herpetol.* 1(2):45–53.

Kramer, D. C. 1973. Geophagy in *Terrapene ornata ornata* Agassiz. *J. Herpetol.* 7:138–39.

Langtimm, C. A., C. K. Dodd, Jr., and R. Franz. 1996. Estimates of abundance of box turtles (*Terrapene carolina bauri*) on a Florida island. *Herpetologica* 52:496–504.

Latham, R. 1917. Studying the box turtle. *Copeia* 1917:15–16.

———. 1972. Eastern box turtle eats green oak gall. *Engelhardtia* 2:1.

Lebreton, J.-D., K. P. Burnham, J. Clobert, and D. R. Anderson. 1992. Modeling survival and testing biological hypotheses using marked animals: A unified approach with case studies. *Ecol. Monogr.* 62:67–118.

Lee, J. C. 1996. *The Amphibians and Reptiles of the Yucatán Peninsula*. Ithaca, N.Y.: Comstock Publishing Associates.

Leftwich, R. L. 1970. *Arts and Crafts of the Cherokee*. Cherokee, N.C.: Cherokee Publications.

Legler, J. M. 1958. Extra-uterine migration of ova in turtles. *Herpetologica* 14:49–52.

———. 1960. Natural history of the ornate box turtle, *Terrapene ornata ornata* Agassiz. *Univ. Kansas Publ. Mus. Nat. Hist.* 11:527–669.

Leidy, J. 1888. Bot-fly larvae in the terrapin. *Proc. Acad. Nat. Sci. Phila.* for 1887:393–94.

Lemkau, P. J. 1970. Movements of the box turtle, *Terrapene c. carolina* (Linnaeus) in unfamiliar territory. *Copeia* 1970:781–83.

Levell, J. P. 1985. Some observations on the mating behavior of *Terrapene carolina triunguis*. *Bull. Chicago Herp. Soc.* 20:40–41.

———. 1997. *A Field Guide to Reptiles and the Law*. 2nd ed. Lanesboro, Minn.: Serpent's Tale Books.

Leviton, A. E., R. McDiarmid, S. Moody, M. Nickerson, J. Rosado, O. Sokol, and H. Voris. 1980. Museum acronyms: Second edition. *Herp. Rev.* 11:93–102.

Lieberman, S. 1994. Can CITES save the box turtle? *Endang. Sp. Tech. Bull.* 19(5):1, 16–17.

Lin, N. 1958. Coital movement patterns in pairings of a male *Terrapene carolina bauri* with a female *Terrapene c. triunguis*. *Brit. J. Herpetol.* 2(6):96–97.

Liner, E. A. 1994. Scientific and common names for the amphibians and reptiles of Mexico in English and Spanish. *SSAR Herp. Circ.* 23.

Lipske, M. 1989. Living legacies. *National Wildlife* (June–July): 15–16.

List, J.C. 1951. The ornate box turtle, *Terrapene ornata*, in Indiana. *Amer. Midl. Nat.* 45:508.

Loomis, R.B. 1956. The chigger mites of Kansas (Acarina, Trombiculidae). *Univ. Kansas Sci. Bull.* 37:1195–1443.

Lowe, P. 1996. Box turtles (Genus *Terrapene*). A Colorado Herpetological Society Care Sheet. World Wide Web Site: http://coloherp.org/careshts/boxturtl.htm

Luiijf, W. 1997. CITES and the tortoise and turtle trade. Pp. 125–34 in J. Van Abbema (ed.), *Proceedings: Conservation, Restoration, and Management of Tortoises and Turtles—An International Conference*. New York: New York Turtle & Tortoise Society.

Lynn, W.G. 1937. Variation in scutes and plates in the box turtle, *Terrapene carolina*. *Amer. Nat.* 71:421–26.

Lynn, W. G., and T. von Brand. 1945. Studies on the oxygen consumption and water metabolism of turtle embryos. *Biol. Bull.* 88:112–25.

Madden, R. 1975. Home range, movements, and orientation in the eastern box turtle, *Terrapene carolina carolina*. Unpubl. Ph.D. diss., City Univ. New York.

Marvin, G. A., and W. I. Lutterschmidt. 1997. Locomotor performance in juvenile and adult box turtles (*Terrapene carolina*): A reanalysis for effects of body size and extrinsic load using a terrestrial species. *J. Herpetol.* 31:582–86.

Mathis, A., and F. R. Moore. 1988. Geomagnetism and the homeward orientation of the box turtle, *Terrapene carolina*. *Ethology* 78:265–74.

Mays, M. L. 1960. A survey of helminth parasites of box turtles in central Oklahoma. Unpubl. M.S. thesis, Univ. Oklahoma, Norman.

McAllister, C. T. 1987. *Phaenicia* (Diptera: Calliphoridae) myiasis in a three-toed turtle, *Terrapene carolina triunguis* (Reptilia: Emydidae), from Arkansas. *Texas J. Sci.* 39:377–78.

McCauley, R. H. 1945. *The Reptiles of Maryland and the District of Columbia*. Privately publ., Hagerstown, Md.

McClure, W. L., and W. W. Milstead. 1967. *Terrapene carolina triunguis* from the Late Pleistocene of southeast Texas. *Herpetologica* 23:321–22.

McCoy, C. J., and N. D. Richmond. 1966. The identity of the Chinese box turtle, *Terrapene culturalia*. *Copeia* 1966:886.

McDowell, S. B. 1964. Partition of the genus *Clemmys* and related problems in the taxonomy of the aquatic Testudinidae. *Proc. Zool. Soc. Lond.* 143:239–79.

McMullen, D. B. 1940. Cutaneous myiasis in a box turtle. *Proc. Oklahoma Acad. Sci.* 20:23–25.

Mertens, R., and H. Wermuth. 1955. Die rezenten Schildkröten, Krokodile, und Brückenechsen. *Zool. Jahrb. (Syst.)* 83:323–440.

Messinger, M. A., and G. M. Patton. 1995. Five year study of nesting of captive *Terrapene carolina triunguis*. *Herp. Rev.* 26:193–95.

Metcalf, A. L., and E. Metcalf. 1978. An experiment with homing in ornate box turtles (*Terrapene ornata ornata* Agassiz). *J. Herpetol.* 12:411–12.

———. 1985. Longevity in some ornate box turtles (*Terrapene ornata ornata*). *J. Herpetol.* 19:157–59.

Metcalf, E., and A. L. Metcalf. 1970. Observations on ornate box turtles (*Terrapene ornata ornata* Agassiz). *Trans. Kansas Acad. Sci.* 73:96–117.

———. 1979. Mortality in hibernating ornate box turtles, *Terrapene ornata*. *Herpetologica* 35:93–96.

Meyers-Schöne, L., and B. T. Walton. 1994. Turtles as monitors of chemical contaminants in the environment. *Rev. Environ. Contam. Toxicol.* 135: 93-153.

Mills, L. 1970. House of Turtles. *Intern. Turtle & Tortoise Soc. J.* 4(4): 20-25.

Milstead, W. W. 1956. Fossil turtles of Friesenhahn Cave, Texas, with the description of a new species of *Testudo*. *Copeia* 1956:162–71.

———. 1960. Relict species of the Chihuahuan Desert. *Southwest. Nat.* 5:75–88.

———. 1965. Notes on the identities of some poorly known fossils of box turtles (*Terrapene*). *Copeia* 1965:513–14.

———. 1967. Fossil box turtles (*Terrapene*) from central North America, and box turtles of eastern Mexico. *Copeia* 1967:168–79.

———. 1969. Studies on the evolution of box turtles (genus *Terrapene*). *Bull. Florida Mus. Nat. Hist., Biol. Sci.* 14:1–113.

Milstead, W. W., and D. W. Tinkle. 1967. *Terrapene* of western Mexico, with comments on the species groups in the genus. *Copeia* 1967:180–87.

Minckley, W. L. 1969. Environments of the Bolsón of Cuatro Ciénegas, Coahuila, México. *Univ. Texas–El Paso Sci. Ser.* 2:1–65.

Minton, S. A., Jr. 1972. *Amphibians and Reptiles of Indiana*. Indiana Academy of Science Monographs 3. 346 pp.

Minx, P. 1992. Variation in phalangeal formulae in the turtle genus *Terrapene*. *J. Herpetol.* 26:234–38.

Minx, P. 1996. Phylogenetic relationships among the box turtles, genus *Terrapene*. *Herpetologica* 52:584–97.

Mitchell, J. C. 1994. *The Reptiles of Virginia*. Washington, D.C.: Smithsonian Institution Press.

Mitchell, J. C., and R. de Sá. 1994. *Terrapene carolina carolina*. (Eastern box turtle): Reproduction. *Herp. Rev.* 25:64.

Monagas, W. R., and R. E. Gatten, Jr. 1983. Behavioural fever in the turtles *Terrapene carolina* and *Chrysemys picta*. *J. Therm. Biol.* 8:285–88.

Montgomery, W. B. 1996. Predation by the fire ant, *Solenopsis invicta*, on the three-toed box turtle, *Terrapene carolina triunguis*. *Bull. Chicago Herp. Soc*. 31:105–6.

Moodie, K. B., and T. R. Van Devender. 1977. Additional Late Pleistocene turtles from Jones Spring, Hickory County, Missouri. *Herpetologica* 33:87–90.

————. 1978. Fossil box turtles (genus *Terrapene*) from southern Arizona. *Herpetologica* 34:172–74.

Mooney, J. 1900. Myths of the Cherokee. In *Nineteenth Annual Report of the Bureau of American Ethnology, 1897–98*. Pt. 1. Washington, D.C.: U.S. Government Printing Office.

Mosimann, J. E. 1958. The evolutionary significance of rare meetings in animal populations. *Evolution* 12:246–61.

Mount, R. H. 1975. *The Reptiles and Amphibians of Alabama*. Agric. Exper. Sta., Auburn Univ., Auburn, Alabama.

————. 1981. The red imported fire ant, *Solenopsis invicta* (Hymenoptera: Formicidae), as a possible serious predator of some native southeastern vertebrates: direct observations and subjective impressions. *J. Alabama Acad. Sci*. 52:71–78.

Müller, L. 1936. Beiträge zur Kenntnis Schildkrötenfauna von Mexiko. *Zool. Anz*. 113:97–114.

Murphy, J. 1976. The natural history of the box turtle. *Bull. Chicago Herp. Soc*. 11:2–45.

Murphy, T. D. 1964. Box turtle, *Terrapene carolina*, in stomach of copperhead, *Agkistrodon contortrix*. *Copeia* 1964:221.

Myers, C. 1952. *Terrapene carolina triunguis* winters in the egg. *Herpetologica* 8:80.

————. 1956. An unusual feeding habit in a box turtle. *Herpetologica* 12:155.

Myers, G. S. 1945. A third record of the Sonoran box turtle. *Copeia* 1945:172.

Neill, W. T. 1948a. Hibernation of amphibians and reptiles in Richmond County, Georgia. *Herpetologica* 4:107–14.

————. 1948b. Odor of young box turtles. *Copeia* 1948:130.

Nichols, J. T. 1939a. Range and homing of individual box turtles. *Copeia* 1939:125–27.

————. 1939b. Data on size, growth and age in the box turtle, *Terrapene carolina*. *Copeia* 1939:14–20.

Nieuwolt, M. C. 1993. The ecology of movement and reproduction in the western box turtle in central New Mexico. Unpubl. Ph.D. diss., Univ. New Mexico, Albuquerque.

Nieuwolt, P. M. 1996. Movement, activity, and microhabitat selection in the western box turtle, *Terrapene ornata luteola*, in New Mexico. *Herpetologica* 52:487–95.

Nieuwolt-Dacanay, P. M. 1997. Reproduction in the western box turtle, *Terrapene ornata luteola*. *Copeia* 1997:819–26.

Noble, G. A., and E. R. Noble. 1940. *A Brief Anatomy of the Turtle*. Stanford, Calif.: Stanford Univ. Press.

Norris, K. S., and R. G. Zweifel. 1950. Observations on the habits of the ornate box turtle, *Terrapene ornata* (Agassiz). *Nat. Hist. Misc*. (58):1–4.

Oelrich, T. M. 1953. A new box turtle from the Pleistocene of southwestern Kansas. *Copeia* 1953:33–38.

Ortenburger, A. I., and B. Freeman. 1930. Notes on some reptiles and amphibians from western Oklahoma. *Publ. Univ. Oklahoma Biol. Surv*. 2:175–88.

Over, W. H. 1923. *Amphibians and Reptiles of South Dakota*. South Dakota Geol. and Nat. Hist. Surv. Bull. 12.

Overton, F. 1916. Aquatic habits of the box turtle. *Copeia* 1916:4–5.

Packard, A. S. 1882. Bot fly larvae in a turtle's neck. *Amer. Nat*. 16:598.

Packard, G. C., M. J. Packard, and W. H. N. Gutzke. 1985. Influence of hydration of the environment on eggs and embryos of the terrestrial turtle *Terrapene ornata*. *Physiol. Zool.* 58:564–75.

Palmer, W. M., and A. R. Braswell. 1995. *Reptiles of North Carolina*. Chapel Hill: Univ. of North Carolina Press.

Parker, J. W. 1982. Opportunistic feeding by an ornate box turtle under the nest of a Mississippi kite. *Southwest. Nat.* 27:365.

Parmley, D. 1992. Turtles from the Late Hemphillian (latest Miocene) of Knox County, Nebraska. *Texas J. Sci.* 44:339–48.

Parsons, T. S., and J. E. Cameron. 1977. Internal relief of the digestive tract. Pp. 159–223 in C. Gans and T. S. Parsons (eds.), *Biology of the Reptilia*. Vol. 6: *Morphology E*. New York: Academic Press.

Patterson, J. 1994. *Box Turtles: Keeping and Breeding them in Captivity*. Neptune City, N.J.: T.F.H. Press.

Paukstis, G. L., and F. J. Janzen. 1988. An additional specimen of *Terrapene carolina triunguis* (Reptilia: Testudines) from southern Illinois. *Trans. Illinois St. Acad. Sci.* 81:283–86.

———. 1993. The status and biogeography of the three-toed box turtle, *Terrapene carolina triunguis*, in Illinois. *Trans. Illinois St. Acad. Sci.* 86:173–77.

Penn, G. H., Jr., and K. E. Pottharst. 1940. The reproduction and dormancy of *Terrapene major* in New Orleans. *Herpetologica* 2:25–29.

Peters, J. A. 1948. The box turtle as a host for dipterous parasites. *Amer. Midl. Nat.* 40:472–74.

Pilgrim, M. A., T. M. Farrell, and P. G. May. 1997. Population structure, activity, and sexual dimorphism in a central Florida population of box turtles, *Terrapene carolina bauri*. *Chel. Conserv. Biol.* 2(4):483–88.

Pilsbry, H. A. 1949. Two overlooked synonyms. *Nautilus* 63(1):36.

Pope, C. H. 1938. *Turtles of the Chicago Area*. Field Mus. Nat. Hist., Zool. Leaflet 14. 24 pp.

———. 1939. *Turtles of the United States and Canada*. New York: Alfred A. Knopf.

Posey, M. H. 1979. A study of the homing instinct in *Terrapene c. carolina* in Maryland. *Bull. Maryland Herp. Soc.* 15:139–40.

Pradel, R. 1996. Utilization of capture-mark-recapture for the study of recruitment and population growth rate. *Biometrics* 52:703–9.

Preston, R. E. 1979. Late Pleistocene cold-blooded vertebrate faunas from the mid-continental United States. I. Reptilia: Testudines, Crocodilia. *Univ. Mich. Pap. on Paleontol.* 19:1–53.

Price, J. W. 1951. A half-century-old boxturtle, *Terrapene carolina carolina* (Linnaeus), from northern Ohio. *Copeia* 1951:312.

Rainey, D. G. 1953. Death of an ornate box turtle parasitized by dipterous larvae. *Herpetologica* 9:109.

Ramus, E. 1997. The well-stocked reptile section. *Pet Business* (May): 48.

Reagan, D. P. 1974. Habitat selection in the three-toed box turtle, *Terrapene carolina triunguis*. *Copeia* 1974:512–27.

Reichman, O. J. 1987. *Konza Prairie: A Tallgrass Natural History*. Lawrence: Univ. Press of Kansas.

Reinert, H. K. 1991. Translocation as a conservation strategy for amphibians and reptiles: Some comments, concerns, and observations. *Herpetologica* 47:357–63.

Rick, C. M., and R. I. Bowman. 1961. Galapagos tomatoes and tortoises. *Evolution* 15:407–17.

Riedesel, M. L., J. L. Cloudsley-Thompson, and J. A. Cloudsley-Thompson. 1971. Evaporative thermoregulation in turtles. *Physiol. Zool.* 44:28–32.

Riemer, D. N. 1981. Multiple nesting by a female box turtle (*Terrapene c. carolina*). *Chelonogica* 2:53–55.

Rodeck, H. G. 1949. Notes on box turtles in Colorado. *Copeia* 1949:32–34.

Rokosky, E. J. 1948. A bot-fly parasitic in box turtles. *Nat. Hist. Misc.* (32):1–2.

Rose, F. L. 1969. Desiccation rates and temperature relationships of *Terrapene ornata* following scute removal. *Southwest. Nat.* 14:67–72.

———. 1986. Carapace regeneration in *Terrapene* (Chelonia: Testudinidae). *Southwest. Nat.* 31:131–34.

Rose, F .L., M. E. T. Scioli, and M. P. Moulton. 1988. Thermal preferentia of Berlandier's tortoise (*Gopherus berlandieri*) and the ornate box turtle (*Terrapene ornata*). *Southwest. Nat.* 33:357–90.

Rosenberger, R. C. 1936. Notes on some habits of *Terrapene carolina* (Linné). *Copeia* 1936:177.

Rossman, D. A. 1965. The ornate box turtle, *Terrapene ornata*, in Louisiana. *Proc. Louisiana Acad. Sci.* 28:130–31.

Russo, P. M. 1972. Behavioral thermoregulation and energy budget of the eastern box turtle, *Terrapene carolina carolina* (Linne). Unpubl. Ph.D. diss., Rutgers Univ., New Brunswick, N.J.

Sammartano, D. V. 1994. Spatial, dietary, and temporal niche parameters of two species of box turtle (*Terrapene*) in microsympatry. Unpubl. M.S. thesis, Southwest Missouri St. Univ., Springfield.

Schmidt, K. P., and D. W. Owens. 1944. Amphibians and reptiles of northern Coahuila, Mexico. *Field Mus. Nat. Hist. Zool. Ser.* 29:97–115.

Schoepff, J. D. 1792–1801. *Historia Testudinum Iconibus Illustrata*. Palm Erlangae. 136 pp. (Issued in 4 parts: 1792, 1793, 1795, 1801).

Schwartz, C. W., and E. R. Schwartz. 1974. The three-toed box turtle in central Missouri: Its population, home range and movements. *Missouri Dept. Conserv. Terrestr. Ser.* 5:1–28.

Schwartz, E. R., and C.W. Schwartz. 1991. A quarter-century study of survivorship in a population of three-toed box turtles in Missouri. *Copeia* 1991:1120–23.

Schwartz, E. R., C. W. Schwartz, and A. R. Kiester. 1984. The three-toed box turtle in central Missouri. Pt. 2: A nineteen-year study of home range, movements and population. *Missouri Dept. Conserv. Terrestr. Ser.* 12:1–29.

Seidel, M. E., and M. D. Adkins. 1989. Variation in turtle myoglobins (Subfamily Emydinae: Testudines) examined by isoelectric focusing. *Comp. Biochem. Physiol.* 94B:569–73.

Seigel, R., and C. K. Dodd, Jr. 2000. Manipulating turtle populations: Half-way technologies or viable options? Pp. 218–38 in M. Klemens (ed.), *Turtle Conservation: A Blueprint for Survival*, Washington, D.C.: Smithsonian Institution Press.

Shannon, F. A., and H. M. Smith. 1949. Herpetological results of the University of Illinois Field Expedition, Spring 1949. Pt. 1: Introduction, Testudines, Serpentes. *Trans. Kansas Acad. Sci.* 52:494–509.

Shaw, C. E. 1952. Sexual dimorphism in *Terrapene klauberi* and the relationship of *T. nelsoni* to *T. klauberi*. *Herpetologica* 8:39–41.

Siefkas, J., T. Farrell, and P. G. May. 1998. Infection by *Mycoplasma agassizii* in a box turtle and its implications for conservation biology. *Florida Sci.* 61(Suppl. 1):18.

Skorepa, A. C. 1966. The deliberate consumption of stones by the ornate box turtle, *Terrapene o. ornata* Agassiz. *J. Ohio Herp. Soc.* 5:108.

Smith, H. M. 1939. Notes on Mexican reptiles and amphibians. *Field Mus. Nat. Hist. Zool. Ser.* 24:15–35.

———. 1958. Total regeneration of the carapace in the box turtle. *Turtox News* 36:234–37.

Smith, H. M., and L. F. James. 1958. The taxonomic significance of cloacal bursae in turtles. *Trans. Kansas Acad. Sci.* 61:86–96.

Smith, H. M., and R. B. Smith. 1979. *Synopsis of the Herpetofauna of Mexico*. Vol. 6: *Guide to Mexican Turtles*, Bibliographic addendum 3. North Bennington, Vt.: John Johnson.

Smith, H. M., R. Humphrey, and D. Chiszar. 1996. A range extension for the box turtle *Terrapene yucatana*. *Bull. Maryland Herp. Soc.* 32:14–15.

Smith, H. M., D. Chiszar, and R. R. Montanucci. 1997. Subspecies and classification. *Herp. Rev.* 28:13–16.

Smith, L. L. 1992. Nesting ecology, female home range and activity patterns, and hatchling survivorship in the gopher tortoise (*Gopherus polyphemus*). Unpubl. M.S. thesis, Univ. Florida, Gainesville.

Smith, P.W. 1955. Presumed hybridization of two species of box turtles. *Nat. Hist. Misc.* (146):1–3.

————. 1961. The amphibians and reptiles of Illinois. *Illinois Nat. Surv. Bull.* 28.1–298.

Sowerby, J. de C., and E. Lear. 1872. *Tortoises, Terrapins, and Turtles Drawn from Life*. London: Henry Sotheran, Joseph Baer and Company.

Spray, D. C., and M. L. May. 1972. Heating and cooling rates in four species of turtles. *Comp. Biochem. Physiol.* 41A:507–22.

St. Clair, R. C. 1995. How developmental environment affects life history in box turtles. Unpubl. Ph.D. diss., Univ. Oklahoma, Norman.

St. Clair, R. C. 1998. Patterns of growth and sexual size dimorphism in two species of box turtles with environmental sex determination. *Oecologia* 115:501–7.

Stickel, L. F. 1950. Populations and home range relationships of the box turtle, *Terrapene c. carolina* (Linnaeus). *Ecol. Monogr.* 20:351–78.

————. 1951. Wood mouse and box turtle populations in an area treated annually with DDT for five years. *J. Wildl. Manage.* 15:161–64.

————. 1978. Changes in a box turtle population during three decades. *Copeia* 1978:221–25.

————. 1989. Home range behavior among box turtles (*Terrapene c. carolina*) of a bottomland forest in Maryland. *J. Herpetol.* 23:40–44.

Stickel, L. F., and C. M. Bunck. 1989. Growth and morphometrics of the box turtle, *Terrapene c. carolina*. *J. Herpetol.* 23:216–23.

Storey, K. B., J. R. Layne, Jr., M. M. Cutwa, T. A. Churchill, and J. M. Storey. 1993. Freezing survival and metabolism of box turtles, *Terrapene carolina*. *Copeia* 1993:628–34.

Strang, C. A. 1983. Spatial and temporal activity patterns in two terrestrial turtles. *J. Herpetol.* 17:43–47.

Strass, P. K., K. J. Miles, B. S. McDonald, Jr., and I. L. Brisbin, Jr. 1982. An assessment of factors associated with the daytime use of resting forms by eastern box turtles (*Terrapene carolina carolina*). *J. Herpetol.* 16:320–22.

Stuart, M. D., and G. C. Miller. 1987. The eastern box turtle, *Terrapene c. carolina* (Testudines: Emydidae), in North Carolina. *Brimleyana* 13: 123–31.

Sturbaum, B.A. 1972. Thermoregulation in the ornate box turtle *Terrapene ornata*. Unpubl. Ph.D. diss., Univ. New Mexico, Albuquerque.

————. 1981. Responses of the three-toed box turtle, *Terrapene carolina triunguis*, to heat stress. *Comp. Biochem. Physiol.* 70A:199–204.

Sturbaum, B. A., and M. L. Riedesel. 1974. Temperature regulation responses of ornate box turtles, *Terrapene ornata*, to heat. *Comp. Biochem. Physiol.* 48A:527–38.

————. 1977. Dissipation of stored body heat by the ornate box turtle, *Terrapene ornata*. *Comp. Biochem. Physiol.* 58A:93–97.

Sturtevant, W. C. 1954. The medicine bundles and busks of the Florida Seminole. *Florida Anthropol.* 7:31–70.

————. 1961. Comment on Gertrude P. Kurath's "Effects of environment on Cherokee-Iroquois ceremonialism, music, and dance." *Bur. Amer. Ethnol.* 180(19):199–204.

Surface, H. A. 1908. First report on the economic features of turtles of Pennsylvania. *Zool. Bull. Pennsylvania Dept. Agric.* 6(4–5):107–95.

Tangredi, B. P., and R. H. Evans. 1997. Organochlorine pesticides associated with ocular, nasal, or otic infection in the eastern box turtle (*Terrapene carolina carolina*). *J. Zoo Wildl. Med.* 28:97–100.

Taylor, W. E. 1895. The box turtles of North America. *Proc. U.S. Natl. Mus.* 17:573–88.

Temple, S. A. 1987. Predation on turtle nests increases near ecological edges. *Copeia* 1987:250–52.

Thomasson, J. R. 1980. Ornate box turtle, *Terrapene ornata* (Testudinae), feeding on a pincushion cactus, *Coryphantha vivipara* (Cactaceae). *Southwest. Nat.* 25:438.

Thompson, W. L., G. C. White, and C. Gowan. 1998. *Monitoring Vertebrate Populations*. San Diego, Calif.: Academic Press.

Tonge, S. J. 1987. Breeding the aquatic box terrapin *Terrapene coahuila* at the Jersey Wildlife Preservation Trust. *Dodo, J. Jersey Wildl. Preserv. Trust* 24:111–20.

Tonosaki, K. 1993. Cross-adaptation to odor stimulation of olfactory receptor cells in the box turtle, *Terrapene carolina*. *Brain Behav. Evol.* 41: 187–91.

Townsend, C. H. 1926. An old tortoise. *Bull. Zool. Soc. New York* 29:217–18.

Trail, C. D. 1995. Natural history and habitat use of the ornate box turtle *Terrapene ornata ornata* at a mixed-grass prairie in southwest Nebraska. Unpubl. M.A. thesis, Univ. Nebraska, Omaha.

True, F. 1884. Bot-flies in a turtle. *Science* 4(96):511.

Tucker, J. K., and R. S. Funk. 1976. Twinning in the Gulf Coast box turtle, *Terrapene carolina major*. *Florida Sci.* 39:238–39.

————. 1977. Eggs and hatchlings of the Gulf Coast box turtle, *Terrapene carolina major*. *Bull. Chicago Herp. Soc.* 12:52–57.

Tucker, J. K., and J. B. Hatcher. 1994. Two further specimens of the three-toed box turtle, *Terrapene carolina triunguis*, from Illinois and a proposal for its inclusion as a member of the herpetofauna of Illinois. *Trans. Illinois St. Acad. Sci.* 87:201–6.

Tucker, J. K., R. S. Funk, and G. L. Paukstis. 1978a. The adaptive significance of egg morphology in two turtles (*Chrysemys picta* and *Terrapene carolina*. *Bull. Maryland Herp. Soc.* 14:10–22.

————. 1978b. Reproductive potential of the Gulf Coast box turtle *Terrapene carolina major*. *Bull. Maryland Herp. Soc.* 14:23–28.

Tuge, H. 1931. Early behavior of embryos of the turtle, *Terrapene carolina* (L). *Proc. Soc. Exp. Biol. and Med.* 29:52–53.

Tully, T. N., Jr., J. M. Morris, and J. D. Carter. 1996. Bacterial conjunctival abscess in a three-toed box turtle. *Reptiles* 4(9):28–29.

Turnbull, H. W., J. F. Scott, and A. R. Hall (eds.). 1959. *The Correspondence of Isaac Newton*. Vol. 1: *1661–1675*. Cambridge: Cambridge University Press.

Vance, J. M. 1985. The tortoise pair. *Audubon* (May): 64–69.

Vogt, R. C. 1981. *Natural History of Amphibians and Reptiles in Wisconsin*. Milwaukee, Wis.: Milwaukee Public Mus.

Ward, J. P. 1968. Presumed hybridization of two species of box turtles. *Copeia* 1968:874–75.

————. 1978. *Terrapene ornata* (Agassiz): Ornate box turtle. *Cat. Amer. Amphib. Rept.* 217.1–217.4.

————. 1980. Comparative cranial morphology of the freshwater turtle subfamily Emydinae: An analysis of the feeding mechanisms and systematics. Unpubl. Ph.D. diss., North Carolina St. Univ., Raleigh.

Warner, J. L. 1982. *Terrapene c. carolina* (Eastern box turtle): Reproduction. *Herp. Rev.* 13:48–49.

Warwick, C. 1993. The decline of North American box turtles. *New York Turtle & Tortoise Soc. Newsnotes* 4(1):15–16.

Webb, R G. 1970. *Reptiles of Oklahoma*. Norman: Univ. Oklahoma Press.

Webb, R. G., W. L. Minckley, and J. E. Craddock. 1963. Remarks on the Coahuilan box turtle, *Terrapene coahuila* (Testudines, Emydidae). *Southwest. Nat.* 8:89–99.

Wever, E. G., and J. A. Vernon. 1956. Auditory responses in the common box turtle. *Proc. Natl. Acad. Sci.* 42:962–65.

Wheeler, W. M. 1890. The supposed bot-fly parasite of the box-turtle. *Psyche* 5(169):403.

Wied-Neuwied, M. A. P. 1865. Verzeichniss der Reptilien, welch auf einer Reise im nördlichen America beobachtet wurden. *Nova Acta Acad. Leopold.-Carol.* 32(1):viii + 146 pp.

Willbern, S. E. 1982. Climbing ability of box turtles. *Bull. Maryland Herp. Soc.* 18:170–71.

Williams, E. C., Jr. 1961. A study of the box turtle, *Terrapene carolina carolina* (L.), population in Allee Memorial Woods. *Proc. Indiana Acad. Sci.* 71:399–406.

Williams, E. C., Jr., and W. S. Parker. 1987. A long-term study of a box turtle (*Terrapene carolina*) population at Allee Memorial Woods, Indiana, with emphasis on survivorship. *Herpetologica* 43:328–35.

Williams, K. L., and P. Han. 1964. A comparison of the density of *Terrapene coahuila* and *T. carolina*. *J. Ohio Herp. Soc.* 4:105.

Wing, E. S. 1968. Animal remains from a midden at Fort Walton Beach. *Quart. J. Florida Acad. Sci.* 30:57–58.

Wood, J. T., and O. K. Goodwin. 1954. Observations on the summer behavior and mortality of box turtles in eastern Virginia. *Virginia J. Sci.* 5(2):60–64.

Wren, K., D .L. Claussen, and M. Kurz. 1998. The effects of body size and extrinsic mass on the locomotion of the ornate box turtle, *Terrapene ornata*. *J. Herpetol.* 32:144–50.

Yahner, R. H. 1974. Weight change, survival rate and home range in the box turtle, *Terrapene carolina*. *Copeia* 1974:546–48.

Yeh, H. K. 1961. First discovery of a box turtle in China. *Vert. Palasiatica* 5(1):58–64.

Yerkes, R. M. 1904. Space perception of tortoises. *J. Comp. Neurol. Psychol.* 2:17–26.

Zangerl, R., and R. G. Johnson. 1957. The nature of shield abnormalities in the turtle shell. *Fieldiana Geol.* 10:341–62.

Zieller, D. 1969. Turtle sanctuary. *Intern. Turtle & Tortoise Soc. J.* 3(6):6–9, 30–31.

Zug, G. R. 1991. Age determination in turtles. *Soc. Study Amphib. Rept., Herp. Circ.* 20, 28 pp.

————. 1993. *Herpetology. An Introductory Biology of Amphibians and Reptiles*. San Diego, Calif.: Academic Press.

————. 1994. North American box turtles: A continuing concern. *Virginia Herp. Soc. Newsl.* 4(2):1–2.

Index of Artists, Collectors, and Researchers

General Index